SAINT WILFRID AT HEXHAM

SAINT WILFRID
AT
HEXHAM

D. P. Kirby

Editor

ORIEL PRESS

First published 1974
by Oriel Press Ltd.
27 Ridley Place
Newcastle upon Tyne NE1 8LH

Printed in Great Britain by
Northumberland Press Ltd.
Gateshead

ISBN 0 85362 155 1

*Publication of this book has been generously assisted by
The Joicey Trust and the Marc Fitch Fund.*

FOREWORD

by The Rt Rev. J. Ramsbotham, Assistant-Bishop of Newcastle.

Dr Kirby sets the scene for the volume as a whole and takes a critical look at what has been called 'the age of the saints' in which Wilfrid lived and at the vicious dynastic politics of the seventh and eighth centuries in Northumbria, arguing that it was Wilfrid's rôle in the dynastic in-fighting which caused many of his misfortunes. Dr Farmer looks more directly at Wilfrid himself as a churchman, an ecclesiastical figure whose links with Rome and Gaul gave him a peculiar awareness of canon law and a sense of the dignity of his ecclesiastical office. He considers the enigma of the man who at one and the same time can attract and repel us. In a review of Wilfrid's actual landholdings in Northumbria, with particular reference to the Liberty of Hexham, Mr Roper sets Wilfrid in his context as a well-endowed prelate whose very wealth made him an object of jealousy. Each of these three chapters tends to see Wilfrid from a different point of view and the reader will probably detect certain differences of interpretation or emphasis which is only natural. Dr Gilbert then unravels the architectural history of Wilfrid's church at Hexham, reckoned in its time by contemporaries to be unequalled north of the Alps, explaining how the building was further elaborated by Acca, bishop of Hexham, Wilfrid's successor, commenting also on the early church at Ripon. It is perhaps the sculpture from Ripon and Hexham which represents the most complete extant evidence of the achievements of Wilfrid's artists, and Professor Cramp supports Dr Gilbert's emphasis on the importance of Roman and Gaulish models. It should be stressed that this is the most detailed survey of early Northumbrian sculpture at Hexham ever published. Similarly, Mr Bailey presents the most systematic analysis to date of early Anglo-Saxon metalwork from Hexham, and the most reliable study of these items, in the course of which he shows how careful one has to be in dealing with the statements of nineteenth-century antiquaries. There are three appendices, a hand-list of sculptured stones from Hexham by Professor Cramp, a consideration of carved Crucifixion scenes at Hexham by Miss E. Coatsworth, and a numismatic analysis of the ninth-century Hexham coin hoard by Mr H. E. Pagan. All those writers who have had occasion to deal with the continental background reveal how important this was for Wilfrid and his religious foundations at Ripon and Hexham. Hexham was no isolated monastic outpost but an integral part of Dark Age Christendom in the West of Europe.

CONTENTS

ABBREVIATIONS

AA	*Archæologia Æliana*
ASC	*Anglo-Saxon Chronicle*, ed. B. Thorpe, 2 vols (Rolls series: London, 1861): trans. D. Whitelock, D. C. Douglas and S. L. Tucker, *The Anglo-Saxon Chronicle* (London, 1961)
Ant. J.	*Antiquaries Journal*
Arch.	*Archæologia*
Arch. J.	*Archæological Journal*
Baldwin Brown	G. Baldwin Brown, *The Arts in Early England*, 6 vols (London, 1903-37)
BIHR	*Bulletin of the Institute of Historical Research*
BMQ	*British Museum Quarterly*
BNJ	*British Numismatic Journal*
Clapham	A. W. Clapham, *English Romanesque Architecture before the Conquest*, vol. I (Oxford, 1930)
Collingwood	W. G. Collingwood, *Northumbrian Crosses of the Pre-Norman Age* (London, 1927)
CS	*Cartularium Saxonicum*, ed. W. de Gray Birch, 3 vols (London, 1885-9: reprinted New York, 1964)
DN	*Trans. of the Architectural and Archæological Society of Durham and Northumberland*
Eddius	*The Life of Bishop Wilfrid by Eddius Stephanus*, ed. and trans. B. Colgrave (Cambridge, 1927)
EHD	*English Historical Documents*, vol. I, 500-1042, trans. D. Whitelock (London, 1955)
EHR	*English Historical Review*
HCY	*Historians of the Church of York and Its Archbishops*, ed. J. Raine, 3 vols (Rolls series: London, 1879-94)

HE	*Historia Ecclesiastica*: edited as *Bede's Ecclesiastical History of the English People* by B. Colgrave and R. A. B. Mynors (Oxford Medieval Texts, 1969)
H & S	*Councils and Ecclesiastical Documents relating to Great Britain and Ireland*, ed. A. W. Haddan and W. Stubbs, 3 vols (Oxford, 1869-78)
Hodges	C. C. Hodges, *Ecclesia Hagustaldensis: the Abbey of St Andrew, Hexham* (Published privately, 1888)
Hodges and Gibson	C. C. Hodges and J. Gibson, *Hexham and its Abbey* (Hexham, 1919)
JBAA	*Journal of the British Archæological Association*
JRSAI	*Journal of the Royal Society of Antiquaries of Ireland*
MA	*Medieval Archæology*
MGH	*Monumenta Germaniæ Historica*
Plummer	*Venerabilis Bædæ Opera Historica*, ed. C. Plummer, 2 vols (Oxford, 1896)
PSAI	*Proc. of the Society of Antiquaries of Ireland*
PSAL	*Proc. of the Society of Antiquaries of London*
PSAN	*Proc. of the Society of Antiquaries of Newcastle upon Tyne*
PSAS	*Proc. of the Society of Antiquaries of Scotland*
Raine	*The Priory of Hexham, its chronicles, endowments and annals*, ed. J. Raine, 2 vols (Surtees Society, 44, 1863)
Savage and Hodges	E. S. Savage and C. C. Hodges, *A Record of all the works connected with Hexham Abbey* (Hexham, 1907)
Ss rer germ	*MGH., Scriptores rerum germanicarum in usum scholarum*
Ss rer Merov	*MGH., Scriptores rerum Merovingicarum in usum scholarum*
Stuart	J. Stuart, *Sculptured Stones of Scotland*, 2 vols (2nd ed., Edinburgh, 1867)

Taylor (H.M.) and Taylor (J.)	H. M. Taylor and J. Taylor, *Anglo-Saxon Architecture*, 2 vols (Cambridge, 1965)
TBGAS	*Trans. of the Bristol and Gloucestershire Archæological Society*
VCH	Victoria County History
Wilson	D. M. Wilson, *Anglo-Saxon Ornamental Metalwork 700-1100 in the British Museum* (London, 1964)
YAJ	*Yorkshire Archæological Journal*

Chapter One

NORTHUMBRIA IN THE TIME OF WILFRID

D. P. Kirby

'*Brunechildis was brought before Chlotar, who was boiling with fury against her. He charged her with the deaths of ten Frankish kings ... She was tormented for three days with a diversity of tortures, and then on his orders was led through the ranks on a camel. Finally she was tied by her hair, one arm and one leg to the tail of an unbroken horse, and she was cut to shreds by its hoofs at the pace it went.*'[1]

THIS WAS in the year 613. Chlotar II was a Merovingian king of the Franks in Gaul, Brunechildis a queen. It was just over a hundred years since the conversion of the Franks to Christianity. That the Franks were capable of appalling acts of violence, especially in the pursuit of dynastic feuds, is a well-known feature of their early history, particularly as described by Gregory of Tours in his *History of the Franks*, written in the late sixth century.[2] Even children of the royal blood might be brutally done to death. It is with something amounting perhaps to a sense of relief that a modern observer turns to the *Historia Ecclesiastica Gentis Anglorum* (the *Ecclesiastical History of the English People*), completed in 731 by the Venerable Bede, born in 673 and a monk of the great Northumbrian monastery of SS Peter and Paul at Monkwearmouth and Jarrow; for, by contrast, it is on the whole a tranquil picture which he presents of early England at the time of the Conversion. Warfare there might have been, and occasional displays of barbarity, but such unbridled ferocity as prevailed in Frankland the English reader may feel could not possibly have existed among the Anglo-Saxons, certainly not after the conversion of the various kingdoms. Was this not, after all, the 'age of the saints' of the early English Church?

In his great work Bede traces the ecclesiastical history of the Anglo-

I

Saxons (or English) from the beginning of their conversion in 597, when St Augustine landed in Kent, and from 635 when the Scottish missionaries, led by St Aidan, came to Northumbria, through the debate concerning the disputed date of Easter which was resolved in favour of the Church of Rome at the council or synod of Whitby in 664, to the archiepiscopate of Theodore of Tarsus at Canterbury from 669 to 690, and the eventual winning over of the Picts and Scots beyond the Forth to the Roman Easter in the period c. 715-17.[3] A halo of sanctity encircles an array of pious kings and saintly churchmen, and Bede glides pleasantly over the peaceful waters of what was for him essentially the golden age of Christianity in England. But oddly enough Augustine, who seems to have been quite at home among the Franks, was almost dissuaded by them from proceeding with his mission to Kent because the Franks said that the Saxons were of such a savage disposition:[4] and the first Irish or Scottish missionary to be sent from Iona in Dál Riata to Northumbria declared that he could achieve nothing among a people so untameable, hard and barbarous.[5] These statements, which occur quite incidentally in Bede's narrative, reflect the jagged edges of a harsher reality beneath the surface of the *Historia Ecclesiastica*. Bede himself, of course, was the product of a dramatic flowering of literature and the arts, not least in Northumbria, which has been termed the 'Northumbrian renaissance' and with which he was strictly contemporary. Above all, Bede was a distinguished Biblical scholar and his extensive commentaries deserve further study. Art historians are divided over which early illuminated manuscripts to assign specifically to Northumbria because the fusion in Northumbria of native English and native Irish designs with Mediterranean styles resulted in 'Hiberno-Saxon' ornamentation which could belong either to Ireland or to Northumbria or to any other area where the fusion was so complete. There is no doubt, however, that the beautiful Lindisfarne Gospels belong to Northumbria. According to the tenth-century colophon entered by the glossator, Ealdred, the Gospels were written out by Eadfrith, bishop of Lindisfarne (689-721), bound by Æthelwald, bishop of Lindisfarne (724-40), and ornamented by Bilfrith the anchorite.[6] So also to Northumbria, and to Bede's monastery of Monkwearmouth and Jarrow, belongs the Mediterranean art of the Codex Amiatinus, produced not long before 716.[7] Despite such cultural activity, however, Bede said little about the Church in Northumbria in his own day in his *Ecclesiastical History*. Instead he directed the attention of his reader to a more distant past about which he knew less but about which he cared deeply. In a way it is as well that he did, for otherwise we would have known almost nothing of the period of the conversion of the Anglo-Saxons in the seventh century: but it is important to remember this fundamental dichotomy in Bede's historical approach.

Recent comment has emphasized that Bede was concerned to present the ideal Christian king in an ideal Christian world: after the arrival of Augustine 'the kingdom of Kent became a microcosm of the kingdom of heaven'.[8] He wrote for and with the approval of Ceolwulf, king of Northumbria (729-37). By contrast, Gregory of Tours intended to indict the Frankish kings by emphasizing personal shortcomings, and not surprisingly he had no royal sanction for his work. 'In sum, the descriptions of kings we meet in Gregory and Bede, though based on authentic information, was never meant to constitute a careful synthesis of all that was knowable about them; they are literary creations ...'[9] In other words, Gregory's picture was too black, Bede's too roseate. If there is a serious imbalance, however, the error of presentation is more on Bede's side than on Gregory's. Perhaps there is a danger in approaching early kings too exclusively as literary creations to serve a didactic purpose that the reality may elude us too. It cannot, for example, be emphasized too much that the 'vendetta-ridden society of the age would have no reason to cherish an ideal of political cohesion'.[10] Gregory was an important Gallo-Roman bishop among the Franks, coming into daily contact with secular life and regular contact with secular rulers, and his picture is not dissimilar from that of Fredegar. Bede, on the other hand, lived all his life from the age of seven in a monastery, in cloistered seclusion. He was not unaware of political tensions in Northumbria by 731 and he knew that on the continent there was the menace of Saracen expansion. It is not likely, however, that he ever witnessed an act of real violence and inconceivable that he experienced royal wrath. He may never even have met a king. By contrast, Eddius' *Life of Wilfrid*, many of the events of which are set in England and in Northumbria, was written by one who had followed his master through numerous stormy encounters

with secular power, and the world which Eddius describes is recognizable more as Gregory's than as Bede's. Like Gregory, Eddius knew
something of the true nature of political life in the Dark Ages. If
Eddius had been the author of the *Ecclesiastical History of the
English People*, England, like Merovingian Gaul, would probably
have had few if any saintly kings. But Bede was a monk, a scholar, a
quietly devout and pious man, writing of a lay world he hardly knew
in praise of kings who appeared to him, from what he was told, to
possess definite virtues as rulers and individuals. This was not simply
the consequences of Bede's philosophy of kingship: it was a consequence of his unavoidably restricted environment and limited experience. Similarly, Bede's portrayal of the ecclesiastical leaders of the
early English Church is controlled. Merovingian ecclesiastics, including Gregory of Tours, frequently found themselves involved in the
political troubles of the times, and some actively participated. Eddius'
Life of Wilfrid is a classic and unique description of the career of an
Anglo-Saxon ecclesiastical figure in the same kind of setting. The
serenity which Bede brings to the ecclesiastical personalities of the
period of the Conversion does not derive necessarily from their individual lives, nor is their apparent mildness and humility purely the
result of Celtic piety or Roman devotion: it is a mirror of the peace
and charity of Bede himself and of the timeless quiet of his own life,
the melodious unison of plainsong and the contemplative observance
of the canonical hours during which, as Bede believed (and a delightful belief too), angels visited the congregations of the brethren.

It must be emphasized that Bede was indeed almost totally dependent for his knowledge of the early history of the Anglo-Saxon
Church, even of Northumbrian affairs, on what he was told. He had
little in the way of written materials, though he possessed copies of
one or two conciliar documents, a handful of papal letters and regnal
and episcopal lists. Some would argue that he had access to primitive
annals in Easter Tables, but this is debatable. He knew Eddius' *Life
of Wilfrid* and the anonymous Lindisfarne *Life of Cuthbert* (upon
which he based his own *Life* of the saint), and he probably knew of
the existence of the Whitby *Life of Gregory* (the pope who directed
the mission of Augustine to Kent), a *Life* which also contained useful
material on Edwin, former king of Northumbria. But Eddius, the

author of the Lindisfarne *Life of Cuthbert*, and the Whitby writer
for his English material, had based their work on oral tradition: and
the vast mass of Bede's information was similarly derived from oral
tradition, handed down in cathedral chapters, monastic cloisters and
royal courts, oral tradition which we have only begun to evaluate for
ourselves. Such communities created instant legend. The panegyrical
nature of oral tradition, designed to glorify not denigrate a remembered and (in their own circle) beloved abbot, bishop or king, nun,
abbess or queen, was essentially initially destructive to some extent of
historical truth. The community on Lindisfarne, for example, would
not wish to stress any weakness in Cuthbert's character or even call
attention to it. The members of the various branches of the Northumbrian royal family, like all royal families, had no desire to display
ancestors and former kings in an unfavourable light. Furthermore,
oral tradition was extremely localized. A community, whether secular
or religious, was basically only interested in its own affairs. There is
no evidence that there was any significant body of tradition at Lindisfarne about Cuthbert's time at Melrose before he went to Lindisfarne.
The monks of Lindisfarne were only interested in what Cuthbert did
there. The kings of Northumbria did not celebrate the deeds of the
kings of Kent, nor would they know a very great deal about them.
And not only was oral tradition localized, it was fragile. It could only
be preserved by a self-perpetuating community like a nunnery, a
monastery or a royal court. It was susceptible to deliberate manipu-
lation, if not falsification. Even under favourable conditions, it could
fragment and disintegrate in less than a hundred years. Bede, however much he strove to write history according to truth as he saw it,
was very much at the mercy of oral tradition. To question Bede's
reliability, in some circles of Anglo-Saxon scholarship, seems tanta-
mount almost to sacrilege. A distinguished historian has recently commented on Bede's account of the conversion of the Northumbrians by
Paulinus in the reign of King Edwin (617-34),[11] though significantly
without reference at all to the British claim that Edwin was baptized
by a British missionary, Rhun map Urbgen:[12] he has argued that any
attempt to adjust Bede's narrative so that apparent difficulties can be
overcome is to impugn the veracity of Bede by supposing that 'he was
ill-informed about what was for him perhaps the most important

single event in the history of his own Northumbria'.[13] But that Bede could be 'ill-informed', regrettable though it may seem to many, is the conclusion to which we are inexorably drawn. No matter how much the details of the mission of Paulinus mattered to Bede, no matter how passionately he cared, he could only reconstruct the history of that mission from the materials available, imperfectly transcribed letters of Pope Boniface V and defective dynastic tradition. Boniface's letters were so transcribed that the name of a king in Kent, understood by Bede to have been Eadbald and so generally understood, could be variously rendered as *Adulualdi* (which is not the name Eadbald) or *Audubaldi* (which is close but remarkably archaic):[14] nor were the letters adequately dated. Furthermore, already by 714 at the latest, oral tradition about Edwin was assuming different forms, stories were being narrated differently and there was even a suspicion that some might lack authenticity.[15] Bede could not correct or even check oral tradition except in certain, probably rare, instances when he might have had more than one source of informationtion or even known some details personally. For example, he would remember Wilfrid. He had known Wilfrid. But he would probably not have been able to provide, unaided, a detailed account of Wilfrid's career. The main body of tradition about Wilfrid was obviously preserved only at Wilfrid's major foundations of Ripon and Hexham. Eddius was urged to write his *Life of Wilfrid* by Acca, bishop of Hexham and former companion of Wilfrid, and Tatberht, Wilfrid's kinsman and abbot of Ripon.[16] Not long before his death, as they were riding along together one day, Wilfrid gave Tatberht a full account of his life.[17] But who was to say that Wilfrid correctly remembered all that had happened or told the truth about it, or that Tatberht accurately reported what Wilfrid had said? Our knowledge of what happened in England in the seventh century or in Northumbria in the time of Wilfrid is by no means as secure as we might at first imagine.[18] Wilfrid was seventy-five years old when he died in 709, a great age when approximately 90 per cent of the population was dead by the age of fifty. He was born in 634 in the kingdom of the Northumbrians. Northumbria was originally two kingdoms, in 634 recently and imperfectly fused into one: Deira to the south of the Tees and Bernicia to the north.[19] The year 634 was a catastrophic one

for the Northumbrians. In that year King Edwin, from the royal
house of Deira, was slain in battle by the pagan Mercians under King
Penda in alliance with the North Welsh led by Cadwallon, king of
Gwynedd. On the death of Edwin, Paulinus, bishop of York, returned
to Kent, taking with him Edwin's Kentish queen and her surviving
children. For a year apostate kings ruled in Northumbria. In 635
Oswald, of the royal house of Bernicia, raised his Christian cross at
Heavenfield, and at Hallington near Hadrian's Wall defeated Cadwallon in battle and slew him in flight at *Denisesburn*, a tributary of
Rowley-water,[20] not all that far from the Roman ruins at *Hagustald*
or Hexham.[21] By this victory, Oswald was able to make himself
master of all Northumbria. He invited missionaries from among the
Scots, with whom he had been in exile, to reconvert the Northumbrians: and so it was that Aidan came from Iona, the great church of
St Columba in Scottish Dál Riata, to establish his episcopal see on the
island of Lindisfarne (Holy Island) near the Bernician royal stronghold of Bamburgh. For Bede, Aidan seemed the personification of all
Christian virtues. He admired him greatly. From this time on, until
the synod of Whitby, the evangelization of Northumbria was con-
ducted by Scottish missionaries whose influence spread south even into
Mercia and Essex. Oswald was slain in battle at Old Oswestry in 643
by Penda, probably in alliance with the Welsh, and for a time Oswald's
brother and successor, Oswiu, was very much on the defensive. At
first he failed to control all Northumbria and it was not until he over-
threw Penda at the battle of the river *Winwæd*, near Leeds, in 656
that he emerged as the powerful ruler of a united kingdom. Edwin,
Oswald and Oswiu are numbered by Bede,[22] among the seven kings
who controlled England south of the Humber and in the *Anglo-
Saxon Chronicle* each of these kings is described as *bretwalda* 'ruler
of Britain'.[23] *Bretwaldas* were clearly powerful military overlords. It
is usually thought that they established themselves by brute force. A
recent attempt to demonstrate that a *bretwalda* was recognized as
commander-in-chief by the agreement of his contemporary rulers has
challenged a number of assumptions normally taken for granted but
may not, in view of what could be regarded as a rather strained interpretation of the evidence, often *ex silentio*, receive unqualified acceptance.[24] Following his victory at the *Winwæd*, Oswiu was for a time

master of southern England, but it was northwards that he directed
the main forces of his arms. He marched against the Picts and sub-
jected very many of them to his overlordship. His son and successor,
Ecgfrith (671-85) defeated a Pictish revolt *c.* 672 and seems to have
secured recognition of his imperium even from the Scots of Dál Riata
and the Britons of Strathclyde: but in 685 he was slain in battle at
Nechtanesmere (Dunnichen) in Pictland, and from that time, according to Bede, the hopes and strength of the Northumbrians began to
'ebb and fall away'.[25]

In the meantime, Wilfrid had studied as a youth on Lindisfarne
from 648 for a year or two in the lifetime of Aidan. But when he
resolved to look instead to Rome and St Peter for spiritual guidance,
particularly on differing points of observance, he found much in the
magnificence of the Merovingian episcopate and in the splendour of
the papal court that was far more congenial to his proud nature. By
the 660s in Northumbria the differences in observances between the
Scottish missionaries and the representatives of the Roman Church
were becoming increasingly apparent. The crucial issue, as contemporaries saw it, was the question of the validity of Holy Orders in the
Celtic Church where there were no metropolitans and episcopal con-
secrations were not according to the canonical rites of the Roman
Church, thereby calling into question the validity of the sacraments.
In public discussions, however, at least as represented by Bede, it was
the differences over the dating of Easter, the greatest festival in the
Christian year, which brought matters to a head. The community of
Lindisfarne under the successors of Aidan, retained a more ancient
method of dating Easter which the Church of Rome had now abandoned. As a party favouring the new Roman dating consolidated in
Deira around Oswiu's queen, Eanflæd (who was Edwin's daughter)
(see Pedigree I, page 18) and the king's son (possibly by a former
marriage to Riemmelth, grand-daughter of Rhun map Urbgen), Alchfrith, joined by Wilfrid on his return from Rome, the division became critical. In 665 the Easter of the Scottish missionaries and the
now official Roman reckoning would diverge quite dramatically.[26] In
664, therefore, at a council at Whitby, where Wilfrid argued vigor-
ously on behalf of Rome's position, King Oswiu pronounced in favour
of the Roman calculation.[27] The consequences of this decision were

far-reaching, perhaps more far-reaching than Oswiu anticipated. Not only did it result in the departure of the Scottish clergy who would not conform (together with some Saxons), but the unexpected death of Tuda, a Scot prepared to accept the new ruling and intended by Oswiu as an ideal choice to be bishop of Lindisfarne, left the way open for Alchfrith to have the zealot, Wilfrid, quickly consecrated in Gaul as bishop of York. Lindisfarne temporarily ceased to be a bishopric, and those Scottish missionaries who did continue to wander over England now had no centralized direction. From 669 when he was confirmed in his office as bishop of York by Theodore of Tarsus, archbishop of Canterbury, Wilfrid, with his own great monastic foundations at Ripon and Hexham, dominated the Northumbrian Church until he quarrelled with King Ecgfrith in 678. At this point he was driven out of Northumbria and his immense diocese partitioned: and though he travelled many times to Rome to appeal against his eviction and carried on a substantial campaign for the vindication of his rights, Wilfrid never recovered sole mastery of the Northumbrian Church. In his last years he lived unobtrusively at Ripon and Hexham. The fall of Wilfrid in 678 paved the way for the creation of smaller dioceses in Northumbria under the direction of Archbishop Theodore at Hexham and in Lindsey (Lincolnshire). Eata, bishop of Hexham, had been one of the first pupils of Aidan and subsequently abbot of Lindisfarne, and he represented the dominant party of moderate ecclesiastics within the Northumbrian Church. In 681 there was further reorganization. Lindisfarne and Ripon emerged as separate sees, and Abercorn was founded on the Firth of Forth for the Picts. Lindsey, Ripon and Abercorn were shortlived, but Lindisfarne and Hexham survived as episcopal sees until the coming of the Vikings in the ninth century. Lindisfarne was administered for a brief period after 685 by Cuthbert. John of Beverley, educated at the Scottish foundation at Whitby, was bishop of Hexham from 687 to 704 when he was appointed to York. On the death of Wilfrid in 709, his devoted companion, Acca, succeeded as bishop of Hexham.[28]

These outlines of Northumbrian history during Wilfrid's lifetime are fairly familiar. Perhaps this is now an appropriate moment to attempt to look deeper, if possible, beneath the surface of recorded events and to sound more accurately the veracity of our picture of these years which is so essentially Bede's picture. Against Bede's tapestry of events, Eddius' *Life of Wilfrid* tends to make Wilfrid appear as a political and ecclesiastical trouble-maker who shattered the calm of the Church in Northumbria in the seventh century. He was unable to come to a lasting peace with Ecgfrith's half-brother and successor, Aldfrith (685-704), and on Aldfrith's death Wilfrid alienated his successor, Eadwulf. This episode is particularly interesting. Aldfrith left only an eight-year-old son, Osred, and it must have seemed very unlikely indeed that he would succeed to the kingship. Only Eddius mentions Eadwulf, and nothing is known about his antecedents but it seems probable that he was a scion of the royal house of Bernicia. His son was with Wilfrid at Ripon and Wilfrid was obviously disposed to support Eadwulf, but for some reason Eadwulf rebuffed him and threatened the bishop's life if he had not departed from the kingdom in six days. We must take cautiously the implication by Eddius that it was solely Eadwulf's failure to conciliate Wilfrid which led to the expulsion of Eadwulf after two months and to the victory of a party fighting on behalf of the young Osred: but Wilfrid obviously joined the conspiracy against Eadwulf and played a significant enough role to emerge not only in possession of Ripon and Hexham but also with King Osred as his adopted son. In this dynastic dispute, Wilfrid was certainly not politically negligible, and it is difficult to see why Eadwulf did not accept his offer of an alliance and why Wilfrid was in a position to be of such apparent value to his former enemies. What the account of these events does reveal is a Wilfrid deeply involved in Northumbrian dynastic and political affairs even towards the end of his life.[29] In his younger days, he must have been extremely formidable. The poor wretched woman who tried to conceal her first-born seven-year-old son, promised to Wilfrid as an infant when Wilfrid appeared to have brought the child back to life, by hiding him among Britons can have had no idea of the power she was hoping in vain to resist.[30] Here was a bishop who was, in the words of his biographer, second to none in largesse,[31] and whose retinue of armed followers was considered by Iurminburh, the queen of King Ecgfrith, to be the equal of a king's.[32] As F. M. Stenton commented, 'He combined the passion of an evangelist with a natural power of leadership, and he could move among the rulers of his day as one of their kind.'[33] Indeed, in addition to southern English and continental rulers he had met in the course of his travels, when Wilfrid died in 709 he had lived through the reigns (not counting Edwin) of five important Northumbrian kings, two Deiran rulers, and the brief reign of Eadwulf, and he was now on familiar terms with King Osred. While bishop of York, at the request of Frankish envoys, he had had the Merovingian prince, Dagobert (subsequently Dagobert II (676-9)), brought back from Ireland through Northumbria and despatched to Gaul: and when Wilfrid was later held to account in Gaul for Dagobert's alleged misdeeds he declared that he had raised up Dagobert not to do harm but to be a Christian ruler.[34] This was Wilfrid the king-maker, in no way a subservient tool of princes. And it is his regal disposition which appears to separate Wilfrid off from the majority of his ecclesiastical contemporaries who apparently kept out of politics and seemingly accommodated themselves so well and so obligingly to the secular royal world. To some extent, of course, Bede's narrative is deceptive. If we look at particular episodes, it is clear that there were recurring crises, and that Wilfrid was not alone in his conflict with secular authority.

In the first place, it was essential for the successful bishop to establish a *modus vivendi* with his king. There can be little doubt that Aidan must have reacted to the assassination of Oswine, king of Deira and a member of the royal family of Edwin, by Oswiu in 652 for Aidan had apparently favoured Oswine and had anticipated his death.[35] Rather interestingly, Cedd, one of Aidan's disciples from Lindisfarne and a missionary first to the Middle Angles and then to the East Saxons, was closely associated with Œthelwald, son of King Oswald, who established himself in Deira on the murder of Oswine: Cedd must have been at least in indirect contact with the Mercians through Peada, son of Penda, ruler of the Middle Angles, and Œthelwald joined forces with King Penda in the great attack on Oswiu which resulted in the Mercian defeat at the *Winwæd* in 656.[36] Cedd, we know, was, like Wilfrid, quite a terrifying figure. He did not hesitate to rebuke Sigeberht, king of the East Saxons, so severely for visiting the house of an excommunicated thegn (or nobleman) that Sigeberht flung himself at Cedd's feet to beg for mercy. Prodding the prostrate body of the king with his pastoral staff, Cedd pronounced words of dire foreboding and stalked away. It came as no surprise to many that Sigeberht was subsequently assassinated in the same house as Cedd had allegedly prophesied he would be.[37] These 'Celtic' saints, monks either Celtic by birth or trained by the Scots, could evidently be forbidding and intractable, and it is difficult to resist the suspicion that Cedd, who also acted as interpreter at the synod of Whitby, was deeply involved in the political events around him. In his relations with King Sigeberht he affords an excellent example of a prelate who emerged as too powerful a figure. The kings could not afford to be so dominated and most of them took great care not to be. Aidan must have trod an uneasy tight-rope between Oswine and Oswiu in the period which culminated in Oswine's assassination. Shortly before 664 a king in Wessex, Cœnwalh, expelled his bishop, Agilberht, and Oswiu himself did not hesitate to break the influence of the Scottish community at the synod of Whitby. Ecgfrith did not shrink from ejecting Wilfrid in 678. At about this time Wulfhere, king of Mercia, son and successor of Penda, drove out his bishop, Winfrith of Lich-field, and Winfrith's appeals to Rome were even less successful than Wilfrid's.[38] Tunberht, bishop of Hexham (681-5), was deposed for disobedience and it is probable that he had offended Ecgfrith.[39] Those bishops who came into office after 678 were those who, with the pre-sumable exception of Tunberht, were prepared to co-operate with Ecgfrith. As before under Aidan, on the whole a period of harmony was established between kings and Church. Apart from the continu-ing nuisance of Wilfrid, so stable was the situation under Aldfrith (685-704) that F. M. Stenton could observe of Aldfrith

'He was undoubtedly one of the most learned men in his own king-dom, and it is probable that his influence on the development of Northumbrian learning was much greater than appears on the surface of history. He is the most interesting member of the remark-able dynasty to which he belonged, and he stands beside Alfred of Wessex among the few Old English kings who combined skill in warfare with desire for knowledge.'[40]

But again, it is necessary to remind ourselves of the darker side of kingship in the early Middle Ages and in Northumbria in the time of Wilfrid. The Merovingian king, Chilperic, father of Chlotar II, composed hymns but he was still a ruthless murderer. Everything we know from the continent and of the Franks in particular (though on the continent they by no means possessed a monopoly of violence) indicates that the actual process of conversion to Christianity imposed a tremendous psychological strain on kings and folk alike, but perhaps particularly on the kings who had to lead the folk in peace and war. Not only did they have to adjust, and encourage their people to adjust also, to the strange new world of Christian ritual in the Church[41] but they had to break as much as possible with a pagan past and long-established traditions rooted in the mists of antiquity: in fact it is clear that the break was neither quickly nor completely made during the period of the Conversion.[42] Pagan thought and pagan magic in a Christian guise underlies many of the 'miracles' of the saints. By the late sixth century the Church had the measure of the strength of Germanic paganism and there was an awareness that progress would be slow and concessions would have to be made. The kings had to reconcile the traditional heroic ideals of the warband and the pursuit of the blood-feud between rival kindreds with Christian morality, which was virtually impossible. Sigeberht, king of the East Saxons, is said to have been slain by his own kinsmen because he was too apt to forgive his enemies.[43] It did not do for a king to take the Gospel teaching on forgiveness too literally. Not that the Church demanded obedience to a pacific religion. It went some way towards making Christianity a viable proposition for pagan Germanic kings. Pope Gregory I, who sent the Augustinian mission to Kent, also recommended the use of warfare as a means of spreading the faith 'so that the precept to forgive one's foes is conspicuous only by its absence from OE literature'.[44] When the Church adopted this attitude to warfare, it made Christianity relevant to the pagan rulers by claiming that, through Christ, a king could expect greater victories and a posthumous fame more glorious than that of his ancestors:[45] and so linked itself to the forces of death and destruction. A Christian king expected that he would conquer. He expected that he would rule successfully and be celebrated by his descendants. He even expected that his heirs would inherit his kingdom and glory. As Bede observes, it was only fitting that a great predecessor should have a worthy kinsman to inherit his religion and his kingdom.[46] The Church undoubtedly disapproved of the blood-feud by which rival kindreds could harass and slay each other across the generations,[47] but the blood-feud, which could be incurred by slaying an enemy on the battlefield or simply by defending one's lord, was inextricably linked to the warfare of the age and on this issue too the Church had frequently to compromise. The Church might seek to associate in the Anglo-Saxon mind the more commendable virtues of the heroic warband, the retinue or *comitatus* of a king, by representing Christ in terms of the leader of a *comitatus* to encourage a close personal bond and a warmth of feeling between the individual and the Christian God as his lord,[48] but the *comitatus* might sometimes turn on its lord, even the king, and the warband was so much a part of a savage world that it is not surprising that the beasts of the battlefield, the raven and the grey wolf, creatures of Woden, figure prominently in heroic verse. The missionary Church in England, therefore, was not faced with an easy task, as is frequently implied,[49] in converting the Anglo-Saxons. Rather it was confronted with the constant necessity to compromise. Pope Gregory I urged a policy of moderation and in a famous letter to Augustine at Canterbury suggested that pagan shrines or temples be converted into churches and that animals, previously brought for sacrifice there, should still be brought but slain only to provide food for those assembled.[50] Aidan realized that he was going to a barbaric people and that the moral precepts of Christianity could only be slowly propagated.[51] If we are to accept Bede's idyllic picture of Aidan co-operating effectively and peacefully with the Northumbrian kings, we must conclude either that these kings never offended against the Church's teaching in any way, unlike their Merovingian counterparts, or that Aidan was able to live with them on their own terms. There is an initial difficulty of source material. By the time Bede was writing, traditions about Aidan on Lindisfarne had been obscured by the subsequent cult of Cuthbert, and Bede found it difficult to discover anything directly about Aidan. The stories he does recount in which Aidan figures were derived from royal families, the royal families of Oswald and Oswiu in Bernicia and of Oswine in Deira. Their primary purpose was to represent the Northumbrian kings as saints. Aidan was a figure of only secondary importance in them. Bede used this material, however, to serve a purpose for which it was not originally devised, to fill in the gaps in his account of Aidan.[52] These stories throw little light on Aidan's real attitude to the kings with whom he dealt. He clearly sensed the latent treachery of Oswiu to Oswine. Even King Oswald left much to be desired. Bede might charm his readers with a description of how Oswald acted as interpreter for Aidan at the royal court or how he ordered a large silver dish to be broken up and given to the poor,[53] but Oswald was also aggressive enough to make himself *bretwalda*, and he was hated by the men of Lindsey as an alien conqueror.[54] Bede does claim that neither respect nor fear made Aidan keep silent about the sins of the rich,[55] but there is reason to suppose he allowed Oswald considerable latitude. There was probably much in Oswald that was still very pagan. It has recently been suggested that his manner of praying with the palms of his hands turned upwards on his knees[56] indicates 'a ritual attitude perhaps used by his pagan predecessors in offering intercession for the folk, particularly in view of the hand and the knee as sacral objects associated with fertility'.[57] As a consequence of the care of his family, or the benevolence of a church, well-disposed perhaps as a result of generous donations, any king, however apparent his personal shortcomings in life, could be cultivated posthumously as a saint. Cenwulf, king of Mercia (796-821), a man of violence so far as can be seen, prepared to hound for the last five years of his reign, even if for reasons he considered justifiable, Wulfred, archbishop of Canterbury,[58] was still venerated as a saint, probably primarily at the monastery of Winchcombe with which he was closely associated.[59] From Northumbria we have the case of King Osred (704-16), the son of Aldfrith. John of Beverley, bishop first of Hexham (688-704) and then of York (704-14), apparently enjoyed such good relations with Osred that the king was later remembered at Beverley as a religious man.[60] But St Boniface, writing from the continental mission field in 746-7, regarded Osred of Northumbria and Ceolred of Mercia as steeped in sin, in debauchery and adultery with nuns, and viewed Osred's assassination as the just judgement of God: he declared that Osred was driven by the spirit of wantonness and fornication in the nunneries of virgins consecrated to God,[61] a view corroborated by Æthelwulf, a monk in a dependent cell of Lindisfarne, writing between 803 and 821, who states that Osred knew not how to subdue wanton senses and did not

fittingly worship Christ.[62] Bede says nothing of Osred's vices, recording only that he was killed.[63] This is a useful indication of the way in
which Bede could exclude or suppress details. The point is not that
these details were irrelevant to Bede's narrative but that they are now
relevant to the historian of this period. It should never be assumed
that Bede tells the whole story even if he knew it. It is unlikely that
Osred was the first Northumbrian king to have undesirable tend-
encies. His father, Aldfrith, was illegitimate. Just as Boniface saw the
death of Aldfrith in Northumbria in 704 as the beginning of evil, so
later Alcuin saw the death of Ælfwold, king of Northumbria, in 788
as the beginning of evil. But really such men were speaking of what
appeared to be a deterioration from the days of their youth. Distance
in time lent enchantment, as it did to Bede. In reality there never was
any 'beginning'. The good and the bad had always co-existed and
always would. Only rarely, however, and then generally from a safe
distance, were kings denounced for evil ways by leading churchmen.
As William of Malmesbury in the early twelfth century remarked, to
relate the crimes of contemporaries is attended with danger, as a consequence of which the historian ignores any disgraceful transaction,
however obvious, through timidity, and for the sake of approval
feigns good qualities where there are none.[64] One way or another,
John of Beverley must have brought himself to tolerate King Osred's
licentious disposition. Other prelates surely behaved similarly on
other occasions. They had little choice if they were concerned at all
for the well-being of their churches or monasteries, for in the final
analysis, except in rare instances of weak kings, the king possessed the
greater power. King Ecgfrith had been able to imprison Wilfrid,[65]
apparently even to plan his death,[66] while King Aldfrith not only
threatened him with an army but planned to deprive him of every
single possession in Northumbria,[67] and all Wilfrid's clergy and
abbots found themselves ostracized by Church and society.[68] It is
not surprising that Wilfrid was prepared to associate closely with
Ceolred, king of Mercia (704-16),[69] whom Boniface condemned equally
with Osred of Northumbria for the immorality of his life, in order to
safeguard his possessions in Mercia, or that in his final bequests Wilfrid gave a substantial part of his treasure to the abbots of Ripon and

Hexham so that they might possess something with which to secure the favour of kings and bishops.[70]

Secondly, it was essential for a successful bishop to align himself effectively with the dominant family in the royal kindred. Perhaps one driving force was uppermost in the minds of these early kings in the domestic affairs of their kingdoms, and that was to keep control of the royal succession within their own family. Much of the internal history of the Anglo-Saxon kingdoms, therefore, and Northumbria is an excellent example, revolved around dynastic power-politics. This helps to explain much of Merovingian history, where the division of the kingdom among all the sons of the deceased king encouraged brother to slay brother or nephews. In Anglo-Saxon England, as in the Celtic lands, the royal succession did not normally pass from father to son but from brother to brother, cousin to cousin, by collateral right within the prescribed generations of the royal kindred, which, so far as we can see, numbered seven among the Anglo-Saxons. For princes as much as seventh in descent from a royal ancester to possess a claim on the kingship meant that there was at any one time a profusion of collateral lines in competition with each other. What happened was that one of the more powerful families within the kindred would attempt to frustrate the ambitions of other collaterals either by intimidation or assassination. Wessex, in the eighth century, particularly between 721 and 756, seems to have witnessed a veritable purge of collateral princes. Mercia under Offa (757-96) witnessed a similar phenomenon, when Offa strove to guarantee the succession for his son, Ecgfrith. The ecclesiastical leaders accepted dynastic blood-letting as an inevitable aspect of the political scene, and for the historian to recognize it also is to make much more sense of the seemingly random and bizarre violence of events in this period. Wilfrid could enjoy harmonious relations with Cædwalla, king of the West Saxons (685-8), who not only suppressed rival lines in Wessex,[71] but set out deliberately to exterminate the royal family of Wight: and one quarter of the island he then gave to Wilfrid.[72]

In Northumbria, the seventh century and early eighth is characterized by the dominance of one branch of the royal kindred. It was Æthelfrith (593-617), great-grandson of Ida, founder of the kingdom of Bernicia, who united Bernicia and Deira to form the kingdom of

PEDIGREE I : the immediate family of King Oswiu

K = King

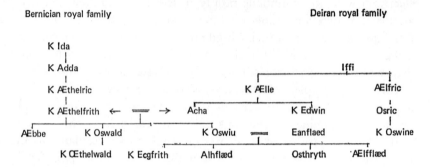

Bernician royal family

Deiran royal family

Other family of Oswiu not by Eanflaed.

the Northumbrians. It is possible that his father, Æthelric, had slain Ælle, king of Deira, the father of Edwin,[73] and in battle Edwin subsequently slew Æthelfrith who had been hounding him. But power was not destined to remain in the hands of the Deiran royal family. Following Edwin's death in battle in 634, Oswald, son of Æthelfrith, eventually mastered Northumbria. This Bernician family was determined to exclude the rival Deiran princes. Oswald was actually Edwin's nephew because Æthelfrith had taken as his second wife, Acha, daughter of Ælle[74] (cf., Pedigree I, above), perhaps in an attempt to provide his own family with a claim to Deira or to alleviate the tension,[75] and Oswald and Oswiu were sons of this marriage. Yet Bede makes it clear, probably unintentionally, that Oswald would have killed Edwin's young son (his own cousin, therefore) and the infant son of Osfrith, an older son of Edwin by a previous marriage (but again still a cousin of Oswald) had he caught them.[76] This touch of Merovingian harshness in the reputedly saintly Oswald would account for his political success. Oswiu attempted a further marriage alliance by taking Edwin's daughter, Eanflæd, as his bride,[77] but when he attacked and treacherously slew Oswine of Deira in 652, Oswiu too was removing a rival kinsman, for Oswine, as the son of a cousin of Edwin's,[78] would also be bound to him by kindred ties. Eanflæd was a strong enough personality to prevail upon her husband (and cousin) to found a monastery in expiation at Gilling in Yorkshire, where Oswine was slain; and the first abbot, Trumhere, was also a kinsman of Oswine.[79] But not every victim of dynastic in-fighting was so commemorated. Apart from suppressing the Deiran royal family—to which it had linked itself by marriage ties, the descendants of Æthelfrith needed to contain potential dynastic rivals from within their own Bernician royal kindred, the collateral ramifications of which must have been multiple. The prolonged domination of this single family in Northumbria is really quite amazing. Oswald and Oswiu clearly intended to keep the kingship in their own immediate family circle, and it is possible that Oswald even intended to exclude Oswiu. It seems likely, from the rebellious actions of Œthelwald, son of Oswald, that Oswald planned that his son should succeed him;[80] but Oswiu, though he could not exclude Œthelwald altogether, at least held on to Bernicia. The fact, however, that he failed to secure Deira immediately by the murder of Oswine and that Œthelwald helped to place him at great risk at the battle of the *Winwæd*, must have made Oswiu more sensitive than ever to matters of dynastic policy. On Oswiu's death in 671, the succession seems to have passed peacefully to his son, Ecgfrith, but concern for what would happen on the death of Ecgfrith, who had no sons, and the determination of this family to retain the kingship, is revealed by the question put to Cuthbert, shortly before he became bishop of Lindisfarne, by Ælfflæd, abbess of Whitby, the daughter of Oswiu and Eanflæd, concerning who would succeed her brother.[81] Cuthbert's answer reveals him as deeply committed to this family. It is salutary to note the political, dynastic alignment of even this apparently eremitical figure. Cuthbert was far more than the recluse of hagiographical tradition.[82] He reminded Abbess Ælfflæd of the existence of Aldfrith, illegitimate son of King Oswiu by Fína, princess of the great Irish royal family of the (Northern) Uí Néill, a son at that time resident among the islands of Britain.[83] Though descent from the Uí Néill was perhaps impressive, there must have been many legitimate sons of other male collateral lines who could have succeeded. The prestige of Oswiu's family, or else its capacity for intimidation, must have been very considerable for Aldfrith to return and rule, so far as we can see, in domestic peace. There was a second and more serious crisis, however, looming over Aldfrith and his half-sister, Abbess Ælfflæd, for Aldfrith fell fatally ill while his sons were still only children. This time there was a rival claimant, Eadwulf, determined to make himself king. It is most unfortunate that we do not know his relationship to the family of Oswiu. Perhaps (and this is conjectural) he was descended from Œthelwald. Again, that Ælfflæd's party, with which Wilfrid came to associate himself, should have succeeded in 704-5 in securing the kingship for the eight-year-old Osred, son of Aldfrith, in the face of Eadwulf's opposition is the measure of their incredible power. But under Osred, the tide turned. Osred was quite aware of the perils of the situation. When he was slain in 716,[84] he was only about twenty years old. He would have had to have held on with determination to survive long enough to have a son of an age to succeed unchallenged: and there is evidence that the situation was becoming critical. Osred, we are told, did not honour his nobles, but destroyed many by a pitiable death and compelled others to receive the tonsure, that is to enter a monastery.[85] It is highly likely that these nobles were in many cases at least royal kinsmen. Those who were banished to a monastery were fortunate. The accession of Cœnred (716-18), a representative of a hitherto obscure line of Bernician aristocrats but a descendant in the ultimate seventh generation of Ida and therefore a collateral, set the pattern for the whole of the eighth century (see Pedigree II, page 21). The monopoly of royal power by the descendants of Æthelfrith had at last been broken. Osric (718-29) may have restored authority temporarily to the old line, but he nominated Ceolwulf, brother of Cœnred, as his successor.[86] Ceolwulf (729-37) experienced a turbulent reign, according to Bede.[87] It must have been extremely galling for Ceolwulf, to whom the *Ecclesiastical History* was dedicated, to have to read so much laudatory material about previous Northumbrian kings who belonged to a different branch of the royal kindred and whom he probably heartily detested. Yet the man who succeeded Ceolwulf when Ceolwulf abdicated and entered the monastery of Lindisfarne in 737 was his own cousin, Eadberht (737-58). Ceolwulf had previously been deposed and tonsured in 731 but had regained the kingship: the second time, presumably, he thought it wiser to enter a monastery voluntarily. Eadberht appears to have embarked on a purge of collaterals, but half a century of fierce

PEDIGREE II : the principal known collaterals of the Bernician royal family

K = King

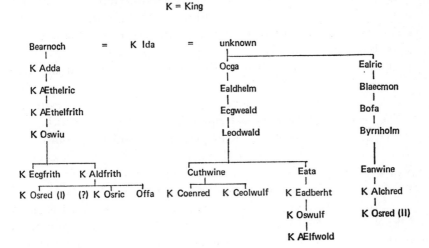

internecine strife followed among surviving rival branches. This period of in-fighting was all the more savage because so many collateral lines were now implacably resolved to secure the kingship. The prolonged dominance in the seventh century of the house of Æthelfrith had meant that the collateral lines had become very distended, and by the eighth century most of them were nearing the critical seventh generation.

It must have been, therefore, a highly pressurized situation which Oswald, Oswiu, Ecgfrith and Aldfrith had managed to keep under control. The methods they used are largely hidden from us but the very fact that they succeeded for so long makes it certain that these contemporaries of St Wilfrid were no less unscrupulous than their eighth-century successors. The involvement of women in the politics of the period confirms this. Abbess Ælfflæd, who was obviously a decisive force in the succession first of Aldfrith and then of Osred is a case in point. She is unusual in the sense that, although a princess, she had from infancy been consecrated to Christ 'in perpetual virginity' as Bede puts it[88] in the double-monastery at Whitby. She had always been a nun. Many queens took the veil on the death of their husbands, rising quickly to the rank of abbess. Oswiu's queen, Eanflæd, entered the monastery at Whitby on Oswiu's death. Oswald's queen, whose name apparently was Cyneburh, similarly entered a nunnery or monastery. But it should not be thought that they necessarily did so willingly and their subsequent political power was possibly less than Ælfflæd's. Cyneburh is said to have been virtually compelled to take the veil by Osthryth, King Oswiu's daughter (see Pedigree I, page 18).[89] What is striking is that it was considered a desirable expedient to remove the ex-queen in this way. Northumbrian royal ladies could be extremely formidable. Iurminburh, Ecgfrith's queen, played a prominent part in securing the expulsion of Wilfrid from Northumbria, and her influence reached even as far as Wessex where her sister was queen, while Wilfrid could find at first no security in Mercia because Osthryth, Ecgfrith's sister, was married to Æthelred, king of Mercia.[90] Peada, son of Penda, who became a Christian in order to marry Alhflæd, another of Oswiu's daughters, in the period just before the battle of the *Winwæd*, was murdered—foully, Bede goes so far as to say—by the treachery, so it was alleged, of Alhflæd, actually at Easter in the year 657,[91] probably as part of Oswiu's attempt to control Mercia after Penda's death. Perhaps it was part of the working out of a blood-feud, deriving from this incident, which resulted in the murder in 697 of Queen Osthryth, Alhflæd's sister, wife of King Æthelred, in Mercia.[92] Bede gives no further details. It is as well to remember, however, that it was not only the Merovingians who murdered their queens. From the poverty of our information generally for Anglo-Saxon England in the seventh century, we cannot be sure that Osthryth was the only queen to perish violently. Again perhaps those who gained the security of a nunnery were the fortunate ones. This was the world in which Wilfrid lived and moved, a world in which the very air was alive not only with the powers of magic[93] but also with the sound of violence.[94]

Wilfrid, for his part, was an excellent example of how not to succeed in the political and ecclesiastical world of the seventh century when an accommodating and compromising disposition together with guile and a flair for skilful intrigue were prerequisites for professional or personal survival. It was only by great strength of character that Wilfrid weathered the vicissitudes of ill-fortune. A central character though he may appear in Eddius' *Life of Wilfrid*, after his fall from power in 678 the rulers of Northumbria probably regarded him as little more than a petty irritation despite his many appeals to Rome. It was not Wilfrid's appeals to Rome which made him relevant again to Northumbrian politics, for these appeals were treated with contempt. It was when Wilfrid intervened in a dynastic conflict in 704 that he assumed significance once more and this was because dynastic issues were at the very heart of political life in the several kingdoms of the Anglo-Saxon heptarchy. If we wish to understand the actions of kings in England at this time we must appreciate fully the immense importance of these dynastic issues: and we must realize also that the Northumbrian kings, whatever the posthumous reputation for personal sanctity of individual rulers, were of necessity violent and vicious men.

It is apparent that Wilfrid was only at his monasteries of Ripon and Hexham for a relatively short period of his life, mainly in his early years and then again in his last years. The whole community at Hexham did not follow its master into exile, and regular monastic life, according to the rule of St Benedict, continued there during his long absences. But it could hardly help being caught up in Wilfrid's affairs. How the community reacted to the rule of Bishop Eata (678-81) or Bishop John (688-704) we do not know. Wilfrid regarded such men as usurpers.[95] Eata certainly tried to hand Hexham over to Cuthbert in 685, but Cuthbert preferred Lindisfarne and Eata returned to Hexham (685-6).[96] He was buried at Hexham and his relics were subsequently greatly venerated there. There was obviously trouble of some kind at Hexham under Bishop Tunberht (681-5), for Tunberht was deposed. Tunberht was a former abbot of Gilling and a friend of Wilfrid,[97] and this alone must have been sufficient to compromise his standing in the eyes of King Ecgfrith. It should not be inferred from this connection between Wilfrid and Tunberht that Wilfrid's dynastic alignment was with Oswine and the Deirans. Hild, first abbess of Whitby, a kinswoman of King Edwin, was among Wilfrid's earliest opponents.[98] It was Alchfrith, son of Oswiu, who was responsible for the advancement of Wilfrid's career, and in the end it was Ælfflæd, daughter of Oswiu, who eventually brought about a final settlement with Wilfrid. And yet it was also with this family, with King Ecgfrith and King Aldfrith, that Wilfrid was primarily at loggerheads. Where, it may be asked, did Wilfrid really stand in the Northumbrian dynastic politics of his day?

It may be that part at least of the answer is to be found in the interests of Acca, bishop of Hexham (709-32) and in those of the community at Hexham. There is no doubt that Acca felt very strongly about Wilfrid. He had been Wilfrid's chaplain in the last years of his life and a close companion, and he encouraged the writing of the *Life* by Eddius.[99] He extended and enriched Wilfrid's church at Hexham,[100] gathering relics of apostles and martyrs, collecting a library, instructing with the aid of a professional teacher the community at Hexham in church music, and expounding the catholic faith as a distinguished theologian.[101] Bede had the greatest admiration for Acca and to him, as his diocesan, Bede dedicated many of his own biblical commentaries, at times producing them specifically at the request of Acca.[102] Despite his commendable ecclesiastical ability, however, Acca was expelled from his see in 731 or 732, nor did he ever recover it for, though he lived until 740, a successor, Frithuberht, was consecrated in 734 or 735.[103] It is difficult to resist the conclusion that Acca's expulsion in some way and to some extent was connected with the attempted deposition of King Ceolwulf at the same time. Once again, a bishop of Hexham was involved in some kind of dynastic conflict. In view of Acca's connection with Bede and Bede's contact with the court of Ceolwulf, it seems almost certain that Acca was a loyal supporter of Ceolwulf and that he fell from power when the king did. On his restoration, Ceolwulf was probably still too insecure to reinstate his former sympathizers. It is not impossible that Acca was even related to Ceolwulf. The problem is whether it is this particular affiliation which sheds light on Wilfrid's personal predilection. The answer is probably not. With the accession of Cœnred, brother of

Ceolwulf, in 716, and then with that of Ceolwulf in 729, Northumbria was controlled by a new family and the situation was very different from what it had been in Wilfrid's day. Religious communities had to be flexible in their loyalties as royal families rose and fell. Ceolwulf, in fact was the last of his line. Eadberht, as his cousin, represented another collateral line, and this family managed to hold on to royal power for a time in the second half of the eighth century, with some success though with much difficulty ending in terrible disaster. Eadberht's son, Oswulf, reigned only for a year before he was slain, but Oswulf's son, Ælfwold, survived as king from 779 to 789. Ælfwold was probably no better or worse than any of his predecessors or successors, but he was assassinated by his own nephew on Hadrian's Wall, and his sons, Œlf and Œlfwine, were drowned by yet another dynastic rival, Æthelred, in 791. This was apparently the end of Eadberht's line. The community at Hexham, however, in 789, was not to know that this was virtually the end for this branch of the royal family. The body of Ælfwold was taken to Hexham by a great company of monks and with the chants of the clergy, and buried with honour in the church. A light from heaven was said to have been shining on the exact spot where Ælfwold had perished, and there the faithful in that district built a church.[104] A spontaneous cult of the saintly king seems to have generated at Hexham. This development reflects a new alignment with the family of Eadberht which is what is to be expected under the circumstances of the expulsion of Acca. Not every church in Northumbria was loyal to Eadberht's family, however: the church of Lindisfarne provoked the wrath of Eadberht by giving shelter to Offa, son of Aldfrith, in 750, and in 793 Ealdorman Sicga, who had slain King Ælfwold, was buried on Lindisfarne. The loyalties of the church at Lindisfarne obviously lay elsewhere than with the family of Eadberht. After 750, Lindisfarne probably supported yet another collateral line which produced King Alchred (765-74) (see Pedigree II, page 21) and probably the 'patrician' Osbald, who made an unsuccessful bid for the kingship in 796 and then fled to the Picts from Lindisfarne with some of the brethren. The loyalty of Hexham was probably valued, therefore, but with the eclipse of Eadberht's family it was no doubt necessary for Hexham to seek a new affiliation. It is interesting, therefore, to find Ripon giving aid and sustenance to Ealdorman Eardwulf in 790, carrying him to sanctuary with Gregorian chants (note the parallel with events at Hexham in 789), after the failure of an assassination attempt by King Æthelred.[105] In 796 Eardwulf, whose ancestry is unknown, became king of Northumbria. It seems not unreasonable to suppose that Ripon, and with Ripon the church of Hexham also, gave Eardwulf their support. Dynastic divisions in Northumbria, as, for example, between King Æthelred and King Rædwulf in the ninth century, or between King Osberht and King Ælla persisted until the capture of York by the Vikings in 866-7. It should not be assumed that every deposition or assassination represented the forces of irresponsibility, but the dynastic preoccupation was probably always constant. The ability to accommodate new regimes, to be flexible in loyalties, to adjust rapidly to the appearance of a new branch of the royal family, was clearly a prerequisite of success for the leader of a religious community in early England and in Northumbria in the eighth century. To be caught supporting a king whose position was insecure could be disastrous, as the case of Acca appears to demonstrate. It may be that one of the reasons for Wilfrid's uneasy career was that he did not prove flexible enough.

What Acca's interests do make possible is an important connection between Wilfrid and the cult of St Oswald. It is a feature worth noting that the whole of Ecgfrith's family was not united in its antagonism to Wilfrid in the 670s. When Wilfrid was a prisoner of Ecgfrith, it was Æbbe, abbess of Coldingham, Ecgfrith's aunt, who procured his release.[106] Why should Æbbe have been well disposed? She was Oswiu's sister, according to Eddius, but this would make her Oswald's sister too. It may be Oswald who provides the clue. Acca and the community at Hexham were devoted to the memory of Oswald. Acca told Bede two miracle stores about King Oswald, one narrated originally by the missionary, Willibrord, a former pupil of Wilfrid at Ripon,[107] and the other relating to an episode at Wilfrid's foundation at Selsey in Sussex.[108] The association, direct or indirect, with Wilfrid is striking. The head of Oswald was buried on Lindisfarne and his dismembered hands and arms at Bamburgh, but the church of Hexham by 731, when Bede wrote, had long made it their custom to go to Heavenfield, near Hexham, where Oswald had erected his cross before the conflict with Cadwallon in 635, on the vigil of St Oswald's Feast, that is the day before that on which he was killed, namely 4 August. On the actual day of his death they offered up holy sacrifice on Oswald's behalf, and, as Bede wrote, had lately built a church there so that the place had become still more sacred.[109] In view of the already established interest of Wilfrid and Acca in the miracles of Oswald, it seems a justifiable inference from the fact that this was a long established pilgrimage to Heavenfield to carry the observance back to Wilfrid's own time at Hexham. Nor was Oswald soon forgotten at Hexham. When a church was built on the site of King Ælfwold's assassination, it was dedicated to SS Cuthbert and Oswald.[110] The cult of Oswald was obviously deeply ingrained in the religious experience of Hexham. But it was perhaps more than a religious experience. Royal saintly cults implied dynastic pre-dispositions. Abbess Æbbe would have every reason to feel sympathy for a bishop so devoted to the cult of her brother, Oswald. She clearly felt less sympathy for Ecgfrith, son of her brother Oswiu, and Ecgfrith's queen, Iurminburh. It is not inconceivable that Wilfrid had met King Oswald as a child, for his father was on familiar terms with the king's companions.[111] In temperament at least, Wilfrid and Cedd were not unalike, and Cedd and his brother, Chad, to whom Wilfrid was remarkably well disposed,[112] were close confidants of Œthelwald, son of Oswald. Œthelwald disappears after the battle of the *Winwæd* in 656, and it is not known if Wilfrid ever met him, but what we also do not know is how long Œthelwald survived *Winwæd* or whether or not he had any children. Wilfrid's loyalties on his return from Rome certainly appear to have been first to Alchfrith, son of Oswiu, but Alchfrith ceases to be mentioned soon after the synod of Whitby. Bede states that Oswiu was attacked not only by Œthelwald but also by his own son, Alchfrith.[113] Alchfrith married a daughter of Penda.[114] He cannot have been a son of Oswiu by Eanflæd, for he was old enough to fight at the *Winwæd* and Oswiu and Eanflæd were not married until after 643: so he must have been either illegitimate (as Aldfrith was) or the son of the former marriage of Oswiu to Riemmelth, a British princess.[115] In either case, he might have felt that his chances of succession were prejudiced by Ecgfrith, son of Oswiu and Eanflæd. Alchfrith wished to go to Rome in 665,[116] but Oswiu refused permission, so that this experience was barred to him. Such a situation could well have culminated in rebellion in which Alchfrith perished. It was, after all, Alchfrith who had played a prominent part in the crisis which had resulted in the synod of Whitby. Again, we do not know if Alchfrith had any children. But the intense interest of Hexham in the cult of St Oswald suggests that, after Alchfrith had faded from the scene or had been violently removed, Wilfrid, perhaps as part of an intense reaction against Oswiu and Ecgfrith, committed himself more to Oswald's family. It is only by chance that we know anything of Œthelwald, son of Oswald, so that the possibility that there were either other brothers or descendants of Œthelwald cannot be dismissed. The Eadwulf, who appeared in 704, could have been one such descendant. Indeed, the connection between Wilfrid, the champion of the Roman Church, and Oswald, the patron of Aidan and the Scottish missionaries, is so peculiar that it seems most reasonable to explain the vitality of Oswald's cult at Hexham in terms of Wilfrid's support of otherwise unrecorded descendants of Oswald against the collateral line of Oswiu and Ecgfrith. This would explain the venom of Ecgfrith and Iurminburh towards Wilfrid and the continuing hostility of Aldfrith, together with Wilfrid's original plan to support Eadwulf instead of Osred, son of Aldfrith. Wilfrid was a powerful prelate, and if this reconstruction is correct, Ecgfrith and Iurminburh would have every reason to rid themselves of a political menace. The essentially dynastic nature of the politics of the period would set Wilfrid and his downfall in an appropriate and natural context. Furthermore, that no descendants of Oswald did emerge to vindicate their right to the kingship and the final rejection of Wilfrid by Eadwulf, a possible descendant, explains why Wilfrid remained for the rest of his life totally or partially in eclipse and barred from the effective or permanent resumption of high office. He evidently proved incapable of transferring his allegiances with the same agility subsequently displayed after his death by his own great monasteries of Hexham and Ripon: and this essentially was his undoing.[117]

To have good credit and standing with the king of the moment was the secret of success in Wilfrid's Northumbria. However imperfectly we can now perceive it, the ecclesiastical leaders of Northumbria in his time had their dynastic and political alignments. Subservience to the will of the ruler was vital but there was a necessity also for skilful intrigue. If this study has indicated a picture of unscrupulous kings and ecclesiastical politicians who were either obsequious or scheming or both, the emphasis is undeniably very different from Bede's. Bede, however, was not concerned with the fundamental realities of political and ecclesiastical power: it was his desire rather to describe and emphasize Christian virtues and the merits of faith and charity, not only in the past but even in 'the happy peace and serenity of the present'.[118] By 734, when he wrote to Ecgberht, bishop of York, he was growing increasingly disillusioned and maintained that the state of the Church in Northumbria had deteriorated since the death of King Aldfrith. He urged Ecgberht to safeguard the flock committed to his charge from the audacity of attacking wolves.[119] The historian has every reason to suspect that even before the death of Aldfrith, Christ's sheep had been intimidated, harassed and savaged by attacking wolves. Wilfrid affords a significant example in his own person. If not even the apparently other-worldly Cuthbert was uninvolved in the dynastic power-politics of his day, the really unusual feature of Wilfrid's life is not that he was involved in secular affairs but that he failed so conspicuously to manipulate his reactions to the force of circumstance. The monastic houses of Northumbria presented Bede with the idealized portraits of many men, of Oswald, Cedd and Cuthbert. The affection and loyalty of Eddius meant that he set Wilfrid in as favourable a light as possible. But Eddius also knew personally the difficulties and demands of life beyond the cloister. When we gaze deeper through the surface waters of Bede's *Ecclesiastical History* we find the scene darkens, currents swirl, and dimly we perceive in the black abyss of time the savage mien and baleful deeds of more fearsome beings.

Notes

[1] This translation is taken with the permission of the Clarendon Press, Oxford, from *The Fourth Book of the Chronicle of Fredegar*, ed. and transl. J. M. Wallace-Hadrill (Nelson's Medieval Texts, 1960), 35.

[2] *The History of the Franks By Gregory of Tours*, transl. O. M. Dalton, 2 vols (Oxford, 1927).

[3] For a study of Bede's knowledge and account of the Pictish Church, see D. P. Kirby, 'Bede and the Pictish Church', *Innes Review* xxiv (1973) 6-25. H. Mayr-

Harting, *The Coming of Christianity to Anglo-Saxon England* (London, 1972), discusses the period of the conversion, and Peter Hunter Blair provides a general survey of *The World of Bede* (Cambridge, 1970).

[4] *HE* I, 23.

[5] *HE* III, 5.

[6] T. D. Kendrick, *et al.*, *Evangeliorum quattuor Codex Lindisfarnensis*, 2 vols (Urs Graf Verlag: Olten Lausanne, 1960).

[7] R. L. S. Bruce-Mitford, 'The Art of the Codex Amiatinus', *Journal of the British Archæological Association* 32 (1969), 1-21.

[8] J. M. Wallace-Hadrill, 'Gregory of Tours and Bede: their views on the personal qualities of kings', *Frühmittelalterlich Studien* 2 (1968), 31-44 (p. 40).

[9] *ibid.*, 43: cf., more extensively, the same author's *Early Germanic Kingship in England and on the Continent* (Oxford, 1971).

[10] J. M. Wallace-Hadrill, *The Long-Haired Kings* (London, 1962), 147, 240.

[11] The chronology followed in this chapter is that proposed by D. P. Kirby, 'Bede and Northumbrian Chronology', *EHR* 78 (1963), 514-27.

[12] For one consideration of this problem and of Bede's whole account of Edwin, see N. K. Chadwick, The Conversion of Northumbria', *Celt and Saxon: Studies in the Early British Border*, ed. N. K. Chadwick (Cambridge, 1963), 138-66.

[13] Peter Hunter Blair, 'The letters of Pope Boniface V', *England before the Conquest: Studies in Primary Sources presented to Dorothy Whitelock*, ed. Peter Clemoes and Kathleen Hughes (Cambridge, 1971), 5-13 (p. 11).

[14] contrast *HE* II, 8 with II, 10 and 11.

[15] *The Earliest Life of Gregory the Great*, ed. and trans. Bertram Colgrave (Lawrence, 1968), 48, 98-9.

[16] Eddius, chapter LXV.

[17] Eddius, chapter LXV.

[18] For a more detailed treatment of the problems associated with the nature of oral tradition and Bede's narrative, see D. P. Kirby, 'Bede's Native Sources for the *Historia Ecclesiastica*', *Bulletin of the John Rylands Library* 48 (1966), 341-71.

[19] Peter Hunter Blair, 'The Origins of Northumbria', *AA* 25 (1947), 1-51, and 'The Boundary Between Bernicia and Deira', *ibid.*, 27 (1949), 46-59: cf., D. P. Kirby, 'Bede and Northumbrian Chronology', 523-7.

[20] Raine, I, xi-xiii.

[21] *ibid.*, x-xi, 8.

[22] *HE* II, 5.

[23] *ASC* A, *s.a.* 827 (recte 829).

[24] Hanna Vollrath-Reichelt, *Königsgedanke Und Königtum Bei Den Angelsachsen* (Köln, 1971). A crucial re-interpretation of Bede's reference to Rædwald as the fourth *bretwalda* (*HE* III, 5), for example (pp. 80-4), may not commend itself to all Latinists.

[25] *HE* IV, 26.

[26] C. W. Jones, *Bedæ Opera De Temporibus* (Massachusetts, 1943), 103.

[27] Eddius, chapter X: *HE* III, 25.

[28] On the bishops of Hexham, see Raine, I xxiii ff., C. E. Whiting, 'The Anglian Bishops of Hexham', *AA* 24 (1946), 119-66, and H. S. Offler, 'A Note on the Last Medieval Bishops of Hexham', *AA* 40 (1962), 163-9. E. John, in a paper, 'The Social and Political Problems of the Early English Church', *Agricultural History Review* 18 (1970) Supplement; *Land, Church, and People: Essays presented to Professor H. P. R. Finberg*, ed. Joan Thirsk, 39-63 (pp. 42 ff.) takes a different view of Tuda's election and the events immediately following the synod of Whitby, arguing that Oswiu intended Tuda to be bishop of York: but he does consider that Oswiu was eventually 'pretty well forced to accept Wilfrid' (p. 50). On the problem of the circumstances surrounding Wilfrid's election to York, cf. *infra*, pp. oo. Though Alchfrith seems to have been involved in some kind of unrest after the synod of Whitby, Mr

John's argument that he rebelled for a separate kingdom of Deira and that Wilfrid was involved (p. 50) seems tenuous. M. Gibbs, 'The Decrees of Agatho and the Gregorian plan for York' *Speculum* XLVIII (1973), 213-46, emphasises rather Wilfrid's preoccupation with the metropolitan dignity of York.

²⁹ Eddius, chapters LIX, LX.

³⁰ Eddius, chapter XVIII.

³¹ Eddius, chapter XXI.

³² Eddius, chapter XXIV: cf., the comment of Pope Agatho, chapter XXI (*infra*, p. 48).

³³ F. M. Stenton, *Anglo-Saxon England* (3rd ed., Oxford, 1971), 145.

³⁴ Eddius, chapters XXVIII, XXXIII.

³⁵ *HE* III, 14.

³⁶ *HE* III, 14, 23, 24.

³⁷ *HE* III, 22. This was too much for Bede who believed that Sigeberht genuinely wished only to forgive the thegn, according to Gospel precepts, a most charitable interpretation and Bede deserves credit for including this episode which he obviously found distasteful. He declared that the king's death, which resulted from his piety and observance of the commands of Christ, increased rather than diminished his merits: but this was certainly not how Cedd saw the matter.

³⁸ Eddius, chapter XXV: *HE* IV, 6. The expulsion is attributed by Bede to Archbishop Theodore, but it is unlikely that Theodore could have acted in this way unless Wulfhere was already ill-disposed to his bishop.

³⁹ C. E. Whiting, 'The Anglian Bishops of Hexham', 126.

⁴⁰ F. M. Stenton, *Anglo-Saxon England*, 89.

⁴¹ For a fascinating analysis, from contemporary documents, of exactly what was involved in the acceptance of Christianity by a non-Christian people, see R. F. Sullivan, 'Khan Boris and the Conversion of the Bulgars', *Studies in Medieval and Renaissance History* III (1966), 55-139.

⁴² Though not all historians of this period would accept all the inferences and conclusions, W. A. Chaney, *The Cult of Kingship in Anglo-Saxon England: The Transition from Paganism to Christianity* (Manchester, 1970) brings a great deal of material together and sets it in a new light. A brilliant and highly technical semantic study of pagan and Christian interaction in a Germanic context and the methods used by the Church in the conversion of the Germanic tribes is provided by D. H. Green, *The Carolingian Lord* (Cambridge, 1965), a book which will be used with profit by specialists in many fields.

⁴³ *HE* III, 22.

⁴⁴ D. H. Green, *The Carolingian Lord*, 296-7.

⁴⁵ *HE* I, 32.

⁴⁶ *HE* III, 6.

⁴⁷ D. H. Green, *The Carolingian Lord*, 308 ff.

⁴⁸ D. H. Green, *The Carolingian Lord*, 300 ff.

⁴⁹ cf. R. I. Page, *Life in Anglo-Saxon England* (London, 1970), 33.

⁵⁰ *HE* I, 30. Subsequently, permission to marry within the Christian prohibited degrees was allowed to the Anglo-Saxons and this permission spuriously inserted into Pope Gregory's replies to specific questions on procedure from Augustine in the *Libellus Responsionum*, question V (*HE* I, 27): see, most recently, P. Meyvært, 'Bede's text of the *Libellus Responsionum* of Gregory the Great to Augustine of Canterbury', *England before the Conquest*, 15-33.

⁵¹ *HE* III, 5.

⁵² D. P. Kirby, 'Bede's Native Sources for the *Historia Ecclesiastica*', 351-2.

⁵³ *HE* III, 3, 6.

⁵⁴ *HE* III, 11.

⁵⁵ *HE* III, 5.

[56] *HE* III, 12.

[57] W. A. Chaney, *The Cult of Kingship*, 115-20 (p. 116).

[58] F. M. Stenton discussed Cenwulf's relations with Wulfred in *Anglo-Saxon England*, 229-30: but N. Brooks will be considering the quarrel at length in his forthcoming *The Early History of the Church of Canterbury*.

[59] *Florentii Wigorniensis Monachi Chronicon ex Chronicis*, ed. B. Thorpe, 2 vols (London, 1848), I, 65; cf., *Willelmi Malmesbiriensis Monachi De Gestis Regum Anglorum*, ed. W. Stubbs, 2 vols (Rolls series, London, 1887, 1889), I, 94-5; and *Willelmi Malmesbiriensis Monachi De Gestis Pontificum Anglorum*, ed. N. E. S. H. Hamilton (Rolls series, London, 1870), 294-5.

[60] *HCY*, ed. J. Raine, 3 vols (Rolls series, London, 1879-94), I, 254: cf., H. Howarth, *Golden Days of the Early English Church*, 3 vols (London, 1917), II, 505. Bede welcomed him on his accession as a new Josiah: *Bedas Metrische Vita sancti Cuthberti*, ed. W. Jaager (Leipsig, 1935), ii, 554-5.

[61] This letter is no. 79 in *Epistolæ selectæ*, i, *Mon. Germ. Hist.* (Berlin, 1916), ed. M. Tangl: and it is translated in *EHD* I, 751-6 (p. 755).

[62] This important ninth-century Northumbrian source *De Abbatibus* is edited by A. Campbell, *Æthelwulf De Abbatibus* (Oxford, 1967): cf. pp. xxiii, xxvi, 4-7.

[63] *HE* V, 22.

[64] *De Gestis Regum Anglorum* II, 357.

[65] Eddius, chapter XXXIV.

[66] Eddius, chapter XXVII.

[67] Eddius, chapter XLVII.

[68] Eddius, chapter XLIX.

[69] Eddius, chapter LXIV.

[70] Eddius, chapter LXIII.

[71] D. P. Kirby, 'Problems of Early West Saxon History', *EHR* 80 (1965), 10-29.

[72] *HE* IV, 16. Other lesser royal families were probably similarly suppressed. There is a possibility that some members of the royal family of Wight did survive, for the last king, Æthelberht, son of Aistulf, is said to have died in the time of King Alfred (871-99): 'The Chronicle Attributed to John of Wallingford', ed. R. Vaughan, *Camden Miscellany* 21, vol. 90 (London, 1958), 38.

[73] D. P. Kirby, 'Bede and Northumbrian Chronology', 526-7. It is possible Æthelfrith was only the grandson of Ida but this seems, on the whole, less likely.

[74] *HE* III, 6.

[75] Dorothy Whitelock, *The Beginnings of English Society* (Pelican History of England 2: reprinted 1971), 42 quotes from the poem *Beowulf*: 'Normally it happens rarely that the slaughterous spear lies quiet even for a short time, after the fall of men, though the bride be fair,' meaning that diplomatic marriages under such circumstances did not in fact usually bring peace.

[76] *HE* II, 20.

[77] *HE* III, 15.

[78] *HE* III, 1, 14.

[79] *HE* III, 24.

[80] *HE* III, 14, 24. Oswald was not to know that he would perish so soon, at Old Oswestry.

[81] *Two Lives of St. Cuthbert*, ed. and trans. B. Colgrave (Cambridge, 1940), 102-5, 234-7.

[82] Cf., further D. P. Kirby, 'Bede and the Pictish Church', *Innes Review*, 10 ff. Note also that Cuthbert was with Queen Iurminburh at Carlisle, and obviously a very close confidant when news came of the death of King Ecgfrith, *Two Lives of St. Cuthbert*, 122-3, 242-5.

[83] *Two Lives of St. Cuthbert*, 104-5, 236-7.

[84] William of Malmesbury has a tradition that he was slain at the instigation of

Cœnred who ruled after him: *De Gestis Regum Anglorum* I, 58. Cœnred was a distant collateral: see Pedigree II, p. 21.

[85] *Æthelwulf De Abbatibus*, ed. A. Campbell, 6-7.

[86] *HE* V, 23. Bede simply records that Osric departed this life, meaning died. William of Malmesbury associated him with Cœnred in the murder of Osred in 716 and alleges that both Cœnred and Osric similarly perished violently (*De Gestis Regum Anglorum* I, 58). There seems no way of testing the reliability of this statement. It is not certain how Osric was related to other Northumbrian kings. It could be that he was a second son of Aldfrith as Symeon of Durham states: *Symeonis Monachi Opera Omnia*, ed. T. Arnold, 2 vols (Rolls series, London, 1882, 1885), I, 39, 11, 340. C. Taylor, 'Osric of Gloucester', *Trans. of the Bristol and Gloucester Archæological Society* 26 (1903), 308-25 (pp. 311 ff.) suggests that he was a son of Alchfrith, son of Oswiu, but the evidence is insubstantial, and the idea that Osric had ruled over the Hwicce in Mercia before becoming king of Northumbria is also rejected by H. P. R. Finberg, 'Princes of the Hwicce', *The Early Charters of the West Midlands* (Leicester, 1961), 167-80 (p. 175).

[87] *HE* V, 23.

[88] *HE* III, 24.

[89] *Symeonis Monachi Opera Omnia* I, 349: cf., H. P. R. Finberg, 'The Early History of Gloucester Abbey', *The Early Charters of the West Midlands*, 153-66 (p. 165). It is unfortunate that the inscribed stone at Whitby, once thought to read CVNVBVRGA, who could have been the wife of Oswald, is now 'too fragmentary to be meaningful': E. Okasha, *Hand-List of Anglo-Saxon Non-Runic Inscriptions* (Cambridge, 1971), 125 (no. 134).

[90] Eddius, chapters XXIV and XL. This would seem to qualify E. John's hypothesis, 'The Social and Political Problems of the Early English Church', 51 and 60, that Wilfrid's unpopularity with Ecgfrith stemmed fundamentally from 'his powerful Mercian connections' and the 'Mercian orientation of Wilfrid's *familia*'.

[91] *HE* III, 11, 24.

[92] *HE* V, 24. H. P. R. Finberg, 'Princes of the Hwicce', 176-7, suspects that she might have been involved in intrigue with a Hwiccian ruler, but possibly a blood-feud alone could explain her death.

[93] *HE* I, 25.

[94] *Two Lives of St. Cuthbert*, 122-3.

[95] Eddius, chapter XXX.

[96] *HE* IV, 28: *Two Lives of St. Cuthbert*, 110-11, 238-9. Bede says that Eata died at the beginning of Aldfrith's reign: *HE* V, 2.

[97] Plummer I, 388-9.

[98] Eddius, chapter LIV.

[99] Eddius, preface and chapter LVI.

[100] Eddius, chapter XXII. See also, *infra*, pp. 81 ff., 115.

[101] *HE* V, 20.

[102] W. F. Bolton, *A History of Anglo-Latin Literature 597–1066*, I, 597–740 (Princeton, 1967), 107 ff.

[103] *Bede's Ecclesiastical History of the English People*, ed. B. Colgrave and R. A. B. Mynors, 572-3: *Symeonis Monachi Opera Omnia* II, 32. When Acca died he was buried at Hexham, and his grave marked by two great crosses (see *infra*, p. 127). When his remains were found in the eleventh century it was discovered that his vestments were well-preserved and that on his breast was an inscribed portable altar (see *infra*, p. 141).

[104] *Symeonis Monachi Opera Omnia* II, 52.

[105] *Symeonis Monachi Opera Omnia* II, 52.

[106] Eddius, chapter XXXIX: cf., also *HE* IV, 19.

[107] *HE* III, 13: and Bede makes it clear that this was just one story among several.

[108] *HE* IV, 13.

[109] *HE* III, 2.

[110] *Symeonis Monachi Omnia Opera* II, 52.

[111] Eddius, chapter II. The period indicated would cover the reign of Oswald as well as that of Oswiu.

[112] *HE* IV, 3.

[113] *HE* III, 14.

[114] *HE* III, 21.

[115] K. H. Jackson, 'On the Northern British Section', *Celt and Saxon*, ed. N. K. Chadwick, 20-62 (pp. 41-2).

[116] Plummer I, 365.

[117] E. John, 'The Social and Political Problems of the Early English Church', 60, is right in seeing ecclesiastical considerations as playing an important part in the complex career of Wilfrid, 'a truly Catholic bishop' possibly more concerned with his monastic foundations than with episcopal rank: but for a study of Wilfrid as a churchman, see *infra*, pp. 35 ff.

[118] *HE* V, 23.

[119] Plummer I, 405 ff.; cf., the translation in *EHD* I, 735 ff.

Chapter Two

SAINT WILFRID

D. H. Farmer

WILFRID HAS always been a controversial figure. In his lifetime he inspired extremes of loyalty and hostility. He quarrelled with kings and archbishops, appealing to the papacy against their decisions and he died as effective bishop over only a fraction of his original Northumbrian diocese. But he was also monastic founder and missionary, a builder and an art-patron of considerable importance. Of his greatness as a pioneer in many fields there can be no doubt, but no doubt also that he was a man who did not fit in, who divided the Church as well as building it up.

Historians of the late nineteenth and early twentieth centuries on the whole gave him a bad press. Too often have facile and over-simple contrasts been made between the 'worldly' Wilfrid and the 'unworldly' Aidan, between the riches and ambition of Wilfrid and the poverty and simplicity of Cuthbert. Anglican writers were unable to forgive him for being the first Englishman to appeal to the pope against an archbishop of Canterbury, while over-zealous converts to Roman Catholicism admired him for the very same qualities and actions: their anachronistic projection of a post-Tridentine papal centralization into Wilfrid's lifetime did nothing to help understanding of the real historical problems. An expatriate German Jew, Wilhelm Levison, shed much more light on the whole matter by emphasizing that the controversies of the seventh and eighth centuries need to be considered in complete detachment from those of the Reformation period. The problems were different, so were the personalities. Nowadays, perhaps, most will agree that the Church in England needed Wilfrid as well as Cuthbert and Aidan, that their achievements were complementary rather than contradictory.[1]

During the Middle Ages, although Wilfrid's feast was widely celebrated, there were few attempts following the work of Eddius and

Bede to re-evaluate his life.[2] One *Life*, written by Eadmer, an utterly committed partisan of Canterbury, performed the difficult feat of praising the constant courage of Wilfrid without reference to the fact that much of his adversity was due to one of Canterbury's greatest archbishops. For Eadmer the villain of the piece was the civil power personified by the kings of Northumbria, while Wilfrid was the champion of the 'liberties of the Church'. He had certainly read Eddius' contemporary biography of Wilfrid, possibly from the copy now in the British Museum and reproduced in Plates I and II, but he omitted much 'inconvenient' evidence, retaining Eddius' partisanship without his authenticity. For Eadmer, because Wilfrid's supposed relics had been translated to Canterbury by Archbishop Oda (942-58), Wilfrid was an honorary Canterbury saint and so to be praised with miracle stories of his altar gleaming at night with gold and precious stones while angelic choirs sung Matins there in his honour. These stories fostered devotion, but threw no light on the historical Wilfrid.[3]

This was left to William of Malmesbury, who devoted just half of the third book of his *Gesta Pontificum* to Wilfrid alone, a high proportion for a book which covered all the northern archbishops and bishops from Paulinus to the twelfth century.[4] Moreover William understood that the problem for all historians of Wilfrid was how to reconcile Eddius' account with Bede's. William used Eddius to complete the picture left by Bede. But his work was also important because it was the principal channel through which full, authentic information about Wilfrid reached medieval readers. Eddius' work was rare in the Middle Ages, William's much more widely diffused. The modern historian, like William, needs to use and criticize both Eddius and Bede, placing both their writings and the life of Wilfrid within their authentic historical context. Even if few facts unknown to either or both will emerge, perhaps the total picture will look somewhat different from the portraits drawn by each of them.

In depicting Wilfrid each achieved much, but each had his limitations.[5] Bede certainly used Eddius' work, but his omissions are surprising. Perhaps these are best explained by considering the aim of his *Ecclesiastical History of the English People*.[6] His intention was to chronicle the origins and progress of the Christianization of Anglo-

Saxon England, the progress from diverse racial and evangelistic origins to a single, united Church. His preoccupation, even obsession about computistics is intelligible if the celebration of Easter by all on the same day is the external sign of real unity. He was personally involved as an able chronologist and computist. A kind of academic hatred for the Irish and British computations warmed his habitual dispassionate detachment. Wilfrid, one would have thought, would have been one of his heroes. Was he not the successful protagonist of the Roman calculation at the synod of Whitby? Was he not also a pioneer of Roman outlook, and of Roman chants, and of the rule of St Benedict? These causes were all dear to Bede. Yet his long notice of Wilfrid, although factual and accurate, lacks warmth, resembling in spirit an obituary in *The Times*. There is no mention of Wilfrid's spirited defence of his life's achievements at the synod of Austerfield, no recording of Eddius' interesting documents to and from the papacy (yet Bede was an assiduous transcriber of other correspondence), and little mention of Wilfrid's monasteries in Mercia. To be sure, we owe to Bede in other passages of his history precious evidence about Wilfrid at Whitby, Wilfrid as an apostle of Sussex and the Isle of Wight, Wilfrid as an inspirer of the Anglo-Saxon mission on the Continent.[7] But, by and large, Theodore, not Wilfrid, is the hero of the *Ecclesiastical History*. Theodore organized and unified while Wilfrid was out of step. His refusal to divide his diocese, his repeated appeals to Rome, his intransigent attitude and partisan followers may have been no less harmful to unity than the other rifts which Theodore tried to heal. Wilfrid did not fit into Bede's theme, so he did not obtain the extended treatment which was his due. Moreover Wilfrid's personality, as distinct from the causes he stood for, was antipathetic to Bede. This detached scholar was out of touch with the violence and power struggles of contemporary politics: he was also critical of some bishops of his day. His Letter to Ecgberht (734) condemned pastors who neglected the apostolate and advocated further divisions of Northumbrian dioceses. New sees, he thought, should be sited in monasteries, even if the monks did not like it.[8] Theodore, not Wilfrid, would have approved of that. Bede admired the pioneer Irish monk-bishops in spite of their paschal aberrations: Wilfrid's episcopal ideal was based on the Merovingian Church, where the bishop was a not-

able landowner and local ruler, his diocese based on the civil organization of the Roman Empire, whose power was such that he could deal
with kings or counts as an equal, admonishing or reproving them if
need be. Bede's Aidan apparently never denounced Northumbrian
kings: he was too gentle for that; and Theodore, Bede's ideal bishop,
never seems to have quarrelled with kings either.

Eddius' portrait of Wilfrid, on the other hand, is one by a devoted
disciple. His *Life* was officially commissioned by Bishop Acca, Wilfrid's successor at Hexham and by Tatberht, abbot of Ripon. Eddius
had both the advantage and the disadvantage of knowing Wilfrid
personally, of sharing some of his journeys—there are 'we' passages
in Eddius as there are in the Acts of the Apostles—and some of his
hardships. Eddius, a monk of Ripon and a church musician from
Kent, wrote within less than ten years of Wilfrid's death in 709 or 710.
He incorporated into his *Life* elements of Acca's and Tatberht's
memories as well as his own. With the exception of the years 692-703,
the coverage is reasonably continuous. Eddius had the disadvantage
of writing about fifteen years before the *Ecclesiastical History* was
completed: his general knowledge of the historical background of
Wilfrid's life was far inferior to Bede's.

Frequent criticism of Eddius as partisan has obscured his real
achievement.[9] This was to write the first commemorative biography
in Anglo-Saxon England. For fullness of detail and authentic information it far surpasses the work of contemporary biographers like the
Whitby *Life of Gregory* or the anonymous *Life of Cuthbert*. As an
historical document it deserves comparison with Bede's *Lives of the
Abbots of Wearmouth and Jarrow*.[10] Eddius not only lists Wilfrid's
achievements as bishop and monk, missionary and church-builder,
he also gives an authentic portrait of the able and attractive young
man, fluent and persuasive, winning his ecclesiastical spurs at Whitby,
of the lordly bishop with his large retinue, of the munificent patron
who obtained from friendly kings and queens lavish endowments for
the Church; of the courageous fighter who travelled far to obtain
justice from the highest authority in the Church; of the old man,
facing his enemies like a stag at bay, recalling his many achievements
and later, on his deathbed, dividing his treasures among his followers.
For these details and many more Eddius is responsible; but while

many of his readers admire his Wilfrid, few of them can love him.

Why then has Eddius' account repelled as well as attracted those who read it? Principally because he identifies too closely with his subject, because he presents Wilfrid as always right and his enemies as always wrong. The cause of goodness is associated too closely with Wilfrid's necessarily human and limited outlook. But there are also inaccuracies and mistakes in Eddius' *Life*. These have often been pointed out. Nowadays historians, on the whole, are less likely to think that where there is divergence between Bede and Eddius, Bede is always right and Eddius always wrong. Certainly Eddius presents us with a Wilfrid who comes to us through his own limited and limiting vision: Wilfrid was greater than Eddius could make him. Eddius, for example, makes Wilfrid more like an Old Testament prophet on occasion than a Christian saint. He could fulminate and threaten like the prophets certainly and work miracles like theirs. His buildings were compared to the Temple at Jerusalem. His king-making activities again seem modelled on those of some of the prophets.[11] It is important to distinguish Wilfrid from Eddius' semi-biblical account of him, and not to hold Wilfrid responsible for Eddius' errors. There is no better example of this than Eddius calling the Irish Quartodecimans, when Wilfrid himself, as Bede recalls, carefully and explicitly avoided any such imputation. Again Eddius' set speeches put into Wilfrid's mouth are much less likely to be exactly accurate than examples of literary convention from the Classical age, tailored to the occasion and liberally injected with more or less authentic detail.

All this means that care must be taken to sift and criticize Eddius carefully. He was a lesser man than Wilfrid, but he emphasized the heroic and spectacular in Wilfrid's life rather than the more humdrum, but no less exacting, characteristics of sanctity. At least in his prime Wilfrid, although a monk and monastic founder of great importance, was active and extrovert rather than contemplative; the qualities revealed by his life were courage, independence, organizing ability, persistence, and intransigence rather than the 'monastic' qualities of humility, obedience, love of poverty and silence. In his early manhood he was perhaps more like a *grand seigneur* or a prince-bishop than a monk: heredity and temperament made him unlikely to be content with the narrow confines of the monastic round of duties in a subordinate position. This born leader of men needed and obtained a wider scope for his talents. In this way he was like Ealdred, archbishop of York, or Henry of Blois, bishop of Winchester. But later in life Wilfrid's monasteries seemed to matter more to him than his diocesan jurisdiction: he mellowed in old age and found, one hopes, peace and happiness during his last years in his favourite monastery of Hexham.

Wilfrid was born in 634 of a noble family.[12] His mother died young, and the harshness of his stepmother was a part cause of his leaving home for the Northumbrian court at the age of fourteen. Handsome and intelligent, he soon found favour with Oswiu's queen Eanflæd. But when Cudda, one of the king's closest companions, retired in ill-health to become a monk at Lindisfarne, Wilfrid went too to look after him. He also learnt to read and soon knew the psalter by heart. Although attracted to the monastic life, he was not tonsured; he wanted rather to go to Rome to see for himself the ecclesiastical and monastic life there. To us, this seems like a criticism of Lindisfarne: Bede however said that some of the Lindisfarne monks encouraged this desire.[13] Even in the lifetime of Aidan (whom Wilfrid must have met) there was some realization of the larger world beyond Lindisfarne, which ties up well with the certain Mediterranean influences in the later Lindisfarne Gospels.[14] Queen Eanflæd also encouraged Wilfrid in the same direction, securing hospitality for him with her kinsman, Earconberht king of Kent, until his hazardous journey to Rome could be arranged. He set out from Kent for Rome in 653 with another Northumbrian nobleman, Benedict Biscop, the future founder of Monkwearmouth and Jarrow, as his companion. Few could then have foreseen the prominent part to be taken by these two in the English Church of the seventh century.[15]

Wilfrid, seldom in a hurry, spent a year at Lyons, while Biscop pressed on to Rome. Lyons was the oldest see in Gaul, an important civic and trading centre of the late Empire and now ruled by Count Dalfinus, brother of Annemundus, its archbishop. Annemundus received him kindly and even offered him the governorship of part of Gaul with the hand of his niece in marriage. But Wilfrid refused this attractive offer and reached Rome. Once again he was received with favour, this time by Boniface, archdeacon of Rome, who instructed him in the sacred sciences. These included the Four Gospels (perhaps by heart) with the Roman method of calculating Easter and 'many other rules of Church discipline'. This was when Wilfrid learnt the elements of Canon Law which he was to exercise in his later appeals to the Holy See.[16]

In the seventh century Rome was the most important centre in the West for collections of Canon Law. Gelasius (492-6) and Hormisdas (514-23) had laid the foundations, but by Wilfrid's time the 'Dionysiana' was the dominant collection. Over the next century or so the Roman tradition, as amplified especially in Spain, was to supersede the rival regional collections of Gaul and Ireland: thus the context of Wilfrid's struggle was larger than at first appears. One element of Christian tradition affirmed in the Romano-Iberian collections was the papal primacy: the popes claimed the office of safeguarding the deposit of faith, of declaring the universal law, and of being the supreme court of appeal. The main sources of these conclusions were Councils (Ephesus, Chalcedon, Sardica) and the Letters of St Leo, together with other decretals of the fourth and fifth centuries. These did not of course imply a day-to-day interference with the ordinary running of distant churches, but did imply the exercise of at least occasional supremacy in special circumstances, which was recognized by all, including the Irish.[17]

Wilfrid again stayed at Lyons on his return journey, this time completing his education 'from very learned teachers' for three years. Now were formed Wilfrid's episcopal ideals, based on the example of Annemundus and other Merovingian bishops. They had inherited from the Roman Empire a tradition of public service; they had also acquired considerable lands with the power, prestige and patronage which such wealth could bring. They were aristocrats who could mix with dukes and counts as their equals, who could use their power for pastoral purposes, withstanding and correcting kings, founding monasteries, relieving the poor and educating the young. At its best this life of munificence could be combined with a private life of holiness and austerity, as in Patiens, bishop of Lyons (praised for his feasts by the king and for his fasts by the queen); at its worst it could degenerate into a combination of ambition and violence little different from those of secular rulers. This was not surprising when the bishops came from the very same families and were suddenly promoted to bishoprics as rewards for political services and without any proper ecclesiastical training. The splendid examples of Ambrose of Milan and Paulinus of Nola in the late Roman Empire inspired the best, but reproved the worst, of the Merovingian bishops.[18]

The consequences of political involvement were brought home to Wilfrid when Annemundus was killed in a palace revolution instigated by Ebroin, the Mayor of the Palace. Wilfrid narrowly escaped the same fate through being a foreigner. Lyons was now clearly no place for him, so he went home. Through Cœnwalh, king of Wessex, he was introduced to Alchfrith, son of Oswiu and sub-king of Deira. Once more Wilfrid made an excellent impression with his fine bearing, his eloquence and his wide knowledge. Alchfrith's favour began Wilfrid's career in England. It took the concrete form of the gift of an estate of ten hides at *Ætstanforda*, followed by the monastery of Ripon with thirty hides. Here Wilfrid displaced a community of Irish-trained monks from Melrose, which included Eata and Cuthbert, both future bishops. Wilfrid was installed as abbot and in 663 Agilberht, bishop of Dorchester, ordained him priest. His promotion, which enabled him incidentally to dispense alms on a more lavish scale than before, was due to the sub-king Alchfrith and to a king and bishop from Wessex.[19]

The synod of Whitby soon afterwards provided Wilfrid with a wonderful opportunity as the principal spokesman on the Roman side.[20] Its immediate occasion was the disunity in Northumbria over the celebration of Easter. This was due to the different calculations favoured by Irish-trained missionaries on the one hand and by those trained in Rome, Kent or Gaul on the other. Things had come to a head when King Oswiu celebrated Easter on the same day that his Kentish queen, Eanflæd, and her followers were celebrating Palm Sunday. Evidently such a state of affairs could not continue indefinitely, as not only was the date of Easter involved but also by consequence those of Septuagesima, Lent, Ascension Day and Pentecost. Moreover in some years the difference in the calculations resulted in a date for Easter different not by one but by several weeks. The problem was specially acute in Northumbria because of the presence in the same area of priests trained in, and tenacious of, the traditions of different regions. In parts of Britain where there was no Anglo-Saxon penetration such as Wales and Cornwall and no continental priests the Celtic calculation survived long after Whitby, but well before this the Southern Irish had conformed to Roman usage: only Iona and its Northern Irish dependencies were out on a limb against the rest. In the long run they would surely have to conform, but when?

Although Whitby was primarily a Northumbrian gathering, Oswiu, who summoned it, was also *bretwalda* of England and the participants included bishops from Wessex and Essex with their followers, the Irishman Ronan as well as Colman, bishop of Lindisfarne, and Hild, abbess of Whitby. The principal speakers were Colman for the Irish side and Wilfrid for the Roman, who was chosen partly for his eloquence in the vernacular.

Wilfrid's main point was that the Roman calculation of Easter was that accepted by the council of Nicæa and was the fixed rule of the Apostolic See, of the other regional Churches and of their own predecessors in the faith. Colman appealed to the teaching of Columba, who propagated a tradition supposedly descended from St John the Evangelist. Oswiu's half-humorous summing-up preferring the power and favour of the heavenly doorkeeper to those of an Irish saint, however venerable, settled the matter but left much unsaid. Eddius' insistence that the whole synod concurred may indicate that the result was a foregone conclusion, a victory for universalism over provincialism. Bede, as a scholar wholeheartedly Roman in matters of computistics, stressed the emergence of moderates like Cedd, Tuda, Eata and Cuthbert, Anglo-Saxons educated in Irish traditions who realistically conformed after Whitby. Only Colman and a handful of reactionaries retired to Ireland; at Lindisfarne first Tuda and then Eata and Cuthbert led the monastic community into conformity, but the days of Lindisfarne's predominance were ended. What happened next to the bishopric is not entirely clear: Bede and Eddius have each told us only part of the story.

At this time the normal system of church government by bishops established in territorial sees was not yet established over the whole of England. To be sure, Canterbury, Rochester and London, all founded by Augustine, were sees on the continental model. Elsewhere the power of bishops was largely coterminous with that of particular kings: the kingdom rather than the city was in fact the ecclesiastical unit, and the power of a bishop could become more, or less, extended as a king gained or lost territory. This was due to the tribal organization of the Anglo-Saxons and to the need of bishops to work in close concert with the kings. In Northumbria the situation was complicated by the double dynasty of Deirans and Bernicians: the former were the older established tribe, whose king, Edwin, had invited Paulinus to Northumbria where he had worked mainly in the York and Lincoln areas, but the Bernician dynasty, to which Oswald and Oswiu belonged, became the dominant one, and its members had received their Christianity, as it so happened, from the Irish or Scots in Iona. This double political power resulted in some ecclesiastical dualism.

Wilfrid's principal patron had been Alchfrith, sub-king of Deira. Oswiu, king of all Northumbria, who resided for part of his time at least at Bamburgh and was more concerned with northern affairs, appointed Tuda to succeed Colman, presumably at Lindisfarne. Alchfrith sent Wilfrid to be consecrated in Gaul by Agilberht, formerly of Dorchester and now of Paris. The ceremony was particularly splendid, with twelve co-consecrating bishops, recalling the twelve apostles, and the carrying of the new bishop to the sanctuary on a golden chair. It was in complete contrast with the consecration of Chad. Alchfrith rebelled against Oswiu and was exiled or killed during Wilfrid's absence: and on the death of Tuda, Oswiu chose Chad to succeed him, who, during a Canterbury vacancy, was consecrated by the simoniac Wine of Wessex, assisted by two British bishops of doubtful orthodoxy. When Wilfrid returned, therefore, he found Chad in control of the Northumbrian Church; and with his own patron gone, he could do nothing else but retire to his monastery at Ripon. Here he took the important and far-reaching step of introducing the rule of St Benedict, hitherto unknown in Northumbria.[21]

Ironically, in view of what was to follow, it was Theodore the new Greek archbishop of Canterbury, who restored Wilfrid in 669. Chad, of whom all (including Eddius) spoke well, was transferred after reconsecration to Mercia, where he established his see at Lichfield. Wilfrid chose York as the centre of his Northumbrian diocese: its importance in Roman times, its association with Paulinus, its size, security and accessibility and the desirability of a change from the leadership of Lindisfarne all made it the obvious choice. His jurisdiction presumably extended over the whole of the Northumbrian kingdom, *i.e.* over the modern Yorkshire, Durham, Northumberland with those parts of the north-western counties not controlled by the Britons of Cumbria together with the parts of southern Scotland ruled by Oswiu. One of Wilfrid's first achievements was to restore Paulinus' old church at York, adding a lead roof, glass windows, altar furnishings and sacred vessels. Even more important, he built up a solid endowment of land which would secure its future.[22]

At Ripon, on the other hand, Wilfrid was responsible for the entire edifice, using dressed stone and pillars (perhaps from Roman ruins) and, for the first time in Northumbria, incorporating *porticus* as in the Kentish churches. The dedication was a splendid event. Altar hangings and an illuminated Gospel Book written in gold on purple parchment, covered with a gold and jewelled binding, were provided by Wilfrid; in the presence of Ecgfrith, king of Northumbria, and Ælfwine, sub-king of Deira and of other magnates Wilfrid read aloud the royal charters which endowed Ripon with land, including properties held by the Britons before they left Elmet for the West. These former church lands, restored to the church of the Britons' conquerors, included those 'round Ribble and Yeadon, the region of Dent, Catlow and other places'.[23]

The years 669-78 were the most obviously successful ones of Wilfrid's life. The period was one of military glory for Northumbria. King Ecgfrith won spectacular victories with rudimentary cavalry against the Picts in the North and the Mercians in the south. This latter led to the recovery of Lindsey (roughly the modern Lincolnshire) by Northumbria and consequently to the extension of Wilfrid's diocese. During these years the church and monastery of Hexham was built, the most notable of all Wilfrid's buildings, where, under his successor Acca, his memory was kept alive. From Ecgfrith's first wife, Æthelthryth, Wilfrid obtained large estates nearby which provided its endowment, while the church, dedicated to St Andrew, was reputed to be the finest north of the Alps. Happily its crypt survives as one of the most impressive Christian remains in England. Above it stood a large and high church with an apsidal east end, transepts, aisles and *porticus*. There was also a gallery with spiral staircases. As at Ripon, Roman columns were re-used. It measured 165 feet long by 126 feet at the transepts, a very large church by the standards of his day, and the source of admiration to contemporaries and later generations alike. Here he also instituted observance of the rule of St Benedict. Elsewhere I have suggested that the oldest surviving manuscript of the rule of St Benedict, written in uncial and surviving at Oxford (Hatton 48), may well have been commissioned by Wilfrid. While positive proof is still lacking (and probably always will be), the attribution to Wilfrid, based on converging evidence, may be regarded as at least a fairly plausible hypothesis.[24]

The mention of Æthelthryth helps us to understand why Wilfrid's prosperity did not last and why Ecgfrith pursued him with such apparently implacable hatred. She was a daughter of Anna, king of the East Angles, who had been given in marriage first to Tondberht of the South *Gyrwas* and on his death to Ecgfrith. Neither marriage had apparently been consummated; Ecgfrith was only fifteen at the time and Æthelthryth considerably older. Ten years later and now king of Northumbria instead of sub-king of Deira, Ecgfrith wanted normal conjugal relations, but Æthelthryth wished to remain a virgin. Wilfrid supported her in her desire for perpetual virginity: through his influence and help she left her husband to become a nun at Coldingham under Ecgfrith's aunt, Æbbe. A year later she founded the monastery of Ely on land which had been part of her dowry and ruled it as abbess for the rest of her life. Bede, not Eddius, tells us all this: he approved Wilfrid's conduct and must have realized its relevance to his fate, while Eddius, who must have known of Wilfrid's dissolution of this marriage, does not mention it at all.[25]

About five years later followed the controversial division of the Northumbrian diocese. Doubtless the hostility of Ecgfrith's second wife, Iurminburh, towards Wilfrid was a contributory, but not the principal, cause. She intimated to the king with some justification that Wilfrid was a rival: his estates, swollen both by Æthelthryth's gifts and by monasteries making over their lands to him for protection, were enormous and his retinue of followers large. His life-style, based on Frankish Merovingian models, was apparently unique among the English bishops of the day.[26]

Theodore's policy in the matter is understandable, even if his way of implementing it is not. While Whitby had been ostensibly concerned with the date of Easter and the form of the tonsure, the underlying issue was whether England's Christianity should be modelled on that of Ireland or on that of Rome and the rest of western Europe. In Ireland, with its strong tribal structure and absence of towns, monasteries and abbots rather than sees and bishops came to be the real centres of church life and organization. The bishop was often subject to the abbot. Theodore's policy, soon after Whitby, was to establish normal territorial sees throughout England on the usual Western (and Eastern) model. In doing this he respected the rule of kings, avoiding ecclesiastical divisions which cut across political boundaries, but establishing gradually more than one see of moderate size within the confines of the same kingdom. His whole programme, reflected in the decrees of the council of Hertford in 672, aimed at establishing clearly both the rights and duties of sees and monasteries to each other. A monk himself, Theodore safeguarded monastic autonomy, but at the same time discouraged the freelance Irish-type missionary working at a distance from his monastery and independently of the diocesan bishop. At the same council his policy of dividing sees had been outlined, but no agreement was reached. Wilfrid's proctors, unknown by name, may well have been those most opposed to it. In East Anglia, Mercia and later Wessex, Theodore's sees, which respected tribal divisions within these kingdoms, formed the basis of diocesan organization for centuries to come.

But in Northumbria he had Wilfrid to reckon with. The division into three was agreed between Theodore and the king without consultation with Wilfrid, and three bishops were appointed over his head. By now Wilfrid's political situation was insecure. He was out of favour with the king and queen, his former patron Alchfrith was dead, his ostentatious way of life did nothing to placate his critics. Ecgfrith wished to be rid of him and Theodore went ahead with the division of the Northumbrian diocese.[27] He may have been affected by the long Eastern tradition of an imperially-dominated church, but if he expected Wilfrid to submit to virtual deposition without lawful reasons, he was mistaken. Wilfrid's knowledge of Canon Law, together with his pertinacity of character led him to appeal to the papacy for reinstatement against Theodore, whom the same papacy had nominated as archbishop of Canterbury.

On his way to plead his cause in person, he initiated as it were by a historical accident the Anglo-Saxon mission to the Frisians. This apostolate was to be pursued with great success later by Wilfrid's disciple Willibrord, whom he visited there towards the end of his life. But on his leisurely way to Rome he met with several adventures. Ebroin, the Palace Mayor who had been responsible for the death of Wilfrid's patron, Annemundus of Lyons, now tried hard to persuade Aldgisl, king of the Frisians, to hand Wilfrid over to him. He refused, and Wilfrid passed on into the territory of Dagobert II. This king of the Franks now repaid Wilfrid for his help and patronage during an earlier political exile in Ireland. On that occasion Wilfrid had provided him with men and arms, which had helped towards his recovery of his throne. Now, in 679, Dagobert offered him the bishopric of his capital town of Strasbourg. Wilfrid however refused, intent on vindicating his cause at Rome. When he arrived, he found that Theodore's proctor, the monk Cenwald, had preceded him.[28]

Eddius' full account of the case emphasizes that the Apostolic See by the power of the keys claimed jurisdiction and that it found Wilfrid innocent of all canonical crime. His own eloquent plea complained of his being unjustly supplanted by three bishops appointed and consecrated 'from outside' over his head. But he accepted in advance the decision of the Holy See and even the division of his diocese provided that the new bishops were chosen in synod from the local Church. The last point is puzzling: the new bishops had all been trained in Northumbria at either Whitby or Lindisfarne. The only way they could be described as outsiders was that they were not trained at Rome or by Roman missionaries and had not come from Wilfrid's household or monasteries. Theodore had evidently not heeded such a narrow definition, and Wilfrid never attacked the character or the orthodoxy of the intruded bishops. Pope Agatho for his part commended Wilfrid for not opposing his expulsion by force and for appealing for the 'canonical aid of St Peter'. The final decision was in Wilfrid's favour. It restored his bishopric to him and enjoined him to choose new coadjutors at a synod and expel the intruded bishops. For Wilfrid it brought vindication, but for Theodore the decision to divide the dioceses was upheld. Not for the first or the last time, however, Rome had reached a decision on limited information and, moreover, lacked all means of implementing the sentence. Familiar over the centuries with cases like those of Athanasius, whom it constantly upheld, or Melitus, bishop of Antioch, whom it rejected, or more recently with Salonius and Sagittarius of Gaul who had appealed against their deposition by a council of Lyons, Rome decided and could only decide on the case as presented in the customary canonical terms. There is no real evidence that Rome understood the geographical and political situation in Northumbria or realized that the English Church was still not fully organized. But they acted as if it were. Wilfrid skilfully presented his case as a straightforward one of unjust deposition: in the context of the Græco-Roman world of fixed dioceses and the importance in society of Roman law the synod could not but uphold the rights of an innocent man and the rule of law and order.[29]

After satisfying his devotion at the shrines of the saints and packing his bags both with relics and papal letters to Theodore and Ecgfrith, Wilfrid left Rome. Once again he had to pass through hostile territory. His supporter, Dagobert II, had been assassinated and a bishop was sent to intercept him with a small army. Wilfrid courageously withstood him and defended his patronage to Dagobert: 'I helped and fed him as an exile and a wanderer and raised him up for your good, not your harm, so that he could build up your cities, comfort your fellow citizens, counsel your elders and defend God's churches as he had promised.' The military bishop allowed him to go free.[30]

But a worse fate befell him in Northumbria. King Ecgfrith refused to accept the papal decision and imprisoned Wilfrid for nine months at Dunbar, partly in solitary confinement. Once again Wilfrid's courage was equal to the occasion. Moreover his gift of healing, the incapacity of local blacksmiths to make effective chains for him, the nervous breakdown of Queen Iurminburh following her theft of Wilfrid's reliquary, above all the timely intervention of Æbbe, abbess of Coldingham, secured his release, but not his restoration. Æbbe's plea was particularly effective as Ecgfrith and his neurotic second wife were staying in her monastery: it is one more example of the power of noble women in Anglo-Saxon society.

This power was experienced soon after by Wilfrid, but in a hostile way. Wilfrid had gone south to Mercia, where he was received with friendship by Berhtwald, nephew of King Æthelred. It was 681 and Berhtwald gave him land for a monastery for his followers. But Æthelred's queen, Osthryth, was a sister of Ecgfrith and made it impossible for Berhtwald to continue to favour him. So Wilfrid moved on to Wessex, when the same thing happened again, this time due to the machinations of his old enemy Iurminburh who was the sister-in-law of Centwine, king of Wessex.[31]

As so often happened in Wilfrid's career, adversity was the occasion of an important new achievement. This time it was the conversion of Sussex. An outcast from most of the Christian kingdoms, Wilfrid now turned to the last surviving stronghold of paganism both for refuge and for yet another missionary venture. Once again he won the favour of the king, Æthelwalh, who assured him both safety and immunity. Wilfrid lost no time in beginning his apostolate: he preached repentance, the story of the Creation 'to confound idolatry', the Redemption and the Last Judgement. Thousands of baptisms followed: some of them voluntary, others 'at the king's command'. Æthelwalh gave him one of his own manors, adding later eighty-seven hides in Selsey, where Wilfrid founded yet another monastery. It was all a far cry from his exciting first contact with Sussex in 666, where on his return from Gaul he was shipwrecked and attacked. On that occasion one of his followers stoned and killed a pagan priest, who was standing on a mound cursing them. In the subsequent skirmish Wilfrid's few Christian followers had routed the numerous pagans. But now, thanks not a little to his skill both as a fisherman and a teacher, Wilfrid won a deeper victory over paganism's last surviving stronghold.[32]

Five years after his successful preaching, Wilfrid befriended an exiled Wessex prince, Cædwalla, and helped him regain his throne in 686. In the course of the fighting Æthelwalh, Wilfrid's former patron, was killed. At this distance we do not know why Wilfrid apparently abandoned his former friend nor if his role in the whole affair was as important as Eddius made it. What is certain is that Cædwalla gave Wilfrid a quarter of the Isle of Wight, as much as 300 hides. Once more Wilfrid converted the people from his base in the port of Brading, if local tradition can be believed. A few years later Cædwalla abdicated, ending his days at Rome as a neophyte in 689. Surely the influence of Wilfrid had been active here.[33]

Meanwhile, according to Eddius, Theodore, now well over eighty years of age, wished to be reconciled to Wilfrid. He acknowledged his fault in consenting to his spoliation by kings and wished him to be his successor as archbishop of Canterbury. Before dismissing this story as partisan propaganda, one should recall that Wilfrid was both the ablest and most experienced bishop in England. He had, after all, preached the Gospel with success in many areas, he had been considered worthy of the bishopric of Strasbourg, and he knew the ways of Rome. Both Dagobert and Cædwalla had owed their thrones, at least in part, to him; if he was not *persona grata* in Northumbria, promotion to Canterbury would be an honourable way both of removing him from the firing-line and of securing peace. In point of fact Theodore lived for another four years and tried his best to effect a reconciliation between Wilfrid and Aldfrith, the new and devout king of Northumbria. To this end he wrote letters to Aldfrith himself, to Æthelred, king of Mercia and to Ælfflæd, abbess of Whitby and sister of Aldfrith. The result was that Wilfrid was restored to York (and Bosa removed) in 686 and he also regained his monasteries of Ripon and Hexham. But by 688 there were new bishops at both Hexham and Lindisfarne: Wilfrid presumably acquiesced in their appointment. This meant that he was restored only to the 'new' see of York, which was a part only of the 'old' see he had once held. In this Eddius' claim that Wilfrid was totally restored and all the Northumbrian bishops set aside cannot be maintained. Moreover the political boundaries of Northumbria had diminished: Lindsey had been reconquered by Mercia in 679 and Abercorn and its neighbourhood by the Picts in 685. In fact Wilfrid's restoration was both partial and, as the event proved, temporary.[34]

Five years of uneasy relations between Wilfrid and the Irish-trained Aldfrith culminated in fresh disputes which resulted in yet another exile. Eddius lists the grievances as follows: 1. that Ripon was despoiled of its lands, 2. that it was changed into an episcopal see and thus lost to Wilfrid, 3. that Aldfrith insisted on obedience to all

Theodore's decrees from the middle and controversial part of his episcopate rather than those of the beginning and end, which were harmonious and peaceful.[35] By now (690) Theodore had died; a long vacancy at Canterbury left the church leaderless and there was no ecclesiastic in England to whom Wilfrid could look for help. The dispute with the king became so bitter that Wilfrid left for Mercia. His long-standing connection with Northumbria's most important rival, destined in fact to supersede her pre-eminence, must have provided his enemies with a plausible excuse to accuse him of subversion or even of treachery.

The next eleven years of his life (692-703) are largely unchronicled. The Mercian centre, where he worked as bishop, was Leicester, not Chad's Lichfield. He soon consecrated Oftfor as bishop of the Hwicce, thus sharing in the policy of 'division of dioceses', and also Swithberht as bishop of the Frisians. Some time during his life he founded at least six monasteries in Mercia: it seems likely that some of them date from these years. There is no definitive list of them, but Peterborough (*Medeshamstede*), Oundle, Evesham, Brixworth, even Wing all have some claim to connexion with Wilfrid, either through written or on archæological evidence. Another monastic contact in these years was with Ely, where in 695 he assisted at the translation of the relics of his old friend Æthelthryth. Ely tradition has it that he also acted as bishop in the Ely area.[36]

Whether or not it is true that it was Wilfrid's enemies who brought things to a head, Berhtwald, archbishop of Canterbury, convoked a national council at Austerfield, near Bawtry, to settle Wilfrid's status and position. We do not know whether other matters also were dealt with, as Bede omits all mention of it. It took place in 703. Eddius presents it as a determined attempt by Wilfrid's opponents to destroy him by sequestrating all his property, especially the monasteries, in both Northumbria and Mercia. Wilfrid was to agree in advance to accepting whatever Berhtwald should decide. The point to note is that now, in contrast to the earlier controversies, his monasteries rather than his diocese formed the principal bone of contention. Some were appalled at the severity of this proposed fate for Wilfrid, and Berhtwald suggested a compromise whereby Wilfrid should voluntarily retire to Ripon, having abandoned all episcopal functions, and agree not to go out of the monastic precinct without the king's permission. Wilfrid rightly rejected such internment, and in a passionate speech recalled all that he had done for Northumbria, how he had brought them to the observance of the true Easter and the Petrine tonsure, to the Roman system of singing with antiphons and responsories, and how he had introduced the rule of St Benedict. In return for all this they had tried to get him to accept in advance any sentence against himself, although he was completely innocent. He refused to accept any decision of the archbishop of Canterbury which was contrary to the decisions of the Holy See.[37] These had included not only vindication in his previous struggle, but also privileges from the popes for his monasteries, confirming his ownership and specifying the lands which they held. Once again then, in his seventieth year, he decided to appeal to Rome in person. He was grudgingly accorded a safe-conduct by the council and strongly supported by Æthelred, king of Mercia, who refused to confiscate the lands of Wilfrid's monasteries. At this time his followers were excommunicated and it was now, probably, that Aldhelm of Malmesbury wrote to them, recommending fidelity and perseverance in persecution.[38]

Wilfrid reached Rome safely and again was well received. In his petition he protested his innocence, asked for protection for the Mercian monasteries and their lands according to the privileges granted by Popes Agatho, Sergius and Benedict, and requested a decision about his claim to be bishop of York and ruler of his Northumbrian monasteries, apart from Ripon and Hexham already safeguarded by earlier papal privilege. This constant appeal to papal precedent, together with the fact that Wilfrid was recognized as the bishop who many years previously had answered in Rome for the orthodoxy of the Church in England obviously did his cause no harm at all. Berhtwald's proctors, for their part, completely failed to prove any charges against him. The result was a papal declaration of Wilfrid's innocence, a letter written to the kings of Mercia and Northumbria saying that the whole question must be settled at a council to be held by Berhtwald and attended by Wilfrid, Bosa, John of Beverley and other interested parties. Peace must be made once and for all either before or during the synod. If this were not possible, the parties concerned must present themselves at Rome and settle matters there. Thus again, although Rome vindicated Wilfrid, it gave the other bishops a full opportunity to state their case. By now, the Northumbrian bishops had been long in office and had exercised their ministry well; Wilfrid was an old man, and although Rome wanted justice to be done, it did not want a total dislocation of the established order in Northumbria. On his way home in 705 Wilfrid suffered what seems to have been a stroke, from which he was apparently cured by an apparition of St Michael. When he reached England, he found that Æthelred of Mercia accepted the papal ruling but Aldfrith of Northumbria refused it. Peace was not made until after Aldfrith's death, when he was succeeded by his son Osred, a child of eight years old.[39]

The synod was held at a site on the river Nidd, in Yorkshire. It was a northern conference, attended by the magnates of Church and State and by Berhtwald, archbishop of Canterbury. First the papal letters were read, then translated and abridged by the archbishop. Next some of the bishops claimed that they had no power to alter the decisions of Theodore and of the Northumbrian kings Ecgfrith and Aldfrith. At this point the abbess Ælfflæd, the late king's sister, intervened, revealing that Aldfrith had intended to obey the papal precepts about Wilfrid if he had lived. Berhtfrith, the king's chief adviser, supported her with his own memories of a siege at Bamburgh when the fighting had taken a dramatic turn for the better after they had vowed to do justice to Wilfrid. After consultation, Wilfrid's best monasteries of Hexham and Ripon were fully restored to him with all their lands and revenues. Bosa, bishop of York, was succeeded by John of Beverley, bishop of Hexham, while Wilfrid was to be bishop of Hexham for the rest of his life. So it was peace and restoration for Wilfrid, but partial restoration only. He retained, however, what counted most to him: his principal Northumbrian and Mercian monasteries together with the exercise of his episcopal office. Even if the final solution displeased extremists on both sides, it must have satisfied the moderates. It left enough power in Wilfrid's hands, it brought him back in peace to his native Northumbria; he was for the rest of his life no longer an exile and a wayfarer, but a respected and still wealthy old man, who, if not broken in health, at least had received some premonition of the end soon to come. The papal decisions had at last been received and, in their final modified form, obeyed. Much has been made of the earlier disobedience of the Northumbrian kings; not often enough has the point been made that the papacy (in spite of Eddius) did not entirely and absolutely support every claim of Wilfrid. Although the popes gave his monasteries privileges and personally supported him against the vindictive accusations of his worst enemies, and rightly asserted more than once that he was innocent of all crime, it never made him a metropolitan (Ecgberht was the first archbishop of York less than thirty years after Wilfrid's death) nor archbishop of Canterbury. Nor did the papacy give him a formal mission as it did to his disciple, Willibrord, in Frisia or, more explicitly and on a larger scale, to Boniface. Perhaps if Wilfrid had lived fifty years later, he too might have fulfilled his ideals by being a papal missionary like Boniface. As it was, his personal and roving apostolate seemed to belong to an earlier stage of the development of the Church in England. In his early life he had been a reformer, but by the time of his death his monastic empire, cutting across the division of the country into kingdoms and dioceses, must have seemed anachronistic to some and, paradoxically, to resemble more closely the Irish system which he opposed when he was younger than the stable, localized diocesan system in force in his later years. Into this he eventually fitted as bishop of Hexham. It was a comparatively small role to fill in comparison with his grandiose position of earlier years.[40]

A pioneer is often greater than the men who replace him, but a pioneer's fate is to be superseded. Both these remarks apply to Wilfrid. Perhaps we should see him as an early example of the papal supporter whose intransigence sometimes embarrassed the papacy itself. In this connexion one may compare him with St Thomas Becket. At all times the papacy has realized the importance of the kingly power and knew very well, not least in the seventh century, that the Church had to work in and through the kings and could get nowhere without them. In this way Wilfrid's disputes were something of a liability to the papacy; it is to its credit that more than once it insisted that justice should be done in Wilfrid's case, although it lacked all physical means of enforcing it. In the end it depended on the recognition of its jurisdiction and moral authority by its subjects and ultimately this was obtained.

What of Wilfrid's private life? In a life so full of conflict and incident, so concerned with power and politics, this seems to receive less than adequate treatment from Eddius, and certainly less than the biographers of Cuthbert devoted to their subject. In the last analysis, it eludes us. One can say that Wilfrid's persistent courage in adversity is worthy of the highest praise, that the reverses he so often met in fact resulted in new achievements for this extraordinarily gifted and many-sided personality, that at the end of his life he was very far from empty-handed in the multitude and importance of his achievements. One might compare him with Bernard for his belief in himself as God's chosen instrument, with Athanasius for his refusal to admit defeat and his ability to conquer persecution, with Boniface for his able versatility and complete devotion to the papacy. Reading between the lines of Eddius' tantalizingly reticent pages, one can sense a certain development and change in Wilfrid's outlook and personality towards the end of his life. Whereas in 703 at Austerfield the old lion had roared again with great effect, by 705 and after there seems more peace and resignation. The illnesses (or strokes) may have been spiritual as well as physical turning-points. After the second of these in *c*. 708 he opened his treasure at Ripon in the presence of two abbots and eight monks. It included gold, silver and precious stones. At his command it was divided into four parts. One part was to be offered at Rome to the churches of St Peter, St Paul and St Mary. This was in lieu of his own plan to end his days in Rome, as Cædwalla of Wessex had done. The second part was to be given to the poor. The third part would be given to the abbots of Ripon and Hexham so that 'they may be able to purchase the friendship of kings and bishops'. The fourth part was for his followers who had shared his exile, and for whom he had not been able to provide land. These four bequests fittingly sum up four great causes of his life. The first represents his interest in Rome and his conviction that the Church in Northumbria and in the rest of England had much to learn from the centre of Christendom. The second reminds us that he had a social conscience, both as an ecclesiastic and a nobleman: the proportion of one quarter agrees exactly with Gregory's

recommendation to Augustine. The third bequest has most often
been remarked upon, and shows that Wilfrid was a realist to the last
and knew very well that his abbeys would need financial help to
maintain the continuity and independence of their monastic life in
face of royal and episcopal pressure. The fourth bequest showed his
concern for those who had suffered through loyalty to himself, the
generous and princely prelate recognizing that lordship implied
obligations as well as rights.[41]

He also took steps to secure the future government of his monasteries. Tatberht, his kinsman and companion, was to be abbot of
Ripon. The Mercian monasteries were to be ruled by a new abbot to
be elected by a named group of abbots. In making these arrangements Wilfrid was using his founder's rights up to the end. Like
many other monastic founders he did not think that the time had
yet come for his monasteries to elect their abbots in accordance with
the procedure of St Benedict's rule.[42] Nevertheless the monasteries
he left behind were surely distinguished for their 'Benedictine'
liturgical splendour, their skilled craftsmanship and their learning.
Certainly all that we know of Hexham, ruled by Wilfrid's nominee
Acca, supports this claim.[43] Wilfrid died at last in his monastery of
Oundle, in his seventy-sixth year and the forty-sixth of his episcopate.
It was 12 October 709 or 710. For his heroic life and his multifarious
achievements his praise, as Eddius says, remains for ever. Of all the
remarkable figures in the conversion of the Anglo-Saxons he must be
reckoned as one of the giants. Of all the churches he founded Hexham and Ripon must have been the greatest: his memory lives on
there, most of all in his crypts, which with their re-use of Roman
materials aptly symbolizes Wilfrid's Roman tastes and personal com-
mitment to the building of the Christian Church on the ruins of the
old Roman Empire.

Additional Note
This chapter was written before the publication of Dr Marion Gibbs'
'The Decrees of Agatho and the Gregorian Plan for York', *Speculum*
XlVIII (1973), 213-46. While the present writer is not in agreement
with all the arguments and conclusions of this scholarly article, he

would like to draw attention to the view that Bede's selective treat-
ments of Wilfrid represents an attempt to reconcile centres in
Northumbria hostile to Wilfrid (above all, Whitby) with Wilfrid's
own followers (at Hexham and Ripon). As such, Bede's account of
Wilfrid is a compromise statement, summarised by Wilfrid's
epitaph. Dr Gibbs also stresses that the papacy did not (or could not)
give Wilfrid everything he wanted, especially, she believes, metropolitan status for York.

Notes

[1] G. F. Browne, *Theodore and Wilfrith* (London, 1897); F. W. Faber, 'St. Wilfrid,
Bishop of York' in J. H. Newman, *Lives of the English Saints*, 1844 and 1902; W.
Levison, *England and the Continent in the Eighth Century* (Oxford, 1946).

[2] Wilfrid's two feast days are 12 October (death) and 24 April (translation).

[3] Eadmer, 'Vita Wilfridi' and 'Breviloquium Vitæ S. Wilfridi' in *HCY* I, 161-237.
At least Eadmer made intelligible the tenth-century Canterbury verse *Life*, ed. A.
Campbell, *Frithegodii Breviloquium* (Zürich, 1950).

[4] *De Gestis Pontificum Anglorum*, 211-44.

[5] Eddius Stephanus, *The Life of Bishop Wilfrid*, ed. B. Colgrave (Cambridge, 1927).
Other editions are by W. Levison, *MGH Scriptores rerum Merovingicarum* VI, 163-
263 and H. Moonen, *Eddius Stephanus het Leven van Sint Wilfrid* (1946). Of
Eddius' work only two manuscripts survive, one of which is a collection of Saints'
Lives for liturgical purposes.

[6] Recent studies of Bede include J. Campbell, 'Bede' in *Latin Historians*, ed. T. A.
Dorey (London, 1966), 159-90, and P. Hunter Blair, *The World of Bede*. Recent
studies of Wilfrid include E. John, 'The Social and Political Problems of the Early
English Church', 40 ff., and H. Mayr-Harting, *The Coming of Christianity to the
Anglo-Saxons*, 129-47. Sir Frank Stenton's treatment in his *Anglo-Saxon England*,
123-47 is, as usual, a model of scholarly clarity.

[7] The main section on Wilfrid is *HE* V, 19; other material is in III, 25; IV, 2, 12,
13, 15, 16, 19, 23.

[8] *Epistola Bede ad Egbertum Episcopum*, 10 (Plummer, I, 413).

[9] Cf., B. W. Wells, 'Eddi's Life of Wilfrid', *EHR* 6 (1891), 535-50; R. L. Poole,
'St. Wilfrid and the See of Ripon', *Studies in Chronology and History* (Oxford, 1934),
56-81.

[10] Cf., B. Colgrave, 'The Earliest Saints' Lives Written in England', *PBA* 44 (1958),
35-60.

[11] Cf., Mayr-Harting, *op. cit.*, 140-2.

[12] In matters of chronology I have followed Plummer's dating. To avoid overload-
ing the narrative I have not discussed here some recently suggested revisions of
particular dates, but cf., *supra*, chapter I, n. 11.

[13] *HE* V, 19.

[14] T. J. Brown and R. L. S. Bruce-Mitford, *Codex Lindisfarnensis*.

[15] Eddius, chapters I-III.

[16] Eddius, chapters IV-V. Eddius mistakenly made Dalfinus the archbishop.

[17] P. Fournier and G. Le Bras, *Histoire des collections canoniques en occident*

(Paris, 1931), t. I; K. Hughes in *The English Church and the Papacy*, ed. C. H. Law-rence (London, 1965), 15-20.

[18] Eddius, chapter V; Mayr-Harting, *op. cit.*, 132-4.

[19] Eddius, chapters VII-IX.

[20] Eddius, chapter X; *HE* III, 25, is fuller and complements Eddius at several points.

[21] Eddius, chapters XI-XIV; *HE* III, 28.

[22] Eddius, chapters XV-XVI; *HE* IV, 2.

[23] Eddius, chapter XVII; his description of the public grant of bookland is unique and important: see *infra*, chapter III.

[24] On Wilfrid's building at Hexham, Eddius, chapters XIX-XXII: and *infra*, chapter IV. For the Oxford manuscript of the rule of St Benedict, D. H. Farmer, *The Rule of St Benedict*, Early English Manuscripts in Facsimile (Copenhagen, 1968).

[25] *HE* IV, 19.

[16] Eddius, chapter XXIV.

[27] *HE* IV, 12.

[28] Eddius, chapters XXV-XXVIII. Levison has specially emphasized Wilfrid's importance for the Frisian mission.

[29] Eddius, chapters XXIX-XXXII.

[30] Eddius, chapter XXXIII.

[31] Eddius, chapters XXXIV-XL.

[32] Eddius, chapter XLI; *HE* IV, 13-14. Bede, not Eddius, tells us how Wilfrid taught the men of Sussex to use their eel-nets for sea-fishing.

[33] Eddius, chapter XLII; HE IV, 15-16; V. 7.

[34] Eddius, chapters XLIII-XLIV.

[35] Eddius, chapter XLV. In fact Ripon seems to have 'become a bishopric' only in the sense that a place had to be found for Eadhæth, a bishop exiled from Lindsey; there was no regular succession of bishops at Ripon.

[36] *HE* IV, 19, 23; E. D. C. Jackson and E. G. M. Fletcher, 'Excavations at Brix-worth, 1958' and 'The Apse and Nave at Wing, Buckinghamshire', *JBAA* xxiv (1961), 1-15; xxv (1962), 1-20.

[37] Eddius, chapters XLVI-XLVII.

[38] Eddius, chapters XLVIII-L. *Aldhelmi Opera*, ed. R. Ehwald, *MGH Auct. Antiq.* XV (1919), 500-2.

[39] Eddius, chapters L-LIX.

[40] Eddius, chapters LX-LXI.

[41] Eddius, chapter LXIII.

[42] Eddius, chapter LXIV: to this day in the Solesmes Congregation of the Bene-dictine Order the founding abbot nominates the first abbot of a daughter house.

[43] *HE* V, 20, 23. Bede dedicated several Scriptural works to Acca.

Acknowledgement for illustrations

Plates I and II (MS. Cotton Vespasian D. VI) are reproduced by kind permission of the Trustees of the British Museum.

Chapter Three

WILFRID'S LANDHOLDINGS IN NORTHUMBRIA

Michael Roper

WILFRID'S CAREER as a landholder fell into six distinct phases, each coinciding with one of the major phases of his ecclesiastical career. During the first phase, which extended from his return from Lyons about 659 until his confirmation as bishop of York in 669, he received the first of his territorial possessions from his patron Alchfrith, son of King Oswiu and under-king of Deira, who gave him ten hides at *Ætstanforda* and subsequently the monastery of Ripon with thirty hides. He also received between 666 and 669 lands in Mercia, apparently including Lichfield, as the gift of King Wulfhere and on these he founded a number of monasteries.[1]

The second phase extended from 669 until 678, when he was undisputed bishop of York with the whole of Northumbria as his diocese. He repaired the church which Paulinus had left uncompleted at York and secured for it an adequate landed endowment. From Ecgfrith and his brother, Ælfwine, he obtained a grant of an extensive region in and beyond the Pennines. From Queen Æthelthryth he received the estate at Hexham on which he founded his second great monastery. Many abbots of monasteries subordinated themselves and their houses' lands to him. Who these abbots were is uncertain, but there does appear to have been an early connexion between the monastery of *Ingetlingum* (usually identified with Gilling) and Ripon,[2] and there is a late tradition that St Everildis founded her nunnery in association with him.[3]

The next phase corresponded to the five years of his first exile. An attempt to settle in a small monastery which he received from Berhtwald, a member of the royal house of Mercia, was defeated by the intrigues of his opponents and he moved to Wessex, where he obtained 71 hides at Wedmore and Clewer (Somerset), which he subsequently transferred to Glastonbury Abbey.[4] But it was to Sussex that he finally retired to embark on a successful missionary campaign. His new patron, Æthelwalh, king of the South Saxons, gave him the royal vill of Selsey with eighty-seven hides. This grant was confirmed by Cædwalla of Wessex after his conquest of Sussex and to it was added a further seventy hides at Pagham and ten at Tangmere.[5] Cædwalla also gave to Wilfrid a quarter of the land on the newly conquered Isle of Wight.[6] Less certain are the connexion between Wilfrid and Seaford, where the relics of St Lewinna, one of his first South Saxon converts, are said to have been until 1058,[7] and his possible association with lands in Wessex.[8] On his return to Northumbria in 686 or 687 Wilfrid transferred his Pagham and Tangmere lands to Archbishop Theodore; his possessions in the Isle of Wight he left in the charge of his nephew Bernwini; and Eappa became abbot of the monastery of Selsey. With his return to Northumbria the fourth phase of Wilfrid's career commenced. Reconciliation with Æthelred of Mercia led to the restoration of his Mercian possessions, while in Northumbria he administered briefly the bishoprics of Hexham and Lindisfarne during vacancies before being finally restored to the see of York and the monastery of Ripon. This phase was brought to an end in 691 or 692 by a dispute with King Aldfrith, the outcome of which was a second exile.

This second exile constitutes the fifth phase of Wilfrid's career. Deprived of his Northumbrian possessions, he retired to his Mercian estates. These appear to have included Leicester, where he is said to have been the first bishop.[9] During this period he may have inspired the foundation of the minster at Withington,[10] and he probably now, if not earlier, obtained the monastery at Oundle, where he eventually died. He also visited Sussex and it was probably during this visit that Nothgitha transferred to him land at Lidsey, Aldingbourne, Westergate and North Mundham, which she had received from her brother, Nothelm, king of the South Saxons, for the purpose of founding a monastery.[11]

The sixth and final phase of his career commenced with the restoration by the council of the river Nidd of his own two greatest monasteries of Ripon and Hexham and his appointment as bishop of Hexham. He retained his Mercian possessions with the exception of the see of Leicester. He succeeded in maintaining his position as a major ecclesiastical landholder in Northumbria and Mercia until the end of his life. One of his final acts was to make provision for the future of his several monasteries, in particular appointing his kinsman Tatberht and his protégé Acca as his successors as abbots of Ripon and Hexham respectively.

Wilfrid regarded his lands very much as his personal possessions. Eddius twice calls York his *propriam sedem* and once *sua propria loca episcopatus sui*; he refers to the restoration by King Æthelred of Mercia in 686 of *multa monasteria et regiones propriæ iuris*.[12] In his account of the consecration of Wilfrid's new church at Ripon Eddius tells how Wilfrid stood in front of the altar and read aloud a list of the lands which Ecgfrith and Ælfwine had granted to him, with the agreement and over the signatures of the bishops and all the chief men, and also a list of consecrated places abandoned by the fleeing British clergy. Thus did Wilfrid publicize the grant to him of lands in and beyond the Pennines.[13]

In the case of Ripon and Hexham, Wilfrid went so far as to obtain a papal privilege from Pope Agatho. He was prepared to renounce all his other Northumbrian possessions if he might only keep these two favourite monasteries.[14] His territorial possessions appear to have been at least one source of the troubles with which his career was beset and of the jealousy and enmity among his contemporaries.[15]

Yet Wilfrid's apparent preoccupation with his territorial possessions must be seen within the context of his time. In a period in which the produce and rents derived from land were the major forms of income and wealth, there was no real alternative for the Church but to acquire landed endowments for its support. This had been so from the time of Constantine and by the sixth century the Church in the west had already become conspicuously wealthy.[16] St Benedict took it for granted that a monastery would receive lands for its support.[17] In England the Church had relied on gifts of lands for its endowment from the time of Æthelberht's first grants to Augustine and his companions. Similarly by the sixth century Irish monasteries, both at home and overseas, were being well endowed with lands.[18] Bede, however, reports that the early Celtic missionaries in Northumbria were very reluctant to accept such gifts.[19] Certainly, what records we have of early grants of lands to the Northumbrian Church show them to have been limited in their extent. Hild's first monastery was endowed with a single hide; Oswiu's grant of twelve estates of ten hides to found twelve monasteries as a thank-offering for his victory over Penda of Mercia appears to have been considered as very generous.[20] But after the synod of Whitby the endowments of Northumbrian monasteries became much larger. Take for example the territorial possessions of Cuthbert, reputedly among the most ascetic of early Northumbrian saints and a churchman of the Celtic-Bernician tradition. According to the mid-tenth-century *Historia de S Cuthberto* these included twelve vills in the Bowmont valley granted by Oswiu, fifteen miles around Carlisle, and Cartmel and *Suth-gedling* granted by Ecgfrith.[21] The difficulty in using this source is to distinguish between possessions given to Cuthbert during his lifetime and those made to him as patron saint of Lindisfarne, Chester-le-Street and Durham after his death, but it seems possible that at least those enumerated here were granted to him in life. We can, however, be more certain about the extent of the territorial possessions of one Northumbrian monastery of this period: the twin monastery of Monkwearmouth and Jarrow. The original endowment of Wearmouth seems to have been seventy hides; that of Jarrow forty hides.[22] Three further hides at Wearmouth were given by Aldfrith in exchange for two silk shawls; Aldfrith also gave eight hides on the river *Fresca* in exchange for a book on cosmography and this land Ceolfrith was subsequently able to exchange for twenty hides at *Sambuce*; a further ten hides at *Daltun* were given by Witmær on his entry into the monastery. Thus by 716 Wearmouth/Jarrow possessed at least 143 hides of land. Like Wilfrid, Benedict Biscop, the founder and first abbot of the twin monastery, obtained a papal privilege for his foundation.[23] Outside Northumbria the same accumulation of large landed estates can be seen in the early history of several monasteries, notably Abingdon, where Hæha appears to have acquired some 170 hides.[24] A general concern for the protection of Church lands is evidenced by the rapid spread of the charter in southern England, whoever was responsible for its introduction.[25] A number of monasteries also later exhibited papal privileges which they claimed to have received during this period, although most of them cannot be considered authentic.[26]

The estates of the more important Frankish monasteries were even more extensive than those of the English monasteries of the period, and it has been estimated that the Church in Gaul held about one third of the land under cultivation at the close of the Merovingian period (751). Ten, twenty or even thirty *villæ* were regarded as a suitable initial endowment and this would be expected to grow rapidly as further gifts were added. The size of these *villæ* varied, but it is probable that each would be equivalent to several English hides.[27] Dagobert I is said to have given at various times twenty-three *villæ* to the abbey of St Denis and, although the source is suspect, several of the *villæ* were granted by acceptable early charters, although not all were charters of Dagobert.[28] When Pippin the Short restored to Abbot Fulrad in about 751 lands which had been seized from St Denis by Charles Martel, forty-six *loca* were involved, and there is no reason to suppose that these constituted more than a fraction of the abbey's lands.[29] Other Frankish monasteries were as well endowed. Corbie received ten *villæ* and parts of two forests at its foundation between 657 and 661 and had added twenty-nine more *villæ* by 822.[30] St Wandrille, founded in 650, held lands in 185 places and amounting to 4264 *mansæ* by the end of the Merovingian period.[31] Nor were the holdings of the great Frankish abbeys confined to their own regions: St Wandrille, for example, held land in over twenty-six regions, ranging from Caux and Amienois to Nantais and Provence.[32] An example of the vast estates which a Frankish bishop could amass on his own account is provided by the will of Desiderius of Cahors (630-655), which included bequests of seventy-nine *villæ* and parts of nine others. Like Frankish monasteries, Frankish bishops might have possessions over a wide area. In the sixth century the bishops of Lyons had possessions in Provence; the seventh-century bishops of Auxerre had lands within the diocese of Cahors. A Frankish bishop appears to have had some power over the temporalities of the monasteries in his diocese from early times, but, as a rule, to have restricted his interference in the affairs of those monasteries to spiritual matters. In many cases bishops granted the larger monasteries freedom from interference in their temporal affairs.[33]

At this period the founder of a church or monastery was regarded as having certain proprietary rights in his foundation. This found expression in two ways: hereditary succession and the monastic connexion. Chad's succession to his brother as abbot of Lastingham and Benedict Biscop's specific instructions not to choose his brother as his successor suggest that hereditary succession to monasteries was not regarded as unusual in Northumbria in the late seventh century.[34] Nor was hereditary succession unknown in the Celtic Church (in both the British and Irish branches); indeed Iona was a notable example of a monastery with a long succession of abbots who were at least distantly related to the founder.[35] Similarly on the Continent hereditary succession was not unknown, and even when a blood relation was not available, an abbot would often nominate his successor during his own lifetime and secure the consent of the community to his choice.[36] Thus Wilfrid's nomination of his several successors, including at least two relatives, should not be considered out of keeping with contemporary practices.

The monastic connexion, or *paruchia*, first appeared as a feature of the Irish Church and was introduced to other parts of western Europe by Irish missionaries, such as Columba, Columbanus and Fursey.[37] In the ninth century Lindisfarne, which had originally been part of the *paruchia* of Iona, appears to have exercised supremacy over a group of Bernician monasteries comprising Melrose, Abercorn, Coldingham, Norham, Tynningham and possibly Tillmouth.[38] The connexion with Melrose appears to date from the abbacy of Eata, who had earlier been abbot of Melrose and does not appear to have resigned that office on becoming abbot of Lindisfarne. Melrose at that time appears to have exercised some sort of supervision over Coldingham. Ripon, before its grant to Wilfrid, had also been a dependency of Melrose.[39] Another Northumbrian monastic connexion of the seventh century was that of Abbess Hild, which comprised Whitby, Hartlepool, and Hackness.[40] Outside Northumbria we have the example of Peterborough (*Medeshamstede*), with its daughter houses in southern England.[41] Nor was it unusual in Merovingian Gaul for one monastery to have a proprietary right in another, despite prohibition by the councils. It was, however, rare before the end of the seventh century when Irish influences made themselves felt.[42] Thus here again Wilfrid, in building up a monastic connexion, was acting within the context of contemporary practice.[43]

The extent of the Church's territorial possessions would determine how far it could fulfil its many duties and obligations. We have seen that the rule of St Benedict assumed the existence of a landed endowment for the sustenance of the community. It is not without significance, therefore, that Wilfrid was the first to introduce the rule into Northumbria, if not into England.[44] But similar considerations applied to all monasteries of a settled nature, whether governed by that or by other similar rules.[45] The peripatetic missionary monks who went out from Iona and Lindisfarne could exist on the alms of food and money given by their converts, but after the initial missionary stage and with the establishment of settled monastic communities more permanent provision had to be made for the maintenance of the church and its servants. For with the spread of Christianity and the development of the Church the number of monasteries and monks increased considerably. How many monks were settled in Wilfrid's monasteries is not known but it may be assumed that their number was considerable. In 716 there were over six hundred brethren, although not all necessarily in orders, at Wearmouth and Jarrow,[46] and this need not have been unusual. No other figures are recorded in English sources for the period, but the great Frankish houses certainly numbered their members in hundreds rather than in tens: Corbie was founded for three hundred and fifty monks, with a limit set at four hundred; Jumièges is said to have had nine hundred monks within ten years of its foundation in 654; Lérins had five hundred monks in the early eighth century. Eighth-century Italian monasteries also had large populations, sometimes reaching five hundred.[47] Bede speaks of the British monastery of Bangor-is-Coed as organized in seven divisions, each of three hundred men, and several early British and Irish monasteries are said to have had a thousand or more inhabitants each.[48]

The needs of a monastic community were not confined to the physical sustenance of the monks; it had spiritual needs which also had to be met. This involved church construction and furnishing and the seventh century became, therefore, a period of considerable church building in England. The first church at Lindisfarne had been built 'according to the custom of the Scots' (*more Scottorum*), that is, not of stone but of wood;[49] and many churches throughout the Anglo-Saxon period must have continued to be built of the latter material. From the beginning of Augustine's mission in Kent, however, stone had been used for the more important churches and monasteries and the use of stone spread in varying degrees to all parts of England during the second half of the seventh century. In the larger monasteries it became not unusual to build several churches within the one enclosure. The cost of building in stone in England at this period must have been high. Stone quarrying appears to have been virtually unknown to the Anglo-Saxons, and even when stone and brick from nearby Roman sites could be re-used, as at Hexham, the cost and labour involved in transportation would not have been negligible. Even scarcer and more expensive than the materials would have been the skilled labour necessary to design and build stone churches. It has been assumed that Italian masons were responsible for the earliest Kentish churches, and we know that Benedict Biscop had to import masons from Gaul.[50] Wilfrid was a great church builder. We are told by Eddius of his building work at Ripon, Hexham and York,[51] and traces of his churches at the two former have survived. Eddius also tells us that Wilfrid brought masons and artisans of almost every kind to Northumbria in 666; Richard of Hexham adds that they were from Rome, Italy, Francia and other lands.[52] At York Wilfrid roofed the church with lead and put glass in the windows. This last must have been particularly expensive as there appear to have been no native glassmakers at that time.[53]

The expense of founding a church did not end with the fabric. The furnishing of the interior was as important and probably just as costly. Ripon was adorned with gold, silver and purple; the altar cloth was of purple interwoven with gold; the gospels which Wilfrid presented were written in gold on purpled parchment, illuminated and placed in a case of gold set with precious gems. At Hexham he provided ornaments of gold, silver and precious stones and decorated the altars with purple silk. According to Ailred of Rievaulx he also provided pictures for the edification of the people. On the occasion of each of his appeals to Rome, Wilfrid brought back presents for his churches: in 679 numerous relics and many other things not enumerated by

Eddius; in 704 again many relics and vestments of purple and silk.[54] Except at Ripon, Eddius does not mention gifts of books, but each monastery and church would require its own bibles and service books and at least a few books of theology and chronology in order to fulfil its regular spiritual duties. Wilfrid's contemporaries, Benedict Biscop and Ceolfrith, certainly brought back numerous books from their various continental visits to form the nucleus of the libraries of Monk-wearmouth and Jarrow.[55] There is no reason to suppose that Wilfrid did not do likewise. Certainly some traces of books associated with him are to be found in later medieval sources. Peter of Blois mentions many books of the Old and New Testaments among Wilfrid's gifts to Ripon, where a *textus Sancti Wilfridi* still existed in 1467. Two more *textus Sancti Wilfridi*, ornamented in silver and gold, were at York soon after 1500.[56] The value of books at this period may be judged by the willingness of King Aldfrith to exchange eight hides of land for a single volume.[57]

Moreover, the Church was not purely inward looking. It was the largest and virtually sole dispenser of charity, and bishops in particular were expected to bear their share of this duty. Indeed in Italy it was specifically enjoined upon a bishop that a quarter of his revenues should be given to the poor. In Merovingian Gaul the proportion was left to the discretion of the individual, but the poor were to receive a fair share.[58] Eddius speaks of Wilfrid's munificence towards both laity and clergy and it may be significant that at his death Wilfrid bequeathed a quarter of his wealth to the poor, a division reminiscent of the Italian practice and possibly one which he had followed throughout his life.[59]

Wilfrid's expenses would also have included those arising directly from the exercise of his episcopal office. At this period, before the establishment of the parish system, a bishop was expected to travel continuously throughout his diocese, performing not only those duties which we should regard as more properly the bishop's preserve, but also others which were later to be carried out by the parish priest, most notably baptism. Bede tells us of the problems which could arise in a diocese when the bishop could not or would not travel.[60] Wilfrid is reported to have been diligent in travelling about his diocese and performing the duties of his office.[61] His conception of what befitted the dignity of a bishop was probably influenced by his continental experience, and this may have accounted for the countless army of followers about which his enemies complained, although the practice of travelling with a retinue is found also in the Irish Church of the period.[62] The need for an adequate endowment for a bishopric is demonstrated by the history of the see of Rochester, which was deserted by two successive bishops after 676 'for lack of means' (*præ inopia rerum*).[63] A determination not to find himself in such a situation may have played a part in Wilfrid's opposition to the division of his diocese in 678.

Despite the widespread accumulation of territorial possessions by the Church in the seventh century, Wilfrid's case seems to be one of the few known examples of opposition to the process. Three other English bishops appear to have been expelled from their dioceses in the seventh century as a result of internal disputes: Agilbert of Wessex and Winfrith of Mercia, apparently for refusing to agree to the division of their dioceses;[64] and Tunberht of Hexham for no ascertainable reason apart from his known connexion with Wilfrid, whose protégé he was.[65] But with the exception of Ripon, there are no complaints from this period of despoliation by laymen.[66] In the eighth century the position appears to have changed somewhat. Bede regarded it as a matter of praise that the early Celtic missionaries in Northumbria should have been reluctant to accept grants of land and expressed concern at the great increase in the amount of land which had passed to the Church in Northumbria in his time. Yet the interest which he showed in recording monastic endowments, the praise which he bestowed on the benefactors of churches and monasteries and the importance which he attached to Ceolfrith's care for the lands of Monkwearmouth and Jarrow show that he was not an opponent of ecclesiastical landholding as such. His complaints were more specific: so much land had been given to monasteries that there was not enough to endow new bishoprics; and too many pseudo-monasteries had been established, thereby avoiding the secular services due from the land without any corresponding religious benefit.[67] There is, however, evidence that in other quarters opposition to ecclesiastical landholding was more radical. St Boniface accused

Osred of Northumbria (705-716), Ceolred of Mercia (709-716) and
Æthelbald of Mercia (716-757) of interference with the possessions of
the Church;[68] Pope Paul I reproved Eadberht, king of Northumbria
(737-758), for seizing three monasteries and giving them to laymen.[69]
On the continent, where the accumulation of territorial possessions
by the Church was of much longer standing and had, therefore,
reached even greater proportions, there seems to have been comparatively little lay opposition, at least so far as we can judge from the
absence of complaints of spoliation from the records of the early
Church councils and from the *vitæ* of the saints.[70] Rare instances of
hostility towards ecclesiastical landholding by Chlotar I, by his son
Chilperic and by a follower of another son, Chramnus, are mentioned
by Gregory of Tours, but without any indication that action
followed.[71] In Visigothic Spain complaints against the landholding
of Fructuosus, a seventh-century bishop of Braga, are recorded.[72] Not
until the time of Charles Martel (714-41) was there any large-scale
spoliation of the Church and even here the reason appears to have
been the need to find land for his supporters rather than opposition
to ecclesiastical landholding itself. Perhaps this could be the explanation for some of the seizures of Church land in England at this time.
Eventually in Gaul a compromise was reached whereby the Church
regained its confiscated lands in the form of *precaria*, which remained
in the occupation of the new lay holders, in exchange for a rent and
an acknowledgment of the Church's proprietary right.[73] Queen
Iurminburh's complaint against Wilfrid in 678 was ostensibly aimed
at his 'temporal glories' ... 'his riches, the number of his monasteries,
the greatness of his buildings, his countless army of followers arrayed
in royal vestments and arms',[74] but, as we have seen, the extent of his
landholding and his monastic connexion, his buildings and the other
uses to which he put his wealth, were not unusual in a contemporary
context. One must, therefore, look behind this complaint for a deeper
cause of opposition to Wilfrid. Opposition of the 'Celtic party' to his
'Roman' ways may have existed, but this would not explain the
association in this opposition of Archbishop Theodore. Rather we
should look for political reasons for Wilfrid's troubles.

In a political context Wilfrid's lands and wealth and the use to
which he put them can be seen to have a deeper significance than

simply as a source of jealousy. The wealthier he was, the more in-
fluential politically both inside and outside Northumbria he could
prove to be. This is underlined by Wilfrid's division of his wealth
immediately before his death, when a quarter was assigned to pur-
chasing the friendship of kings and bishops.[75] Recently Mr E. John
has drawn attention to the significance of Wilfrid's Mercian possessions in his stormy relations with the Northumbrian royal house and
the dynastic entanglements in Northumbria in which Wilfrid
played a part have been explored previously in this volume.[76] A not
insignificant strand in this tangled web may be isolated in Wilfrid's
personal connexion with his monastery of Hexham.

The details of his acquisition of Hexham are very largely unrecorded. The grantor was Æthelthryth, wife of King Ecgfrith, whom
she divorced in order to take the veil at Coldingham and subsequently
to become abbess of Ely. The precise date and the extent of the grant
can only be conjectured.[77] Its importance lies in its geographical position, for it was Wilfrid's first known acquisition of property in
Bernicia, the northernmost of the two kingdoms which had become
Northumbria. He was bishop of all Northumbria, and, therefore,
obviously possessed of some considerable influence already, yet
hitherto his Northumbrian possessions had apparently been confined
to Deira. Deiran expansion to the west at the expense of the British
reached the Irish sea and consequently came to a halt by the middle
of the seventh century. Indeed Wilfrid's own acquisition of the trans-
Pennine region must represent a stage in the consolidation of the
westward gains. To the south further advance was blocked by Mercia,
and although Ecgfrith's successful war against Wulfhere resulted in
the annexation of Lindsey,[78] this was temporary and no real sub-
stitute for the kind of rapid expansion and colonization which was in
progress under Oswiu and Ecgfrith on the northern borders of
Bernicia. The advance against the Picts was only halted by Ecgfrith's
death in battle in 685 at *Nechtanesmere*, after which the English
appear to have withdrawn south of the Forth. Although the Picts
then began to raid Northumbrian territory, there is no reason to suppose that the Forth frontier was not held until a much later date.[79]
This northward expansion altered the relative importance of the two
Northumbrian provinces. Alchfrith, Wilfrid's first patron, and his

successor Ælfwine, who met his death in 679 fighting against the Mercians at the battle of the Trent, were the last recorded under-kings of Deira. But before Ælfwine's death we already hear of the first of a series of officials, known variously as *subregulus, præfectus, dux regius* or *secundus a rege princeps*, who had the duty first of extending and later of defending the northern frontier of Bernicia.[80] It was, there-fore, in an expanding Bernicia that the greatest landed acquisitions were probably to be had. In view of the increasing political importance of Bernicia, Wilfrid must have been very pleased to have received a grant there; indeed he may have gone out of his way to solicit the grant. But at the time of Wilfrid's acquisition of Hexham, the final political union of Bernicia and Deira was less than twenty years old and a possible attempt following the synod of Whitby by Alchfrith to separate Deira, in which Wilfrid may have been implicated, had occurred only some five years before.[81] Wilfrid's move into Bernicia could well have appeared as an undesirable intrusion in the then prevailing dynastic and political situation and have thus contributed to the opposition to him. Whatever the circumstances of Alchfrith's rebellion, Bernicia was the stronghold of Ecgfrith's family, and the situation may have been aggravated by the manner of the gift to Wilfrid. Some nineteenth-century historians saw Wilfrid's involve-ment in the divorce of Ecgfrith and Æthelthryth as a key to his down-fall in 678,[82] and in this there could be an element of truth. This is not to suggest that Ecgfrith's hostility towards Wilfrid was motivated solely by Wilfrid's part in Æthelthryth's divorce and entry into Cold-ingham. Indeed Ecgfrith may well have welcomed his freedom from a wife who had been a wife in name only; certainly he does not appear to have waited long before his remarriage to Iurminburh.[83] But the situation was complicated by the fact that Hexham, which Wilfrid appears to have received at about the time of the divorce, had been part of Æthelthryth's dowry (*dos*).[84] The precise legal position of women as landholders at this date is uncertain, although they prob-ably had much greater power to hold land and even to alienate their dowry than they were permitted after the Norman Conquest.[85] Never-theless, Ecgfrith may have had a reasonable expectation of recovering Hexham on the dissolution of his marriage had it not been for the grant to Wilfrid; similarly Iurminburh may have had some expectation of receiving Hexham as part of her own dowry. Thus, when Archbishop Theodore was seeking allies to support him in his desire to divide Wilfrid's extensive Northumbrian diocese, Ecgfrith, his new queen and the dominant Bernician party at the Northumbrian court may have had reasons other than the ecclesiastical merits of the plan for enforcing it on Wilfrid.

According to Bede, the partition of Wilfrid's diocese in 678 involved a twofold division between Bosa, who became bishop of Deira with his see at York, and Eata, who became bishop of Bernicia with his see 'at Hexham or else at Lindisfarne' (in Hagustaldensi sive in Lindisfarnensi ecclesia); at the same time Eadhæd was made bishop of the newly conquered province of Lindsey.[86] The apparent uncertainty of Bede here as to whether Hexham or Lindisfarne was Eata's see is puzzling. Later historians certainly took him to mean that Eata had sees at both places,[87] while William of Malmesbury talks in terms of four dioceses replacing one.[88] Geopolitical considerations may already have required the division of Bernicia into two dioceses; certainly from 681 until the early ninth century Bernicia usually had three and never fewer than two bishops and there were separate sees at Hexham and Lindisfarne. It is not unlikely that the factors which led to the arrangement of 681, when Tunberht became bishop of Hexham and Eata of Lindisfarne only, with a third bishop, Trumwine, for the province of the Picts, were already appreciated in 678. But why, if two dioceses were created in 678, should one bishop have ruled both? A possible answer is that this was not the original intention. Eddius tells us that when, probably in 680, Wilfrid was in prison following his return from his appeal to Rome and his continued refusal to agree to the division of his diocese, he was promised part of his former diocese if he would acquiesce in Ecgfrith's commands and decisions.[89] It is not impossible, indeed if credence is given to William of Malmesbury it is quite probable, that Wilfrid was from the outset intended to retain part of his original diocese and only his own refusal to compromise frustrated this intention. If this was so, then the administration of two sees by Eata could be explained by supposing that one of them was that offered to Wilfrid in 680 and probably in 678 also. In another context, Bede states that Eata was first consecrated to Hexham (cui regendæ primo fuerat ordinatus),[90] but it would be more logical to expect him to have been bishop of Lindisfarne, where he was already abbot, and Wilfrid to have been bishop of Hexham, which was one of his monasteries. A confused Northumbrian tradition, which may be independent of Bede and which goes back at least to pre-Conquest episcopal lists, makes Wilfrid the first bishop of Hexham and Eata only the second, or even in some versions the third after Tunberht.[91] Moreover, it may be no coincidence that Wilfrid's departure into exile and Tunberht's appointment to Hexham both occurred in 681. Despite the extreme measures against Wilfrid which Eddius attributes to Ecgfrith, that Ecgfrith was still prepared in 680 to offer a compromise and was in the end prepared to let Wilfrid go free into exile suggests that Wilfrid yet had supporters in Northumbria whom Ecgfrith was not prepared to antagonize completely. In these circumstances Ecgfrith may have been prepared to permit Wilfrid to retain Hexham as his see, provided he was at the same time deprived of his Deiran possessions. That Wilfrid's supporters continued for some time after his exile to be a significant factor in Northumbrian politics is suggested by the appointment to Hexham of Tunberht, a known protégé of Wilfrid. A former abbot of Gilling, Tunberht had left there following an outbreak of plague to join Wilfrid at Ripon, from where he presumably moved to Hexham, possibly playing there a part similar to that which his kinsman, Ceolfrith, played in the foundation of Jarrow. But in 684 Tunberht was in turn expelled and Eata, leaving Lindisfarne to Cuthbert, returned as bishop of Hexham.[92] This expulsion may mark the final victory of Wilfrid's enemies.

On his return from exile in 686 or 687 it was to Hexham that Wilfrid was first of all restored, but only briefly, for after he had recovered York and Ripon he was replaced at Hexham by John of Beverley. Not until 706 when Wilfrid returned from his second exile was Hexham finally restored to him. He spent the few remaining years of his life as bishop of Hexham, being succeeded in that see by another protégé, Acca. But the turbulent history of Hexham was still not over, for in 731 or 732 Acca was himself expelled from the see, although the sources do not indicate why.[93]

It would be wrong to view Wilfrid's connexion with Hexham in purely political terms. The extensive programme of building which he carried out at Hexham, the association of Hexham with Ripon in the privilege of Pope Agatho and the willingness which Wilfrid expressed in his final appeal to Rome to renounce all his Northumbrian possessions except these two monasteries if the pope so ordered, are all measures of the high regard which Wilfrid had for his foundation. In recording the final restoration of Ripon and Hexham in 706 Eddius may well have been echoing Wilfrid's own assessment when he called them 'the two best monasteries' (duo optima cœnobia).[94]

Notes

[1] Unless other sources are cited, the authority for this preliminary survey is Eddius.

[2] Plummer I, 389.

[3] The York Breviary II, ed. S. J. Lawley, Surtees Society LXXV (1882), 390. I identify the site of this monastery with Poppleton on the evidence of Domesday Book I, 329a2 rather than with Everingham as in the Breviary.

[4] H. P. R. Finberg, The Early Charters of Wessex (Leicester, 1964), nos 362, 363, 366.

[5] HE IV, 13; CS 64, CS 50. I would accept these charters as substantially authentic.

[6] HE IV, 16.

[7] VCH Sussex II, 2.

[8] VCH Hants II, 3, III, 272; Finberg, op. cit., 216.

[9] HE IV, 23; De Gestis Pontificum Anglorum, 307; Chronicon ex Chronicis I, 242.

[10] H. P. R. Finberg, Lucerna (London, 1964), 21.

[11] HE IV, 14; CS 78, CS 79.

[12] Eddius, chapters XV, XXIV, XLIII, XLIV. Compare CS 50: in potestatem propriæ dominationis; and CS 79: in propriam protestatem.

[13] Eddius, chapter XVII.

[14] Eddius, chapter LXII.

[15] Eddius, chapter XXIV.

[16] A. H. M. Jones, The Later Roman Empire 284–602 (Oxford, 1964) II, 894-910, and 'The Western Church in the Fifth and Sixth Centuries' in Christianity in Britain 300–700, ed. M. W. Barley and R. P. C. Hanson (Leicester, 1968), 9-18 (pp. 11-13).

[17] The Rule of St. Benedict, ed. J. McCann (London, 1952), 98-9, 110-11, 116-17, 132-5.

[18] K. Hughes, The Church in Early Irish Society (London, 1966), 75-7, 92.

[19] HE III, 26.

[20] HE IV, 23, III, 24. Iona itself was on an island equivalent to only about five hides (HE III, 4).

[21] Symeonis Monachi Opera Omnia I, 197-200; cf., E. Craster, 'The Patrimony of St. Cuthbert', EHR LXIX (1954), 180-2. On the Carlisle grant, see also Place-Names of Cumberland III, English Place-Name Society XXII (Cambridge, 1952), xxii. At least one visit by Cuthbert to the city is recorded (HE IV, 29; Two Lives of St. Cuthbert, 116-17, 122-5). The charter (CS 66) by which Ecgfrith is said to have granted Carlisle to Cuthbert is an obvious forgery, probably made to support the claims of the bishops of Durham to Carlisle after its annexation by William II in 1092; cf.,

J. N. L. Myres, 'The Teutonic Settlement in Northern England', *History* 20 (1935-6), 245; Craster, *op. cit.*, 181. The grant of Crayke which this charter also purports to contain may not have been made to the Cuthbertine community until much later, for it is possible that the monastery there was not founded until the reign of Osred (705-16). W. Levison, *England and the Continent in the Eighth Century* (Oxford, 1946), 301, n. 1, considered the identification of the monastery which was the subject of Æthelwulf's poem (*Symeonis Monachi Opera Omnia* I, xxxiii-xxxix) with Crayke as very uncertain; cf., *Æthelwulf De Abbatibus*, ed. A. Campbell (Oxford, 1967), xxv ff. The correct reading of *Suth-gedling* given by Craster, *op. cit.*, 181-2, makes identification of that place with the *Ingetlingum* of the anonymous *Life of Ceolfrith* (Plummer I, 388), usually taken to be Gilling, possible if not certain.

[22] Plummer I, 367, 370, 391. The anonymous *Life of Ceolfrith* gives the original endowment of Wearmouth as fifty hides, subsequently increased by other gifts.

[23] *Ibid.*, I, 369, 373, 380; *HE* IV, 18.

[24] *CS* 75, 100, 101 are probably not authentic as they stand, but may be derived from a number of separate genuine charters: cf., F. M. Stenton, *The Early History of the Abbey of Abingdon* (Reading, 1913), 9-19.

[25] Cf., F. M. Stenton, *Latin Charters of the Anglo-Saxon Period* (Oxford, 1955), 31; Levison, *op. cit.*, 232; P. Chaplais, 'The Origin and Authenticity of the Royal Anglo-Saxon Diploma' and 'Who Introduced Charters into England? The Case for Augustine', *Journal of the Society of Archivists* III (1965-9), 49-52 and 526-42.

[26] Those for Peterborough, St Paul's, Chertsey and Evesham are obvious forgeries (*CS* 48, 55, 56, 129); that for Malmesbury and Frome is suspect (*CS* 105); the privilege of Pope Agatho for SS Peter and Paul, Canterbury, seems to have an authentic basis (*CS* 38); Pope Constantine's privilege for the monasteries of Bermondsey and Woking can be accepted as authentic (*CS* 133). Cf., Levison, *op. cit.*, 25, 26, n. 2, 187-90, 201, 218-19; F. M. Stenton, 'Medeshamstede and its Colonies' in *Preparatory to Anglo-Saxon England: being the Collected Papers of Frank Merry Stenton*, ed. D. M. Stention (Oxford, 1970), 185-8; E. John ' "Secularium Prioratus" and the the Rule of St Benedict', *Revue Bénédictine* 75 (1965), 222 n. 1.

[27] E. Lesne, *Histoire de la Propriété Ecclesiastique en France* I (Lille & Paris, 1910), 122-3, 211, 224; L. Levillain, 'Etudes sur l'Abbaye de Saint-Denis à l'époque Mérovingienne' IV (ii) in *Bibliothèque de l'École des Chartes* XCI (1930), 291.

[28] *Gesta Dagoberti I Regis Francorum*, ed. B. Krusch in *Ss rer Merov* II, 413, 415, 418, 420; *Diplomata Imperii*, ed. G. H. Pertz, *MGH* (in folio) I (Hanover, 1872), nos 14, 16, 32, 57. Cf., Lesne, *op. cit.*, I, 225; Levillain, 'Etudes sur Saint-Denis' I in *Bibl. de l'École des Chartes* LXXXII (1921), 87, 116. With other charters which Pertz considered authentic (*op. cit.*, nos 10, 18, 34, 35, 64, 67, 75, 85, 87, 94) they record the donation of some thirty *villæ* to St Denis between 625 and 726.

[29] Pertz, *op. cit.*, no. 23; cf., Lesne, *op. cit.* I, 225.

[30] L. Levillain, *Examen de Chartes Mérovingiennes et Carolingiennes de l'Abbaye de Corbie* (Paris, 1902), 42, 45-8, 199, 214-17.

[31] F. Lot, *Etudes Critiques sur l'Abbaye de Saint-Wandrille* (Paris, 1913), xii-xxvi, 19

[32] E. Lesne, *op. cit.*, I, 214-19; Lot, *op cit.*, xiii-xxv.

[33] *Vita Desiderii Cadurcæ Urbis Episcopi*, ed. B. Krusch in *Ss rer Merov* IV, 586-588; *Vita Beati Nicetii Lucdunensis Episcopi*, ed. B. Krusch in *Ss rer Merov* III, 522; *Desiderii Episcopi Cadurcensis Epistolæ*, ed. W. Arndt in *MGH Epistolæ* III (*Epistolæ Merowingici et Karolini Ævi* I) (Berlin, 1892), 213; Lesne, *op. cit.*, I, 124-5, 127, 137-8, 147-9, 286.

[34] *HE* III, 23, 28: Plummer I, 375. Cf., Plummer II, 262-3. Chad and Cedd also established a quite considerable monastic connexion: cf., *HE* IV, 3.

[35] K. Hughes, *op. cit.*, 76-7, 161-4.

[36] P. Schmitz, *Histoire de l'Ordre de Saint Benoît* I (2nd ed., Maredsous, 1948), 276-7.

[37] K. Hughes, *op. cit.*, 57-102; E. John, *Revue Bénédictine* 75 (1965), 219; D. Greene, 'Some Linguistic Evidence relating to the British Church', *Christianity in Britain*, 84-5.

[38] E. Craster, *op. cit.*, 179.

[39] *HE* III, 26; *Two Lives of St. Cuthbert*, 76-7, 80-1, 174-5, 188-9.

[40] *HE* III, 24, IV, 23, 24.

[41] F. M. Stenton, 'Medeshamstede and its Colonies', 179-92.

[42] E. Lesne, *op. cit.*, I, 140-1.

[43] On the use of something akin to the monastic connexion by the reformers of the English Church in the tenth century see E. John, *Revue Bénédictine* 75 (1965), 223.

[44] Eddius, chapters XIV, XLVII.

[45] The monastery of Monkwearmouth and Jarrow, for example, was governed by a rule based partly but not exclusively on the rule of St Benedict: Plummer I, 374-5. Irish rules envisaged a settled monastic community as a normal alternative to solitude or pilgrimage: K. Hughes, *op. cit.*, 138, 142, 186.

[46] Plummer I, 382, 400.

[47] U. Berlière, 'Les Nombres des Moines dans les Anciens Monastères', in *Revue Bénédictine* 41 (1929), 242, 248, 256, and 42 (1930), 31; Schmitz, *op. cit.*, I, 292; E. Lesne, *op. cit.*, I, 105.

[48] *HE* II, 2; cf., L. Gougaud, *Christianity in Celtic Lands* (London, 1932), 74.

[49] *HE* III, 25.

[50] Plummer I, 368, 390; cf., Clapham I, 41.

[51] Eddius, chapters XVI, XVII, XXII.

[52] Eddius, chapter XIV; Raine I, 20. Continental, especially Gallic, influences have been seen in the surviving fragments of Wilfrid's churches: cf., *infra*, chapter IV.

[53] Plummer I, 368.

[54] Eddius, chapters XVI, XVII, XXII, XXXIII, LV; Raine I, 175. Wilfrid's successor at Hexham, Acca, provided relics, books and furnishings there (*HE* V, 20).

[55] Plummer I, 369, 373, 375, 379. Benedict Biscop also brought back pictures.

[56] J. Leland, *Collectanea*, ed. T. Hearne (Oxford, 1715) III, 110; *Ripon Chapter Acts*, ed. J. T. Fowler, Surtees Soc. LXIV (1875), 245; *The Fabric Rolls of York Minster*, ed. J. Raine, Surtees Soc. XXXV (1858), 223.

[57] Plummer I, 380; cf., *ibid.*, 373, where three hides of land are given in exchange for two silk stoles.

[58] E. Lesne, *op. cit.*, I, 147, 333-5, 370, 375; A. H. M. Jones, *Christianity in Britain*, 12.

[59] Eddius, chapters XXI, LXIII. Cf., Eddius, chapter XI, which, although derived from Isidore of Seville *via* the anonymous *Life of Cuthbert* (*Two Lives of St. Cuthbert*, 112, 331), need not on that account lack relevance to Wilfrid's own career.

[60] Plummer I, 410-11; cf., II, 308.

[61] Eddius, chapter XXI.

[62] Eddius, chapter XXIV; cf., K. Hughes, *op. cit.*, 80.

[63] *HE* IV, 12.

[64] *HE* III, 7, IV, 6; cf., Plummer II, 215-16.

[65] *HE* IV, 28; *ASC* E 685; *Vita S. Eatæ* in *Miscellanea Biographica*, Surtees Soc. VIII (1838), 123: Cf., however, *supra*, p. oo, and *infra*, p. oo.

[66] Eddius, chapter XLV.

[67] Plummer I, 413-17.

[68] *S Bonifatii et Lullii Epistolæ*, ed. M. Tangl, *MGH Epistolæ Selectæ* I (2nd ed., Berlin, 1955), 152, 169-70. E. John, *Land Tenure in Early England* (Leicester, 1960), 64-79, links the complaint against Æthelbald with the imposition on Church lands of the burdens of building bridges and maintaining fortresses rather than with any

actual despoliation. For a contrary view see N. Brooks, 'The Development of Military Obligations in Eighth- and Ninth-Century England' in *England before the Conquest*, ed. P. Clemoes and K. Hughes (Cambridge, 1971), 69-84.

[69] H & S III, 394-5; *EHD*, 184.

[70] E. Lesne, *op. cit.*, I, 149.

[71] *The History of the Franks*, IV, 2; IV, 16; VI, 46.

[72] *Vita S. Fructuosi*, ed. F. C. Nock (Washington, DC, 1946), 90-2, 114-16.

[73] E. Lesne, *op. cit.*, I, 331-2; *ibid.* II (i) (Lille, 1922), 7-8, 41.

[74] Eddius, chapter XXIV.

[75] Eddius, chapter LXII.

[76] E. John, 'The Social and Political Problems of the Early English Church' in *Land, Church and People*, ed. J. Thirsk, 51; cf., also now *supra*, chapter I.

[77] For a fuller study of these topics see Appendix I.

[78] Eddius, chapter XX; *HE* IV, 12.

[79] *HE* IV, 26: cf., Plummer II, 261-2.

[80] Eddius, chapters XIX, LX; cf., P. Hunter Blair, 'The Bernicians and their Northern Frontier', *Studies in Early British History*, ed. N. K. Chadwick (Cambridge, 1954), 170-1.

[81] *HE* III, 14. Cf., Plummer II, 198; E. John, 'The Social and Political Problems of the Early English Church', 50. But see chapter I, *supra*, pp. 30-1 (n. 28).

[82] Plummer II, 235-6; W. Bright, *Chapters in Early English Church History* (Oxford, 1888), 280-3; W. H. Dixon and J. Raine, *Fasti Eboracensis* (1863) I, 64-6.

[83] Eadmer, *Vita Wilfridi* in *HCY* I, 186.

[84] Raine I, 23.

[85] F. M. Stenton, 'The Historical Bearing of Place-Name Studies: the Place of Women in Anglo-Saxon Society' in *Preparatory to Anglo-Saxon England*, 314-24 (pp. 315-16).

[86] *HE* IV, 12.

[87] *Symeonis Monachi Opera Omnia* I, 30; Raine I, 24; Leland, *Collectanea* I (ii), 368.

[88] *De Gestis Pontificum Anglorum*, 220. R. L. Poole, 'St. Wilfrid and the See of Ripon' in *Studies in Chronology and History*, 66-7, argued that the fourth diocese was offered to Wilfrid and comprised Western Deira with Ripon as the see, but except that Eadhæd retired there after the Mercian reconquest of Lindsey in 679, there is no evidence of Ripon as an episcopal see in the seventh century. Cf., E. John, 'The Social and Political Problems of the Early English Church', 42-50.

[89] Eddius, chapter XXXVI.

[90] *HE* IV, 28.

[91] H. Sweet, *The Oldest English Texts*, Early English Text Society 83 (Oxford, 1885), 169; *Chronicon ex Chronicis* I, 245; Raine I, 3, 9, 219.

[92] Plummer I, 388-9; *HE* IV, 12; *ASC* E 681; Raine I, 24-6. For Tunberht's expulsion see the sources cited in n. 65 above; the reference there to *ASC* is to Cuthbert's consecration, which occurred in the year after Tunberht's expulsion.

[93] Plummer I, 361; Raine I, 34-5. See again, however, *supra*, chapter I, p. 24.

[94] For Wilfrid's buildings at Hexham see Eddius, chapter XXII; Raine I, 13-18; H. M. and J. Taylor, 'The Seventh-century Church at Hexham: a New Appreciation', *AA* 39 (1961), 103-34; and *infra*, chapter IV. For the final appeal to Rome and the restoration of 706 see Eddius, chapters LI, LX.

Chapter Four

SAINT WILFRID'S CHURCH AT HEXHAM

Edward Gilbert

OF WILFRID's church at Hexham, dedicated to St Andrew, no certain traces remain above ground. Only the famous crypt can be said without cavil to have been looked on by his eyes and those of his cantor and biographer, Eddius Stephanus. The site of the abbey was royal land, which could have come from a previous British sanctuary, though no historical evidence of this exists. It was donated by King Ecgfrith's queen, Æthelthryth, an East Anglian princess and a close friend of Wilfrid.[1] The monastery was St Wilfrid's second foundation, the first being at Ripon, and in 678 Hexham became a cathedral. It was enlarged by Acca, Wilfrid's priest and successor there as bishop.[2] The see of Hexham came to an end during the first half of the ninth century. According to Ailred of Rievaulx, the abbey was burnt by the Vikings.[3] After the Scandinavian invasions the church seems to have been in the hands of secular priests, serving the immediate neighbourhood as, for example, at Repton. For such a purpose the whole church need not have been restored: the nave could have been neglected, and parts of the church were certainly derelict when Hexham was administered in the eleventh century by Eilaf of Durham. Ailred, his grandson, tells us that trees and shrubs were then growing there, probably actually in the nave. Eilaf I, and his son, Eilaf II, began a restoration which neither lived to finish. Eilaf II died in 1138 and the final re-dedication came in 1154, with a great translation of relics. In spite of this, Richard, prior of Hexham, had no doubt that what he was looking at was substantially the old Anglian cathedral.

Wilfrid clearly introduced a new architecture into England. Eddius says that there was no church comparable to Hexham this side of the Alps.[4] Baldwin Brown and others, in an age which saw Rome's inspiration behind all architecture assumed that St Andrew's, Hexham, had a Roman model.[5] Wilfrid visited Rome on several occasions, but he also spent a great deal of time in Gaul. Since we now know that the cathedrals of Gaul were not simply copies of Roman basilicas,[6] it is at least possible that Wilfrid used a model from Gaul. Eddius' comment can hardly refer to the size of the church which is known not to have been extraordinary for the time, and it is unlikely that it refers to the plan, as Baldwin Brown and Clapham understood.[7] It could refer to the ashlar fabric, unusual at that period, and to the ornamentation. Eddius' statement was probably true for England, less so for North France, still less for South France, and not at all for Spain. Eddius gives us an impression of Hexham church from his description of the foundations, the crypts, the columns and side-aisles, the winding passages and spiral or newel staircases, and the remarkably high walls. William of Malmesbury writing in the early twelfth century was told that Hexham resembled a Roman church,[8] but he does not say in what respect. As he was unlikely after 400 years to be describing an untouched building, and in view of the tendency of the twelfth-century writers to Romanize, concerning which Baldwin Brown has warned us,[9] this helps very little. Apart from additional literary evidence in Bede's nearly contemporary comments, and in the descriptions by twelfth-century writers such as Ailred of Rievaulx and Richard of Hexham, the material evidence for the early abbey at Hexham includes the crypt usually accepted as Wilfrid's, the walls and foundations, notices on the site of the present nave, recorded by C. C. Hodges and discussed in his successive publications,[10] and the various carved stones found on the site. The Romanesque church survived until *c.* 1200 when the present splendid transept and east end were constructed. The nave was not then rebuilt. It was damaged by the Scots in their devastating raid of 1296. Some works of restoration were done in the later Middle Ages, but after the Reformation the nave was apparently abandoned and fell into ruins. The original form of the church is thus to some extent uncertain, but is nevertheless, in the light of available evidence, recognized as being important in the history of west European architecture.

The Nave Crypt

Wilfrid's nave crypt (plate III) is probably the most famous early

crypt still extant in N.W. Europe. It has been described often enough
and by none better than Baldwin Brown. What is more difficult to
do is to understand it. The crypt (Plan I) consists of a barrel-vaulted

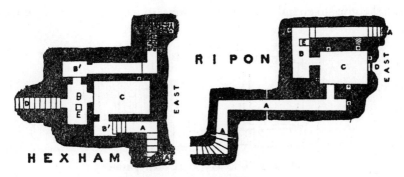

PLAN 1. Hexham and Ripon crypts

chamber (C), with a west antechamber (B), also barrel-vaulted at the
same height. The latter has a west entry of ten steps of which the
top three are modern additions, and the others not necessarily all of
the same date. The entry passage is unvaulted. There are also passages
coming from the east, from the ancient transept, whose entries (AA
on Plan 1) have now been blocked in. Apparently where they met
the original transept west wall, they turned north and south respectively, being at this point actually cut into the ancient east wall of
the early nave. Finally they turn westwards again, closely flanking
the main crypt chamber, and ending in antechambers B^1. From these
the north passage enters the main antechamber, and the south
chamber enters the crypt direct. The passages are vaulted with lintels:
the minor antechambers with triangular vaults.

What type of crypt is this then, and where does it belong in the
crypt sequence of N.W. Europe? These questions are easier to ask
than to answer. The history of the crypt is itself not clear. There was
undoubtedly a period in which mausolea and crypts consisted of a
square or rectangular chamber, half-sunk in the ground and reached
by a single stepped entry from the west. These crypts were presumably
barrel-vaulted. Such structures as at Jouarre (c. 630) or the Hypogée
des Dunes, Poitiers (c. 700) (Plan 2), are of Merovingian date.[11] The

Carolingian crypt was very different, more integrated with the church, consisting typically of a semi-circular or rectangular corridor round the edge of the sanctuary but below it and entered at each end by west doors. At its most easterly point it passed, but did not enter, a small confessio chamber lying to the west, under the high altar of the

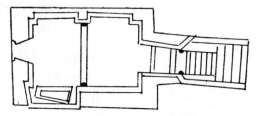

PLAN 2. The Hypogée des Dunes

church. Less well-known are the pre-Merovingian structures, consisting essentially of a square or rectangular sanctum with corridor passages either on three sides or all round. The passages were not primarily means of public entrance, or intended to give views of the chamber; they were a pagan inheritance, and their exact purpose is not clear, but perhaps to provide for simple proximity to the relic or for burials ad sanctos, or both. There is an example in the crypt of Tarrasa,[12] before 600. It is obvious that this type has resemblances to the Carolingian crypt which must have been to some extent a revival.[13] To convert the former into the latter would also not be difficult.

The difficulty with the crypt of St Andrew's, Hexham, is that it corresponds closely to none of these types in its present form. Baldwin Brown, who alone wrestled with this problem, called the crypt a mausoleum of a type common in N.W. Europe from 300 to 600, i.e., a crypt of Merovingian type.[14] He was thinking presumably of the rectangular chamber and the single flight of steps down to it from the west, and virtually ignoring as irrelevant the complex and characteristic north and south passages. The tendency today is to regard it as a highly irregular Carolingian crypt, taking the N-S passages as the relevant corridors. This view is difficult in almost every detail. The altar is at the wrong end, the entries are also at the wrong end, the passageway should not enter the chamber itself, the chamber is remote from the usual Carolingian confessio, and the west steps are untypical. A Carolingian crypt should be under the apse, and such a crypt in England in the 670s is an architectural improbability.

We are thus driven to ask whether the crypt could be an almost unique surviving specimen of the rare Early Christian crypt, even if an exceptionally elaborate and late example. This corresponds better to the facts. As such, the chamber itself is quite understandable and so are the flanking passages on three sides. On the other hand, the west entry is once again an irrelevant intrusion. A crypt with three contemporary entries is very unusual or quite unknown in early Medieval Europe, and it is easier to see the crypt, in spite of superficial appearances to the contrary, as not of one date. It seems unscientific to assume an abnormality without proof. Insertions, by contrast, are not abnormal: very much to the contrary. Nor can insertions always be detected. This has been shown many times.

That Wilfrid built the north and south passages is clear from Eddius' text (*infra*, p. 103) and therefore the probable sequence is that he built the original complex and grandiose Early Christian crypt, and that this was converted, so far as it could be, into the Merovingian crypt noted by Baldwin Brown by the addition of the unvaulted west steps, thus giving the public access to the crypt. Later, when the number of pilgrims increased, it may be that the eastern entrances were opened to the public. It is indeed perfectly possible that the eastern entrances AA did not exist in Wilfrid's Early Christian crypt. The reason for suspecting this is that the south passage ends today where the blocking of passage A begins, in what seem clearly to be the fragmentary remains of a newel staircase (plate IV). This feature corresponds so exactly to Eddius' remarks about passages and newels (or spirals) above and below the floor of the church that the writer is inclined to accept this feature as original. It could have been in the east wall of the ancient nave, and if so probably at its angle. The crypt passages could have communicated with the wall passages of the nave above and the entry for the priests and monks from the transept would then be superfluous. It is possible, therefore, that the entries AA were cut later when, because of increasing pilgrim traffic, the community at Hexham desired to give the crypt a Carolingian form. A similar development occurred at Repton (Plan 3). This would be technically easy. It is a pity, though, that both entries AA at Hexham are now inaccessible. We shall probably never know for

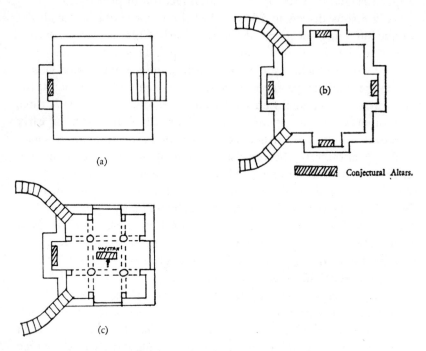

PLAN 3. Repton, development of the crypt
a. Before 700 *b*. 8th century *c*. 9th century

certain the exact history of the crypt at Hexham, but the above sequence at least takes account of observable architectural details, and there is one important piece of literary evidence which supports the thesis that Wilfrid built an Early Christian crypt. This is Eddius' hitherto unexplained, even ignored, statement that Wilfrid built 'according to the wisdom of Solomon'.[15] Solomon's Temple was an outstanding example of a sanctum ringed with passages.[16] Nor is it historically impossible that some contemporary architecture should have been influenced by Jewish architectural ideas, and in particular by the Temple (Plan 4). Assuming that what we have here is basically an Early Christian crypt, modified subsequently to a greater or lesser

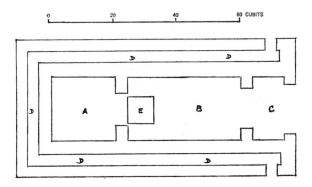

PLAN 4. The Temple at Jerusalem
A. Holy of Holies B. Cult chamber C. Porch D. Wall passages

extent, it may also be noted that it is built in ashlar, here re-used Roman stone.[17]

The position of the crypt under the east end of the nave is irregular. Moreover, a curious fact is that the crypt was not aligned with the present crossing of the church, the axis being about 1′ 3″ to the north. On the other hand, the west entry is so aligned and therefore not central to the crypt (see Plan 5). Hodges records walling running east from the east face of the main chamber, though this is not shown on his Plan 5.[18] These last two facts still await explanation. There are other peculiarities about the crypt at Hexham. The position of the entries suggests an original west-oriented church, as Micklethwaite correctly noted.[19] Remarkable, too, is the extreme plainness of the doors and walls (plate III). There is hardly a vestige of enrichment either of architecture or sculpture. This contrasts strikingly with the Hypogée des Dunes, Poitiers, where even some of the steps down are carved, as are the monolithic jambs of the door of entry and the altar. Then again, a completely sunk chamber would be irregular for the Merovingian age. The sister crypt at Ripon, however, had an east window, and it is doubtful if the Hexham crypt was originally totally underground, as we shall see. But even with all these peculiarities, there can be little doubt that this crypt was first designed as a mausoleum or martyrium. The crypt was always dark: the lighting was by lamps, the recesses for which still exist, and it was plastered, some of the apparently original plaster surviving. One would expect it to be

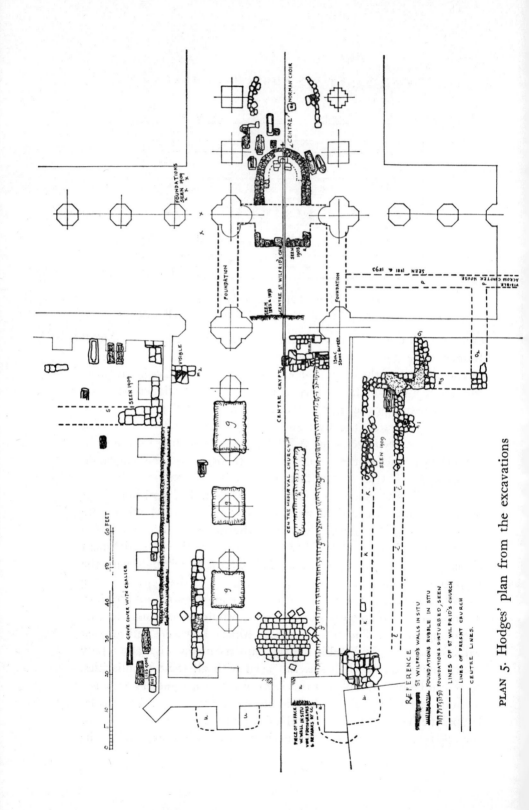

PLAN 5. Hodges' plan from the excavations

for Wilfrid himself, but in that case the idea was abandoned, perhaps when the church was made into a cathedral against his will.

The Upper Church

The upper church is also an enigma. The great difficulty is to reconcile the textual records and the structural remains drawn for us in the plan by Hodges.[20] This plan represents only walls seen casually on the site before 1907 and during an unsystematic excavation of 1905-08. We can accept the walls noted, but not that there were none where none are recorded. The excavators, Hodges and others, interpreted their plan to indicate an original five-aisled basilica, like St Peter's, Rome, with a large transept. Baldwin Brown, conscious of difficulties in this interpretation, virtually ignored most of it, giving priority to the texts which led him to hypothecate a transeptal basilica with columned nave arcades and single aisles (Plan 6). Clapham adopted a similar plan (Plan 7). Taylor rested mainly on Hodges' plan, and took Baldwin Brown to task for ignoring it (Plan 8). In justice to Baldwin Brown it should be said that he did not pretend to do otherwise, and gave reasons for doing so. He stated

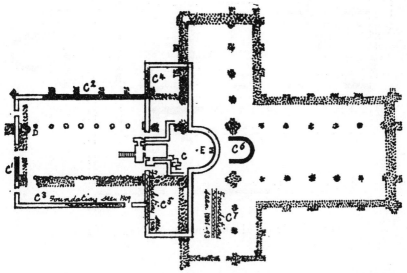

PLAN 6. Restored plan by Baldwin Brown, showing medieval additions

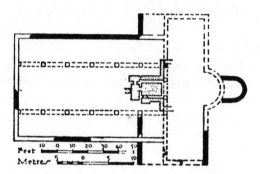

PLAN 7. Restored plan by Clapham

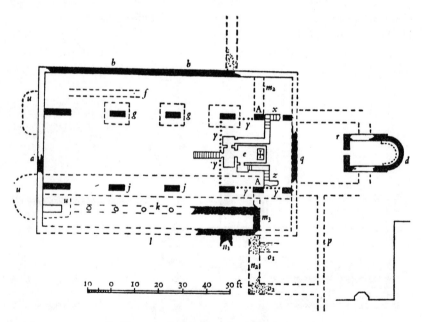

PLAN 8. Restored plan by H. M. and J. Taylor

that, 'A mere record of what has been seen and reported would supply little more than a miscellaneous collection of facts in which no system is apparent.'[21] Taylor's own plan has been criticized on these same lines. If, however, it is remembered that the walls on Hodges' plan were not necessarily all of one date, as has hitherto been assumed, the plan becomes comprehensible and most of these difficulties vanish. Were the walls on Hodges' plan all of one date or not? The crucial textual evidence is that of Bede who tells us that Acca enlarged (or 'rebuilt') (*ampliavit*) the church, enriching it and making separate porticus within the walls (*intra muros*) for the relics of every apostle or martyr he could collect.[22] *Ampliavit* normally means 'enlarged'. It has a secondary meaning of 'adorned' which has usually been taken here. The addition of porticus, however, would be expected to enlarge the church, and since we know from Richard of Hexham that the nave was ringed with porticus (*infra*, p. 103), it is unnnecessary to take the secondary meaning of *ampliavit* here. The architectural evidence also supports the idea of this enlargement. Hodges' plan (Plan 5) shows Wilfrid's nave walls 'g' and 'j' with inner narrow aisles, about 3' wide, and outer wider aisles closed by walls 'b' and 'l'. The thick walls are clearly Wilfrid's nave walls, of about 10' wide, 8' on the plan and 11' according to Savage. Similar thick walls, 9', have been found at Ripon. The natural interpretation is that the narrow inner aisle, bounded by walls 'k' and 'f' is Wilfrid's, and the enlarged outer aisles held Acca's porticus. Such a sequence is far from unknown at the time. Queen Æthelthryth, Wilfrid's friend, built her abbey church at Ely with an original narrow aisle, later widened. The nave wall was here solid, and was only pierced with arches when the aisle was widened by Abbot Ælfsige *c.* 1000.[23] Certainly Æthelwold, bishop of Winchester, restored the church *c.* 970, but the narrow aisle had no parallel then: it is essentially a Merovingian feature, and much more likely to be Æthelthryth's. It is unlikely that Ælfsige would have had to widen an aisle built by Æthelwold only thirty years before.

Bede's statement that Acca's porticus were within the walls (*intra muros*) suggests that St Andrew's similarly had a solid-walled nave originally, and that the arches implied in wall 'g' on Hodges' plan (Plan 5) were pierced by Acca for his porticus. These could not have

been within the walls of Wilfrid's church or they would not have
enlarged it. Porticus before *c.* 700 in England were normally outside the walls, communicating only by doors or very small arches like
a porch, as for example, we find in the mid-seventh century church at
Reculver in Kent. Hence indeed their name. The reason was to provide for burials, not then allowed inside the church. When larger
arches were made, this would bring the porticus *intra muros*, like
those at Brixworth, for instance, with similar arches of entry.[24] Bede
evidently thought the point important, and there is a suggestion that
Acca may have been innovating. If the openings in wall 'g' were
Acca's insertions, then wall 'g' must have been Wilfrid's wall, and
Wilfrid's floor must have been at least 6' down from the present one
for the arches went down to that depth (Fig. 1). A similar depth of

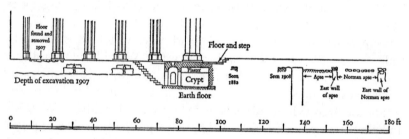

FIG. 1. Hodges' section of the nave. From Taylor and Taylor, Fig. 133

floor is equally implied if the arches were built by Wilfrid. It is also
directly suggested by the fact that the old walling in the crypt entry
stops some 5'-6' below the present floor. Neither this floor nor the
older floor at about the same level are therefore evidence for the
width of Wilfrid's church. That Acca widened the nave is a reasonable supposition. The multiple date of Hodges' walls is also suggested
by the architectural evidence. Apart from the two successive aisles,
there is a clear suggestion of an original south transeptal unaisled
porticus, or transept, bounded by wall 'm$_3$' 'o$_1$' and 'p', which was

later extended to wall 'o₂' to make quite a big transept. The inner
transept would be about 75′ long, as against Peterborough's 82′ and
the lengthened transept about 105′ which is long for an Anglian structure. Both figures are internal. Hodges, Savage, Baldwin Brown and
Clapham all agreed in seeing a transept at Hexham. Krautheimer,
admittedly, thought the evidence insufficient,[25] and the Taylors
thought that Hexham at this time had no transept.[26] Nevertheless
the transept seems probable. Oddly enough, Baldwin Brown (Plan 6)
does not use wall 'p' for its east wall, but Clapham does and is here
followed. Baldwin Brown and Clapham also found square porticus,
probably for towers, at the angles of nave and transept; but this was
the extended transept, so these were probably not present in Wilfrid's
time and they too suggest work here of more than one date. So does
the present north aisle wall at the foot of which are a few beds of
ancient work. This walling, as Savage and Hodges noted, is unlike
that in the crypt and is hardly the magnificent ashlar of Wilfrid to
which Ailred refers (Fig. 2). Furthermore, this walling is in reality

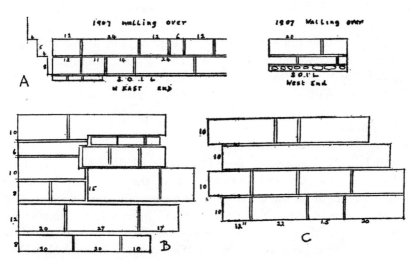

FIG. 2.   A. Ancient walling in nave, west wall
          B. Walling in crypt
          C. Ancient walling in nave, north aisle

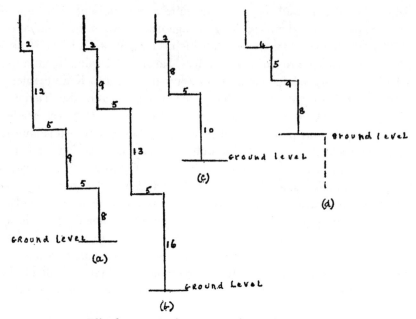

FIG. 3. Plinths at Hexham (a & b) and Repton (c & d)

part of a plinth not unlike those at Repton, and presumably that
shown in Savage and Hodges' Plate XXVI. Such plinths, according
to Baldwin Brown, were unknown before *c.* 700. In any case, we can
hardly see Wilfrid's plinth at the modern ground level.

The Floors

The conclusions drawn here from the evidence conflict with those
offered by Hodges and Savage. They believed the walls on Hodges'
plan unitary in date and original, because, they said, they found the
same mortar in all these walls, in the ancient flagstone flooring, and
in the original crypt. Nevertheless, there is something incorrect in
this reading of the evidence for the flagstone floors concerned certainly
could not have been Wilfrid's. On Plan 5 it can be seen that they
over-ran wall 'k', not to mention wall 'h', a wall which fits into no reconstruction of the church and is usually discreetly ignored. If ever
the existence of a previous British sanctuary at Hexham is proved,
this could be one of its walls.[27]

Ailred of Rievaulx records that his father, Eilaf, relaid the floor of part of the church in cut stone,[28] and there is every reason to suppose that his successors finished the work. The description fits exactly the ancient flooring found by Savage and Hodges. They give the stones as measuring 2′ 6″ × 2′ 3″ × 6″, which is certainly 'cut stone'. The correspondence of the literary and structural evidence seems decisive. These floors were, moreover, almost at, or just above the modern floor level, and this is improbable for Wilfrid's floor (Fig. 4). It follows

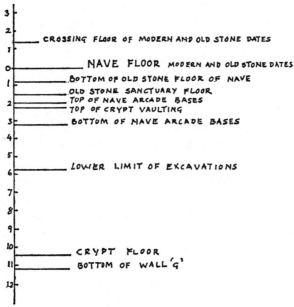

FIG. 4. Heights above and below the nave floor

that the mortar found was not Wilfrid's. Further evidence of this is that it occurred in the north aisle wall just shown to have been later than Wilfrid. This mortar was probably Eilaf's, and its occurrence in the crypt must be secondary. It was made of sand and lime, with too much sand, and was not a very good or indeed typical Saxon mortar. That the flagstone floors were Eilaf's is further suggested by the east end of Wilfrid's apse. This was found ringed with empty tombs including that always traditionally ascribed to Acca. The tombs were

scattered on the ground where they had presumably been exhumed
for the translation of 1154. The exhumation holes are visible in the
photograph in Hodges and Gibson and evidently this ground level
which is about a foot below the flagstone floor, was that of the twelfth
century.[29] If the ancient flagstone flooring was Eilaf's then Wilfrid's
floor, more probably of *opus signinum* than flagstones, must have
been lower, as noted above, presumably below the top of the crypt
vaulting (Fig. 4). This seems to have been the case, however, for when
the flagstone floor buried the crypt there was no earth on the latter.[30]
The crypt, it appears, must have originally carried a kind of podium
in the nave, presumably for the choir. A similar arrangement seems
to have existed at St Martin's of Tours, a church with special relevance for St Andrew's, Hexham.

The Bases Found on the Piers of Wall 'g'

The bases on the piers of wall 'g' found by Hodges, and shown in
his elevation (Fig. 1) were believed by him and Savage to be the
original work of Wilfrid. It is not possible to accept this. Neither
Baldwin Brown, nor Clapham, nor Taylor, nor the present writer
believe that such bases, whether for columns or pillars, could be
original work of the seventh century in England. Only arcades on
piers are known to have existed in early days in England. Taylor,
therefore, supposes that Hodges' 'bases' were in reality piers. Hodges,
however, plainly describes them as bases, and his elevation shows
them as such (Fig. 1). Moreover, piers on sub-piers are equally unknown at the date, and the underlying piers could hardly have been
planned for these bases. They create openings varying from 5' to 18'
wide, and themselves vary from 10' to 14' long (Plan 5). Such an
irregular construction was not made for a regular nave arcade, as
Baldwin Brown and Clapham appreciated, but it agrees remarkably
well with arches cut in the walls for porticus. As to the piers in wall
'g' carrying these bases, Savage and Hodges described them as simply
foundations of cement. They would be such if the bases had really
been Wilfrid's work, but once this hypothesis is discarded they could
be Wilfrid's walls robbed of their dressings. Foundations built in the
form of piers are perhaps not very usual. It would be hard to find
parallels. This point bears on the question of whether the first arcades

1. wall 'g' were built by Wilfrid himself, or pieced by Acca, but this is not very crucial. Probably, for the present, an open mind is best on this matter.

The East End

East of wall 'p', here taken as Wilfrid's east transept wall, there are on Hodges' plan two apses in file (Plan 5). The smaller western one was found ringed with tombs including that traditionally ascribed to Acca, which, as Symeon of Durham tells us was sited at the east end of the church.[31] These facts create a strong presumption that this was the original apse, and it has always been taken as such in popular tradition. Doubts have arisen for various reasons. It is very narrow, and the wall 'r' at the west end makes it look like an independent chapel, as Taylor noted. The first difficulty is explicable if it was a martyrium sanctuary, and the second if this was of two stages as at Repton with a crypt below. The wall 'r' would then belong to the crypt, the upper stage being pierced to unite it with the transept, again much as at Repton. The two-staged sanctuary was common enough in England in early days, as at Repton, Brixworth and other places. There are, moreover, in Hodges' elevation (Fig. 1) signs that the walls of the structure ran down below the floor, and there is moreover a strong tradition at Hexham of there having been a second crypt, which indeed Eddius implies. Savage excavated to try and find it in the cloisters, but found nothing there. No deep excavation has taken place under the sanctuary, though, as noted above, the tombs must have been well down from the cut-stone floor of this structure. The form of the east end, an apsed rectangle, cannot be paralleled in England, but it seems to have existed in Auxerre even before the Carolingian age. If Hexham had a crypt there, which of course is not certain, it would perhaps explain the position of the surviving crypt under the nave, the favourite site for a crypt being pre-empted. Two crypts can and often do exist in one church, as at St Servaas, Maastricht, where there are three, the two oldest being not so unlike that at Hexham.

Parallels

Wilfrid would not have built a church unrelated to contemporary

architecture as Baldwin Brown and Clapham understood perfectly. A
probable parallel in Baldwin Brown's view was the church of the great
Mercian abbey of Peterborough (*Medeshamstede*). He believed that
Wilfrid had some connection with this abbey, most probably when
bishop of the Middle Angles for some years near the end of the century. Bede tells us that Wilfrid died in the province of Oundle (in *pro-
vincia Undalum*) in the abbey of a certain Cuthbald,[32] whom Hugh
Candidus of Peterborough in the twelfth century identifies with Cuthbald, abbot of Peterborough from 673.[33] This identification is not impossible and Peterborough was in the province of Oundle. Eddius
however tells us that Wilfrid died *in Undolum*[34] which is usually
taken to mean 'in Oundle' though the Latin is peculiar, and there is
no other evidence of a monastery at Oundle at that date. The writer
is inclined to believe that Peterborough was Wilfrid's monastery.
Certainly the architectural evidence is plentiful for a monastery of
this date at Peterborough, but totally absent at Oundle. There is even
at Peterborough a stone carving resembling items at both Hexham
and Ripon, and such an affinity could only belong to the time of
Wilfrid. There seems a good reason, therefore, to support Baldwin
Brown's view that the monastery at Peterborough had special
relevance to Hexham (Plan 9). It had a *transept continu* of some size,
a narrow sanctuary about 22′ across, of which the east finish is lost,
and apparently a solid-walled nave for Baldwin Brown is surely right
when he says the plan was non-basilican,[35] *i.e.* without aisles. Bishop
Æthelwold restored the church *c.* 970 but there is no suggestion that

PLAN 9. Medeshamstede (Peterborough) E. End of the Abbey Church

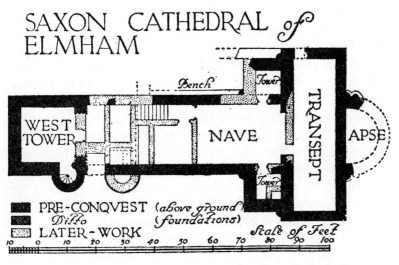

SAXON CATHEDRAL *of* ELMHAM

Bench   Tower

WEST TOWER   NAVE   TRANSEPT   APSE

Tower

■ PRE-CONQVEST (*above ground*)
■ Ditto   (*foundations*)
▨ LATER~WORK   *Scale of Feet*

PLAN 10. North Elmham, the Anglian Cathedral

he replanned it. Æthelwold 'found there in the church, the stalls of cattle and sheep and the whole place filled with foulness ... he straightway began to make the place clean...'[36] This shows what twelfth-century writers meant by 'rebuilding' a church. We should call it restoring. The total destruction of the church to which Hugh refers elsewhere must apply to its obliteration as a centre of worship, not to architectural destruction. It is important to take words as the writer meant them, not as we use them. The plan, one may safely say, is not one of *c*. 970 in England, nor in Europe if the solid-walled nave is allowed. More probably it is that of the first stone church. This stone church could be Wilfrid's if Peterborough was one of his Mercian abbeys, and the very first church built by the Mercian, Sax-wulf, could well have been of wood, like the first York minster. The cathedral of North Elmham, which must have been under construction when Æthelthryth returned to East Anglia, just at about the time that Wilfrid was building at Hexham, is possibly also relevant. North Elmham (Plan 10) had exactly the plan which has been reconstructed for Peterborough and Hexham, a relatively large *transept continu* with a diminutive sanctuary, and a long solid-walled nave. There were certainly porticus at the re-entrant angles of nave and transept, as seems to have been the case at Acca's Hexham. The plan is obviously not Romanesque, whatever the date of the buildings on it. The ideas behind it again could well have been Wilfrid's, if only indirectly, in view of his friendship with Æthelthryth.[37] A church which may have had a similar plan is that of Britford near Salisbury, where there are reasons for supposing an original *transept continu*, and where the surviving solid-walled nave is dateable to *c.* 800 by the openings of the porticus at the re-entrant angles of nave and transept, much like those at North Elmham and suspected at Hexham:[38] and another church suspected of an early *transept continu* and an aisleless nave, with porticus at the angles of nave and transept is at Stow (Lincs.), which could conceivably have had Wilfridian connections.[39]

Important parallels to St Andrew's are provided by the churches at Brixworth and Repton, the former an offshoot of Peterborough.[40] Brixworth has piers and arches in the nave like those implied in wall 'g' at Hexham, though the Brixworth arcades could belong to Acca's time rather than to Wilfrid's.[41] St Wystan's, Repton, where Æthelbald, king of Mercia, was buried in 757, is a very important analogy for Hexham. Like St Andrew's at Hexham, it shows signs of a crypt with a single stepped entrance, later replaced by double entrances, a transept which could formerly have been a *transept continu*, a nave—possibly solid-walled—with a narrow south aisle (4′ 6″ wide), and probably from the beginning a two-staged sanctuary. The latest Anglian work at Repton is now thought to have been in the reign of Wiglaf, king of Mercia, in the mid-830s.[42] Recently, the crypt has been regarded as the work of Æthelbald, king of Mercia (716-57).[43] But Guthlac, the founder of Crowland abbey, was at Repton *c.* 700 when Repton was already a flourishing community.[44] Moreover, this view is obliged to question the validity of the plan by R. Garwood (Plan 11), made during the restorations of 1886-7,[45] part of which, with reference to the transept can still be visibly authenticated, and it ignores the important change of fabric from a red limestone to a whiter one occurring in all the standing Anglian work about 10′ above today's ground level. This evidence seems conclusive (as Baldwin Brown wrote) 'that the upper part of the walling ... is of later date than the red stone part below'.[46] We have to consider also the evidence that the red stone church was of two dates itself, as suspected by Baldwin Brown, both of which were subsequent to the first building of the crypt. The evidence as a whole surely supports the traditional view that the crypt was begun before 700. It is now thought to have been originally a free-standing

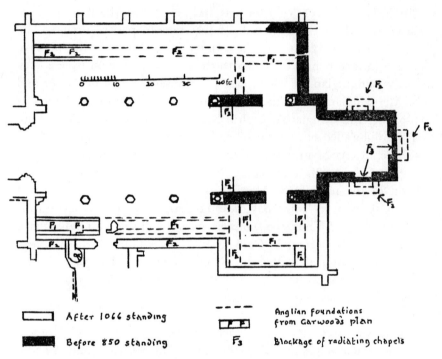

PLAN 11. St Wystan's, Repton; Garwood's plan

martyrium or mausoleum, a fact also favouring this early date.[47] There is therefore a good case for seeing the origins and early development of St Wystan's as about contemporary with that of St Andrew's, Hexham, and therefore as evidence of the sequence at Hexham.[48]

Transepts had long been a feature of church building on the continent. St Martin's of Tours probably had a transept as did the cathedrals, for example, of Le Mans and Clermont before 600. These churches had central towers but apparently lacked the *transept continu*. They have been described as domed basilicas.[49] The main altar was under the crossing and not at the east end. The earliest certain traces of a *transept continu* in Gaul seem to be *c.* 800 at St Generoux Deux Sèvres.[50] St Philibert's church, Jumièges, shortly after 630, had a transept, and, since there is no mention of an altar where the crossing would be, it may be that it was a *transept continu*. Similarly, a *transept continu* may have existed at the Basse Œuvre, Beauvais, where the west wall of the transept partly survives. The date here is not agreed, but the transept is not in bond with the nave which in turn is not in bond with the façade. The main nave is very likely Carolingian, in which case the transept should be earlier and of Merovingian date. The solid-walled nave at St Eusebe, Gennes, is probably Merovingian, though it has been regarded as Gallo-Roman. The solid-walled nave occurred early in Gaul, before 500 at St Pierre de Vienne. At St Eusebe de Gennes, however, it is probably Merovingian. Crozet calls it 'archaic'.[51] It has been suggested as the original form of the nave of St Martin's of Tours, also before 500,[52] and certainly exists at Tourtenay, near Poitiers, which Crozet again calls 'very archaic'.[53] Thus, the *transept continu* and the solid-walled nave were probably current in Gaul when Wilfrid built Hexham abbey. And the church of St Veterin, Gennes, with a similar plan, has an archaic towered porticus at the angle of the nave and transept, placed like those in the English examples discussed above.

Wilfrid's Church : Plan and Superstructure

The conclusion is probably, therefore, that Wilfrid's church had a two-staged sanctuary on the site of the western apse in Hodges' plan. Finality must await further excavations. The transept seems reasonably certain. It was aisleless and probably a *transept continu* from the weight of analogies. It was later lengthened on the south at least. The nave was more probably solid-walled than not, with very thick walls. Traces of these exist underground, but probably not above ground. The nave had extensive wall passages, leading on to an envelope of passage porticus of two stories, both passages and porticus having upper stages reached by newel staircases which existed, probably, at the angles of the nave and possibly elsewhere also. There was probably a west porch of two storeys breaking the wall passages and envelope of porticus. The latter would be reached by doorways from the passages (Plan 12).

For the superstructure of St Wilfrid's church Eddius is an important source, and he describes the church as follows: Wilfrid

'built the bottom of the church in the ground, spread out with crypts (*domibus*) of wonderfully polished stones. Above ground he built a complex church, propped up by many-coloured columns and by many porticus, and ornate with a wonderful length and height of walling, and surrounded by straight passages at right-angles, arranged sometimes above and sometimes below, and with newel staircases....'[54]

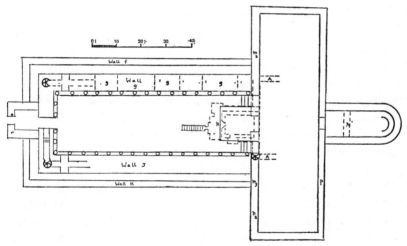

PLAN 12. St Andrew's, Hexham, Restored Plan *c.* 680

The implication that there was more than one crypt should be noted. The reference to columns led Baldwin Brown to posit his columned nave arcades, and Clapham to follow him. This thesis is now abandoned for lack of parallels in England, but this does not explain Eddius' words. A similar problem has dogged the church of St Martin of Tours, where Gregory of Tours' reference to the forty-one columns of the nave is hard to explain. The latest, and surely the best, theory is that of Jean Hubert, who sees the columns as facing the nave walls, perhaps in two orders, as at St Pierre de Vienne, where the number of columns is much the same.[55] This could have been the arrangement at St Andrew's: indeed Eddius' phrase, indicating that the walls were 'propped up' (*suffultos*) by the columns rather than supported by them (*sublatos*), favours it. The columns certainly existed and it is hard to suggest a better arrangement for them. As for Eddius' porticus, the surviving ancient walls of the church show us fairly clearly where these were. These are the lower part of the south nave wall, and part of the nave west wall.[56] Savage and Hodges thought these walls dated to the fourteenth century, but in fact they seem to be Romanesque. Internally they based their conclusions apparently on the base of the respond at the west end of the nave north arcade (plate VI) This and the column bases it carried have the double hollow moulding. Hodges thought this perpendicular.[57] We know now that such mouldings are Early Norman, and would here reflect Eilaf's work. Hodges and Gibson called the plinth under the nave south wall 'ogee'. It is a plain hollow moulded plinth (plate V). Under it is an older plinth of apparently three or four square orders, seen in 1907. This latter plinth appears also on the interior of this nave south wall, and without the hollow moulded order on top of it, proving the latter an insertion (plate V). This interior square-cut plinth itself lies on a wider older walling about 10′ thick. The nave walls above the plinths are 6′-7′ thick.

The exterior west wall, with its restored doorway, has few continuous beds, and is surely a medley. Hodges, for no obvious reason, thought the inferior stonework above the plinth on the south of the doorway, was Wilfrid's original work. A more natural interpretation would be that it was patching of some date (Fig. 2C). Whatever their date, the ancient south and west walls have internal wall passages associated with newel staircases. There is a ground floor passage in the north aisle west wall leading to a newel staircase, some of the walling of which is old, and which is placed at the angle of the nave north and west walls. In the nave west wall is another ground floor passage running south from the doorway and also ending in an ancient newel staircase at the angle of the nave south and west wall. This is clearly visible in one of the photos taken at the time of the rebuilding of the nave (plate VI). The south wall also had a wall passage, not now visible, at its west end. The angle newels and the galleries to which they led can be paralleled in Norman work, but the ground floor passages are unusual, and the whole fits so exactly Eddius' words that there were 'passages at right angles, sometimes above and sometimes below, with newel staircases', that it seems that we have here one of the important harmonies between texts and architectural remains, which have to be accepted as significant. In other words we are looking even today, in these parts of Hexham abbey, at a conservative rebuild of Wilfrid's original work, at first or second remove, but pre-*c.* 1200. These passages must have originally served Wilfrid's porticus, and, if the cross walls are missing from the porticus, possibly they did not exist at ground level. The ground floor of the passages is slightly above the cut-stone floor attributed above to Eilaf, and, if Wilfrid's floors were lower, there could have been a few feet of passageway to fill in. This might explain the mysterious concrete found in wall 'g' which looks inappropriate to a seventh-century wall.

We thus have some evidence that the passages referred to by Eddius were wall passages, a fact already suggested by the great thickness of the nave walls, and that they served for access to porticus of two stages ringing the nave. The arrangements correspond fairly strikingly to those of the 'double-walled' martyria of the fifth century in the East, which consisted of a central nucleus surrounded by outer galleries or a series of chapels.[58] The suggestion is that Wilfrid's nave, with its own crypt, was considered a martyrium in its own right. Since Hodges thought he saw marks of columns on or in the inner aisle walls,[59] it is just possible that Wilfrid's nave envelope could have been, as at St Juan de Baños, Spain, built in 661, a colonnaded portico.[60] In that case, his west entry was probably a single-storeyed porch, as at Baños. The Baños porticos may have had upper storeys as the putlog holes for the floors exist. In our northern climate, however, simple passage porticus would seem more likely. That Richard of Hexham was not looking at any such arrangement is suggested by the form of what he saw. His description runs thus ... 'He surrounded the body of the church with porticus and lean-to rooms, which with marvellous and mystic skill he separated into upper and lower stages, with walls and newel staircases. In and above the newels he built stone steps and curving or dog-elbowed passages....'[61]

The porticus were in tower form, and some still stood in Richard's day. The 'lean-to' room (*appenticiis*) evidently separated the porticus. This vivid description corresponds exactly with the structural remains deduced at the west façade of Brixworth, dating to after *c.* 700.[62] The arrangements flanking the nave would no doubt be similar, and would resemble those seen in the drawing of a Kentish Carolingian church found at St Augustine's, Canterbury (Fig. 5)[63] or visible today in Maastricht. Richard, of course, attributed all this work to Wilfrid,

FIG. 5. A Kentish Carolingian Church, for comparison with Acca's Church

but the concept is not earlier than *c.* 700. No such work exists in Kent before then, and the only comparable features, in the west façade of Reculver church, are known to be an insertion after 700. On the other hand, these structures, involving the wider aisles at Hexham, do sound like the 'astonishing structures' by which Acca enlarged Wilfrid's church. On the whole, therefore, it seems reasonable to ascribe to Acca the enlarged porticus and chapels ringing the nave at Hexham, the lengthening of the transept, and the building of porticus at the angles of nave and transept, and possibly also the eastern entries (AA) to the crypt. This work is itself of historical importance. The 'separate porticus' (*distinctis porticibus*) flanking the nave, to which Bede refers, are probably typical of the English pseudo-aisled basilica, such as Brixworth. The multiple tower scheme implied is proto-Carolingian. There must have been five ringing the nave, two at the angle of nave and transept, and it is not impossible that others covered the transept (Plan 13). This leaves unaccounted for on Hodges' plan, the foundations for two heavy flanking western towers, and the eastern apse. The former are much more likely to be Romanesque in England than early, and probably belong with the double hollow base attached to the nave west wall. The eastern apse would also seem

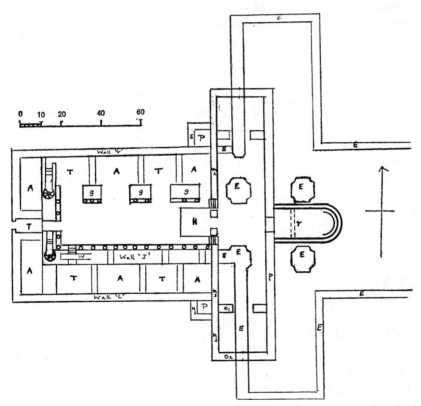

PLAN 13. St Andrew's, Hexham, Restored Plan before 732
A. '*Appenticiis*' referred to by Richard. T. 'Towered porticus' referred to by Richard.
P. Other porticus. E. Medieval work.

Romanesque, and was perhaps a development from Eilaf's original scheme before the rededication of 1154.

Wilfrid's plan and arrangements, if recovered rightly here, belong to the Merovingian age as surely as Acca's are proto-Carolingian. This is hardly surprising if we recall Wilfrid's deep involvement in Frankish affairs in his youth and at the time of the building of St Andrew's, Hexham. St Martin's of Tours, for instance, had most of the features here ascribed to St Andrew's, Hexham. The constant references by Gregory of Tours to the *absida altaris* and the *absida corporis* (or *'tumuli'*, the same thing) do suggest a martyrium sanctuary on two stages at Tours.[64] The transept is vouched for by Conant:[65] the solid-walled nave by Hubert,[66] and the envelope of 'porticus' by Odo of Cluny.[67] Even the raised choir in the nave seems indicated for Odo tells us that the crowd pressed on the *antipodia chori*, which implies a choir on a podium. If this comparison is valid, a relationship between the two churches becomes quite probable, especially when we remember that Wilfrid must surely have visited the church of St Martin during his residence at Lyons, so that St Andrew's, Hexham, could have been intended to reflect the design of St Martin's, to be, that is, a martyrium with transeptal form. It is of course, always possible that the influence of St Martin's came indirectly, via such a church as that of St Philibert at Jumièges, which certainly had a transept, probably *continu*. But Wilfrid's personal association with Gaul in this context is striking, and Martin was the principal saint of the Frankish kings. Office holders took their oath of loyalty on the 'cappa' holding relics of Martin's famous cloak.

The Enceinte

Nothing now remains of Wilfrid's claustral buildings, which need excavation. We can be fairly certain they were on the south like the medieval cloisters. References exist, however, to two associated churches. One was St Mary's, presumably on the site of the medieval church of that name, which may have included some parts of the church of St Mary, known to have been built by Wilfrid shortly before his death. It lay, if so, a little way E S E of the main church. This early church is described by Ailred of Rievaulx as having porticus on each face and being nearly round.[68] Some resemblance to the rotunda at Aachen, which was sixteen sided externally, is indicated. Clapham compared it to the baptistery of the Arians at Ravenna.[69] It is certainly unexpected to find a centrally planned church in west Europe which was not a baptistery, for which it would only have been suitable if the first church were west-oriented.[70] Wilfrid's church of St Mary could have been on a different site.

The other church, dedicated to St Peter, is thought, less certainly, to have stood W N W of the abbey Church.[71] There was, therefore, possibly a triple cathedral, such as was quite common in Merovingian times. In Gaul the churches were usually side by side, but, according to Hubert,[72] in the extreme west they could be in file, as for instance at St Augustine's, Canterbury. The original function of these churches is uncertain. One, the main church, was for the parish. One was usually a baptistery, and the third one, according to Hubert, was originally for catechumens,[73] though not everyone agrees about this. It was probably later used as a private church for monks or canons serving the cathedral. If Acca incorporated a porticus for St John into the main church, this must have released the original baptistery for other purposes. The exact history of all this is hardly recoverable today.

St Peter's Church at Ripon

It is highly regrettable that we do not know more about Wilfrid's first church at Ripon, destroyed by the West Saxons in 948. Like St Andrew's, it is described by Eddius as having many coloured columns and many porticus, and the similarity of the two churches is not to be questioned.[74] The two crypts were similar, the Ripon crypt, which survives, being a slightly smaller and simpler version of that at Hexham. The Ripon crypt is made in fair ashlar, showing that the ashlar work at Hexham was intended and not merely opportunist. The main crypt chamber is the same width as that at Hexham but about 16 per cent shorter. It has a window in its east wall, indicating it was not wholly an underground structure. There is a west entry, as at Hexham, but here entering the main chamber direct from the north. The case for seeing this as an inserted entry is the same as at Hexham. There is, however, only one east passage. One would suppose this to be due to relative lack of funds. The main chamber, as at Hexham, is barrel-vaulted, with thin transverse arches, like pilasters, supporting flat slabs. Traces of blue and gold paint were found under the plaster in this main chamber.

The crypt today is under the crossing of the medieval church, but Peers found by excavation what he thought were the original nave walls, flanking the crypt on both sides.[75] These walls were about 9' thick, giving a nave about 30' wide. Embedded in their west interior angle were column bases. Neither was *in situ* and they were of different material and size. They were too big for wall-columns, but could have carried large triple arcades.[76]

Notes

[1] Eddius, chapter XXII.
[2] *HE* V, 20.
[3] Raine, 173-203.
[4] Eddius, chapter XXII.
[5] Baldwin Brown, II, 149-183.
[6] Jean Hubert, Jean Porcher and W. F. Volback, *L'Europe des Invasions* (Paris, 1967). There is an English translation, *Europe in the Dark Ages* (London, 1969) by Stuart Gilbert and James Emmons.
[7] Clapham, I, 45.
[8] *De Gestis Pontificum Anglorum*, 255.
[9] Baldwin Brown, II, 150.
[10] See in particular Hodges and Gibson, and Savage and Hodges.
[11] *Europe in the Dark Ages*, 57-66.
[12] Puig y Cadafalch, *L'Art Visigothique* (Paris, 1961), 29.
[13] A. Grabar, *Martyria* (Paris, 1943-6), 515.
[14] Baldwin Brown, II, 160-4.
[15] Eddius, chapter XVII.
[16] Cecil Roth, *Jewish Art* (London, 1961), 82.
[17] Baldwin Brown, II, 162.
[18] Hodges, 17 and plan 8.
[19] J. T. Micklethwaite, 'On the crypts of Ripon and Hexham', *Arch. J.*, 39 (1882), 347-54.
[20] Plan 5: Hodges' plan was never printed by him but plan 5 is a copy of it by Oriel Press.
[21] Baldwin Brown, II, 168.
[22] *HE* V, 20: Bede states that Acca 'enlarged his church ... with enrichment on all sides and astonishing structures ... for he did his best to put altars in their honour, making separate porticus within the walls...' (ædificium multifario decore ac mirificis ampliavit operibus. Dedit namque operam ... ut ... in venerationem illorum poneret altaria, distinctis porticibus, in hoc ipsum intra muros ejusdem ecclesiæ.)
[23] Clapham, I, 90 (and n. 1).
[24] *Infra*, p. 100.

[25] R. Krautheimer, 'The Carolingian Revival of Early Christian Architecture', *Art Bulletin* 24 (1942), 1-38.

[26] Taylor (H. M.) and Taylor (J.), 297-312.

[27] For their views on these matters see Hodges and Gibson, 39-42, and Savage and Hodges, 38-40.

[28] Baldwin Brown, II, 158.

[29] For the photograph: Hodges and Gibson, facing p. 82. The floor level is shown in E. A. Fisher, *The Greater Anglo-Saxon Churches* (London, 1962), Fig. 2.

[30] See the plan and elevation in Savage and Hodges, 38.

[31] *Symeonis Monachi Opera Omnia*, II, 33.

[32] Bede *HE* V 19.

[33] *The Peterborough Chronicle of Hugh Candidus*, trans. C. M. and W. T. Mellows (Peterborough, 1941).

[34] Eddius, chapter LXV.

[35] Baldwin Brown, II, 168-71: see also for Peterborough, Taylor (H. M.) and Taylor (J.), 491-4.

[36] *The Peterborough Chronicle of Hugh Candidus*, 15.

[37] For North Elmham, C. A. R. Radford, 'The Bishop's Throne in Norwich Cathedral', *Arch J.*, 116 (1959), 115-32, and S. E. Rigold, 'The Anglian Cathedral at North Elmham, Norfolk', *MA* 6 (1962), 67-108.

[38] A. W. Clapham, 'Britford Church', *Arch. J.*, 104 (1947), 160-1, and Taylor (H. M.) and Taylor (J.), 105-8.

[39] Taylor (H. M.) and Taylor (J.), 584-93.

[40] F. M. Stenton, 'Medeshamstede and its Colonies', reprinted in *Preparatory to Anglo-Saxon England*, ed. D. M. Stenton (Oxford, 1970), 179-92.

[41] Edward Gilbert, 'Brixworth and the English Basilica', *Art Bulletin* 47 (1965), 1-20.

[42] Edward Gilbert, 'St. Wystan's, Repton', *Cahiers Archéologiques* XVII (1967), 83-102.

[43] H. M. Taylor, 'Repton reconsidered', *England before the Conquest*, ed. P. Clemoes and K. Hughes (Cambridge, 1971), 351-89.

[44] *Felix's Life of St. Guthlac*, ed. Bertram Colgrave (Cambridge, 1956), 82-7, 178.

[45] J. T. Irvine, 'Plan of Discoveries Lately Made in Repton Church', *JBAA* 50 (1894), 248-50.

[46] Baldwin Brown, II, 319.

[47] Edward Gilbert, 'St. Wystan's, Repton', 88-91.

[48] For a more detailed discussion, see Edward Gilbert, 'St. Wystan's, Repton: its date and significance', *Cahiers Archéologiques* XXII (1972), 237 ff.

[49] *Europe in the Dark Ages*, 32. Gregory of Tours (II, 16) refers to the church at Clermont as being *in modum crucis*.

[50] R. Crozet, 'L'Eglise St. Generoux et ses parentés', *Symposium sobre cultura Asturiana* (Oviendo, 1967), 21-5; cf. Crozet, *L'Art Roman en Poitou* (Poitiers, 1948), 37-8.

[51] R. Crozet, *L'Art Roman en Poitou*, 275.

[52] *Europe in the Dark Ages*, 27 and Plate 128.

[53] R. Crozet, *L'Art Roman en Poitou*, 39, 119, 125.

[54] Eddius, chapter XXII (cujus profunditatem in terra cum domibus mire politis lapidibus fundatam, et super terram multiplicem domum columnis variis et porticibus multis suffultam, mirabileque longtitudine et altitudine murorum ornatum, et variis liniarum anfractibus viarum, aliquando sursum, aliquando deorsum per cochleas circumductam . . .)

[55] *Europe in the Dark Ages*, 29.

[56] For the following discussion see also Hodges and Gibson, 39-42, and Savage and Hodges, plates XVI to XXVI, and the key to the latter.

[57] Hodges and Gibson, 42.

[58] P. Verzone, in *Encyclopedia of World Art* (London, 1960), II, 766.

[59] Hodges and Gibson, 41.

[60] H. Schlunk, in *Ars Hispaniæ* (Madrid, 1947), II, Figs 290-2.

[61] Raine, 11 f. (Ipsum quoque corpus ecclesiæ appenticiis et porticibus unique circumcinxit, quæ miro et inexplicabili artificio per parietes et cocleis et super ipsas ascensoria ex lapide et deambulatoria et varios viarum anfractus ... machinari fecit...)

[62] Edward Gilbert, 'Brixworth and the English Basilica', 12-16, and H. M. Taylor, 'Corridor Crypts on the Continent and in England', *North Staffs. Journal of Field Studies* 9 (1968), 38: cf. for the west façade at Monkwearmouth, Edward Gilbert, 'Anglian remains at St. Peter's, Monkwearmouth', *AA* 25 (1947), 12-16.

[63] C. R. Peers and S. W. Clapham, 'St. Augustine's abbey Church before the Conquest', *Arch.*, 77 (1927), 201-18.

[64] *The History of the Franks By Gregory of Tours*, II, 14.

[65] J. K. Conant, *Carolingian and Romanesque Architecture* (London, 1959); Restoration Study IB.

[66] *Europe in the Dark Ages*, 27 and plate 128.

[67] Migne, ed., *Patrologiæ cursus completus*, t. 133-4, 709.

[68] Raine, 190.

[69] Clapham, I, 146.

[70] See also Gilbert, 'Some Problems of Early Northumbrian Architecture', *AA* 42 (1964), 65-83 (pp. 73-5).

[71] Taylor (H. M.) and Taylor (J.), 298.

[72] Jean Hubert, *L'Art Pré-Romane* (Paris, 1938), 39.

[73] *Europe in the Dark Ages*, 13.

[74] Eddius, chapter XVII.

[75] C. R. Peers, 'Recent Discoveries in the Minsters of York and Ripon', *Ant.*, II (1931), 113-22.

[76] The writer wishes to acknowledge his indebtedness to the Russell Trust, Edinburgh University, and the Leverhulme Trust in connection with researches in France. He is likewise indebted to Professor R. J. Cramp, and the staff at St Andrew's, Hexham, to Dr D. P. Kirby and to Mr Bruce Allsopp for invaluable suggestions.

Acknowledgements for illustrations

Plan 1 Courtesy John Murray Ltd.

Plan 2 Courtesy Mme May Vieillard-Troiekouroff and *Cahiers Archéologiques*

Plan 3 Courtesy Mme May Vieillard Troiekouroff and *Cahiers Archéologiques*

Plan 5 Traced from the original by J. Blake

Plan 6 Courtesy John Murray Ltd.

Plan 7 Courtesy Oxford University Press

Plan 8 Courtesy Cambridge University Press and Dr H. M. Taylor

Plan 9 Courtesy Oxford University Press

Plan 10   Courtesy Mme May Vieillard Troiekouroff and *Cahiers Archéologiques*

Fig. 1   From Savage and Hodges *A Record of all Works Connected with Hexham Abbey Since January 1899*

Fig. 5   Courtesy *Archaeologia*

Chapter Five

EARLY NORTHUMBRIAN SCULPTURE AT HEXHAM

Rosemary Cramp

THE VERY considerable quantity of carved stone work, in the form of both architectual and funerary sculpture, which has survived from Hexham, is of unique importance for assessing the artistic achievement and influence of the pre-tenth-century foundation. The Gospels written on purple vellum, in letters of purest gold and illuminated, have not survived and only one extant manuscript has been ascribed to one of the *scriptoria* of Wilfrid's foundations.[1] Nor likewise have the great metalwork objects survived, such as the golden shrine for the gospels, or the gold altar cross which are described in his Ripon epitaph as among the treasures of that church. It is primarily from the vestiges of the sculpture and architecture that we must judge the artistic standards of Wilfrid and his successors in the See of Hexham.

The great church of St Andrew at Hexham not only excited contemporary and later admiration for the size and complexity of its structure, but also invoked a rare comment on its decoration. It is difficult sometimes, however, to be sure whether the medieval commentators were describing fresco wall paintings or painted stone reliefs. Eddius mentions only that Wilfrid enriched his church by authenticated relics, hangings of silk and purple and precious metal artifacts.[2] A preoccupation with luxurious hangings and precious metalwork, which is also found in Bede, rather than with the niceties of architectural sculpture perhaps reflects the taste of the aristocratic secular environment. The numerous rich textiles which have been identified as hangings in the Sutton Hoo ship burial substantiate this point. Acca's work at Hexham is also mentioned by Eddius only in terms of the 'magnalia ornamenta ... de auro et argento lapidibusque pretiosis'.[3]

Architectural Sculpture

It is not until Prior Richard's account of the church at Hexham that architectural sculpture is described:

> 'These same, and the capitals of the columns which sustain them, and the arch of the sanctuary he (Wilfrid) adorned with pictures and images and with many sculptured figures worked with relief from the stone, and pictures with a pleasing variety of colours and marvellous elegance.'[4]

This is the fullest medieval description and other writers tend to draw on this text: Symeon of Durham says, 'In this convent are walls adorned with various colours and pictures painted.' These he specifically assigns to Wilfrid but there is no evidence that he is right in this and the decoration which survived to Prior Richard's day could have been added between the late seventh and the late ninth century. Nevertheless, one might expect that carvings connected with the basic structure such as the arch of the sanctuary should belong to the earliest period.

The term *cælatora* used by Prior Richard has a wide semantic range, but it can mean relief sculpture, as has been shown by R. N. Quirk in an extensive discussion of the term.[5] Such sculpure could have been painted (see below (and Appendix II) nos 31 and 32) as has been found in the contemporary church and monastic buildings at Wearmouth.[6] There is to date very little evidence of fresco wall painting in England,[7] although reliefs on both panels and friezes remain a popular mode of church decoration throughout the period. The literary references, therefore, might lead one to expect that there were columns and carved capitals, a particularly elaborate arch, and, from analogy with other surviving monuments, perhaps decorated friezes and panels. We should not expect the surviving archæological evidence to fit too exactly into a scheme which in itself is only selectively recorded. However some interesting relationships do occur between the literary evidence and the surviving fragments of sculpture which can be plausibly considered as part of the structural ornament.

There are nineteen pieces from Hexham which could be considered as imposts, strip work or friezes and thus possibly part of a scheme of decorated openings. It is sometimes difficult, however, to decide upon the function of an individual piece since a number are incomplete and others are built into the modern fabric with only one face visible. Where two carved faces survive I have assumed that the piece could be a slab impost of the type that is known on the Continent in monuments of the eighth and ninth centuries, as at St Pedro de la Nave[8] or St Germigny des Près[9] where imposts with miniature balusters survive as in Hexham, nos 24 to 28 (plate XIV).

The only measurement which invariably survives is the height (cf., Appendix II) and this should be diagnostic in deciding whether pieces are part of the same scheme.

One Hexham group, nos 24-8, are all decorated on the long face by varying combinations of miniature balusters framed by a flat sectioned plain moulding. They are all 5½″ in height and where their find-spot can be determined they were all found in the destroyed Saxon nave. The only complete specimen or section seems to be no. 25, which has an asymmetrical scheme of three balusters at one end, and one at another, separated by single shafts dividing up what appear to be four rails shown in perspective. Traces of paint still adhere to the grooves. A similar asymmetrical scheme of three balusters and a single baluster divided by four 'rails' is seen on no. 28 but these are straight, and the balusters less well cut. No. 26 has also the same type of four horizontal dividers separating two groups of three balusters. It seems clear that variation rather than symmetry of layout is the sculptor's intention: no. 27 has a single baluster and triple baluster group divided by three horizontal bands of alternate facing cables and on the right three grooved 'slots'. A similar type of herringbone is found on the long face of a large complete impost, no. 42 (plate VIIIa) built into the south jamb of the existing west door of the nave and on its shorter face are three balusters and three horizontal 'rails'. It is possible that Hexham 41 and 42 (plate VIIIa and b) also belong to the baluster sequence since they are of the same height, although larger in other dimensions. The profile of 41, with half round moulding at the top and bottom enclosing a projecting triple groove, is possibly derived from Roman prototypes as likewise the double cable ornament of no. 42. Imposts such as this, with differing decoration on each face including balusters and interlace, are found on free standing piers at St Germigny des Près,[10] and these Hexham pieces are certainly wide enough to support piers although, since only two faces are visible, nothing decisive can be said about their function. It is possible that the early church builders reused some Roman imposts and adopted them also as models. Certainly the baluster series, which could imply decoration of one major and other minor openings linked by strip work, fits most happily into the late seventh century in England, although it may have continued for longer on the continent. Free standing large scale balusters have been found at Monkwearmouth, which was founded in 674, with its porch completed by 685. Many other examples have also been found in the excavations of the monastic buildings at Monkwearmouth, some with their original paint. Similar full scale balusters have been found at Jarrow founded in 682, but neither type is of the same shape as those found on the Hexham imposts and friezes. These, as Baldwin Brown was the first to point out,[11] derive from a Roman type with splayed ends, as is found, for example, on the Birrens altar. At Jarrow, however, miniature balusters of precisely the same type are found on friezes now built into the north wall of the north porch[12] (plate VIIIc and d).

The plan and profile of the Jarrow and Hexham pieces, on the other hand, are so dissimilar that they must have had different functions— the Jarrow fragments are clearly chamfered back for setting under wall plaster, although where it can be checked they are dressed flat at the base. These friezes do not divide the balusters with horizontal motifs as on several of the Hexham pieces, but like Hexham 24, are set out in a continuous line. But there are devolved types at both sites as at Hexham 28 (plate XIVc). Hodges compared the Jarrow miniature baluster type with two chamfered imposts from Simonburn which were discovered in 1876 built into the chancel arch of the church (plate XIIa). It is strange that he did not compare these imposts with the slab imposts from Hexham especially as there are other close stylistic links between the two sites as for example the plant scrolls and the geometric motif on the chamfered face of the impost and the end of Hexham 32[13] (plate IXc).

The baluster scheme is clearly linked, therefore, with other Northumbrian churches which like Wearmouth/Jarrow favoured classical ornament and were founded in the seventh century. They could reasonably belong to the seventh-century building[14] and have been derived from either Roman or continental prototypes. It seems, there-fore, as though the group of baluster imposts with their design clearly linked with Roman art and other architectural fragments from early Anglo-Saxon churches should be part of the early construction of the church. Before discussing a potential scheme for this group one should consider other possible imposts or friezes, some of which provide a coherent series and are of similar dimensions with the same high quality of cutting. Notable among these are two animals, a boar and a cow,[15] framed in a wide flat moulding, plate IXa-c. Both are carved in finely dressed sandstone, and both also bear traces of under-coat for paint.[16] The animals are shown in action, and slightly en-croach on their frame. Their eyes are roundish and their bodies solidly conceived. Little details such as the pricked ear of the cow and the marked tusk of the boar provide some animation to what are otherwise rather ponderous beasts. No. 32 is slightly higher than the baluster imposts but of similar depth (see p. 177). The stone on which the cow is carved is much deeper and triangular in shape, presumably to insert into a wall face. It is possible that there was a frieze of animals which terminated in an opening. One other animal, a lion, now built into the west wall of the church, no. 33, might be considered with this group even though it is 2.5 cm higher (plate IXd). It is a rather rougher carving than the other two but depicted like them in move-ment. It faces to the right and the tail is hitched over its back. Its mane is sketchily indicated by hatched diagonal and zig-zag lines. There are traces of the front leg but the head is lost. Its body tapers markedly towards the hip in the manner of lions on Hiberno-Saxon manuscripts like the Lichfield or Echternach Gospels. The Hexham lion was equated by Hodges and Savage with the lion arm rests from Wearmouth. These are as much as 42 cm high and 52 cm long, how-ever, and are carved nearly in the round with extremely sensitive and realistic treatment of the mane and paws.[17] The scale of the Hexham piece is best explained if one considers it as part of an animal frieze of a more monumental type than that which was carved in low relief on the façade of Monkwearmouth porch.[18] The creatures do not seem to have been part of a series of evangelist symbols, but such animal friezes are known in Iranian art and appear in early Christian churches of the Middle East. These eastern traditions which are also to be seen in the smooth skinned animals at Ravenna and St Pedro de la Nave could have been transmitted to England also. One further piece of sculpture, hitherto unpublished, no. 21 (plate Xc), may very well belong to the same ornamental tradition although it is not possible in its fragmentary state to say whether it belongs to a frieze or even perhaps a lintel or step. The fish, as the creature seems to be, has the same plain rounded head and incised rounded eye as the cow and boar, and like them the surface has traces of paint; the skeletal body is conveyed by a divided cable reminiscent of nos 42 and 27. Like them it seems to belong to the possible fitments of Wilfrid's church. Decorated steps with ornament not unlike this are found in the seventh-century Hypogée des Dunes (Poitiers).[19] There are several fragments about which I have found it impossible to make a decision as to whether they are Roman or Anglo-Saxon influenced by Roman (see p. 125). One of these doubtful specimens, no. 29 (plate Xd), is not dissimilar in profile to the fish, but the widely spaced rectangular pellets and finely cut cable can be paralleled on the Roman site of *Corstopitum*, Northumberland.

Within the frieze and impost series there are fragments which clearly have an insular context; nos 34-7. Nos 34 and 35 (plate XIb and c) both have the same scheme of four strand plait enclosed in a plain square sectioned frame. On 34 the cutting is cruder and the figure of eight knots more closely packed, but they are the same as the central knot in 35, although here the pattern appears to have been complicated by an interwoven closed circuit loop. The crudity of this work in comparison with the fine geometric interlace on the imposts now built into the buttresses on the south face of Ripon cathedral (plate XId) destroys the possible argument that Wilfrid's or Acca's craftsmen had no sympathy for insular type of interlace and so produced work on these imposts inferior to those so far discussed. The Ripon traditions in sculpture seem more closely linked with models in insular metalwork than with earlier Roman carvings (see p. 136), but fine geometric interlace seems to be an early feature on sculpture as well. For example, there is fine interlace on architectural fragments from the classically inclined site of Wearmouth, and an impost, possibly contemporary, from Peterborough. The type of interlace on Hexham 34 and 35 with closed circuit loops and widely spaced tight knots is more common on crosses and manuscripts of the ninth to tenth centuries.[20] Similarly the impost no. 36 (plate XIa) where the interlace again has heavy strands and works on the closed circuit principle, should be assigned the same date. It is unfortunate that so little remains of no. 37 (plate Xa) The small serpentine creature is obviously associated with another motif now almost obliterated, but this too would fit best into a context of the tenth century or later.

Collingwood, who is the only writer to have faced the problems of these pieces, dated them to the period of Eilaf's restoration, supposing that he could have used 'old fashioned English craftsmen'. 'The forms are in bold relief; the plaits of i, j, are of the eleventh century; spiral snakes are not seen on pre-Danish monuments.'[21] Nevertheless there are in the church some fine fragments of Norman work in the shape of capitals and stoups so that, if 34-7 are dated to the post-Conquest period, the English workmen must have had more competent workmen alongside them. Today we are less eager to be dogmatic about interlace types in relation to dating, and these pieces could equally well belong to a restoration or rebuilding by incompetent workmen at any time from the ninth to the eleventh century. We see the work of such craftsmen in no. 12 (plate XXIVa and b), and since the community of St Cuthbert at Durham is demonstrably on other sites very conservative in taste it could be that this work represents a conservative restoration of the tenth or early eleventh century in which there was a renewal of some damaged openings, possibly by carvers in Durham and its dependencies who favoured earlier English models.

If we accept that the fragments so far surveyed imply that the church, as at Ripon, used slab imposts, perhaps with strip work extending a short way along the wall face, as at St Pedro de la Nave,[22] one need not accept as a consequence that these imposts were supported on wall shafts, half shafts or columns, although there exist three fragments of shafts now built into the north side of Hexham abbey. These are accepted by the Taylors[23] as possibly part of the fabric of the early church and they suppose that the half round column could have provided enrichment for the soffit face of rectangular piers and the small detached columns part of a triple chancel arch, or the supports of a screen or a gallery. All of these possibilities would be reasonable if one could be sure that these quite plain shafts are pre-Conquest and not post-Conquest (plate XIIIe). There is one piece of evidence which might support the column supposition other than Prior Richard's statement (see p. 116). This is a fragment of what may be a capital, no. 30 (plate XIIc and d). The broadest face although broken shows that it is sufficiently wide to support the fully round columns. Each face is decorated by three zones of geometric ornament enclosed in plain rectangular horizontal bands and a vertical cable moulding. On the wider face the upper zone has two complete curlicues and the beginnings of a third. These spring from a plain band, and below is a double cable of the herringbone type already noted on nos 21 and 42. The lowest zone has three rows of small countersunk chequers. The drawings reproduced in Collingwood and in the Cathedral Guide are inaccurate. The other more fragmentary face has similar curlicues in the upper zone, divided by a single cable from a row of large circles. Below a plain rounded band is a double row of countersunk circles. Although chequers and cable mouldings are known from Roman work (see pp. 125-6, 179), the small size of the chequers, and the idiosyncratic scheme on the two faces makes it highly probable that this is Anglo-Saxon work.[24] Such a heavy support for an impost or capital, could well coexist with what appears to be a free standing rectangular base with curving outline, no. 40 (plate XIIb and e). This very curious piece has one dressed face which could have been the base, tapering to one broken which is shown in the plate as the bottom. Each vertical face has an upper and lower row of deep pellets divided from a central heavy cable by a thick convex moulding. The scheme, although more crudely worked, is not unlike the capping of the shaft of the 'Acca' cross (plate XVIIa). One might see this then as the base of a pier which had been constructed with a slightly rounded face or which had been faced with a half shaft. If the latter were true, Wilfrid or Acca must have made a determined effort to create at Hexham an effect of the antique basilica, especially as at other places where imposts have been preserved, such as at Ripon or Ledsham or Simonburn, no capitals, bases or shafts have survived. It is unfortunate that the church at Ledsham in the West Riding, which might well reflect Wilfrid's work at York or Ripon, was so drastically reconstructed in the nineteenth century. One cannot know, therefore, how closely the original schemes of ornament were copied by its restorers. Nevertheless the chancel arch imposts and their associated strip work (plate XIIIb) bear the 'Visigothic' ornament of triangle and circle already noted at Ripon, Hexham, and Simonburn, and there is built into the north wall two fragments of strip work with interlaced plant scrolls which compare very interestingly with the Hexham cross shafts (plate XIf).

One can see therefore how the Hexham pieces could have been used in openings without postulating a colonnade. None of these pieces can definitively be thought of as part of the decoration of the sanctuary arch: there are no historiated capitals, and no stones shaped as for an arch or hood moulding. The two tiny fragments which were considered by Collingwood, and more hesitantly Taylor, to have been parts of windows, are only doubtfully Anglo-Saxon (see numbers 38 and 50 in Appendix II).

Naturally one need not suppose that the architectural fragments are a fully representative collection of the sculptural decoration of the pre-Conquest church. They were largely found on the site of the nave, and could well represent the austerely classical taste of that part of the church. One might have expected the east end to be more lavishly decorated, but that area, especially under the crossing, has been less disturbed in modern times.

There is however at least one other piece which should rightly find its place in the east end of Wilfrid's church: the stone seat or 'frith stool' which now stands on the floor of the choir above the centre-point of the semi-circular apse where Hodges considered it would best fit, in the midst of the clergy bench.[25] It had originally been set into the wall of the choir. One does not know how early it had been associated with the rite of sanctuary, but it is an important survival of early church furniture. The low seat scooped from a single stone has originally been set into a wall and possibly occupied the central position in the clergy bench. Its restrained incised ornament effectively emphasizes the outlines of the chair both in plan and elevation (plate XIIIa). On the horizontal surface of the arms the widest point between the double incised mouldings is filled by a triquetra which is loosely clasped by a two-strand twist. Such a twist, combined with interlace is found ornamenting the chair on which St Matthew is seated in the Codex Aureus. A.135, fol.q v[26] and the same motif is on the lintel supporting the arch above. We know of ornamental metal inlays on wooden furniture of the eighth century, and the simple twist and triquetræ are possibly derived from metal work motifs. Their simplicity and restraint tend to incline one towards an early, *i.e.* late seventh century, date, but with ornament so simple it is impossible to be sure.

One other fragment, no. 39 (plate XIe), now unfortunately lost, might have been part of a piece of furniture in the church although it was considered by Hodges as possibly one of the pilasters of a stone choir screen.[27] Enclosed within a fine double round moulding is a delicate four-strand interlace found also on the Codex Aureas chair.[28] It seems impossible to say anything more now that the fragment is lost, however, except to remark that this interlace type is not common in Northumbrian stone carving but the widely spaced loops seem to be copied in a cruder form in the impost no. 35 discussed above.

There are three other groups of high quality carving which have been considered as part of the decoration of the sanctuary area of Wilfrid's church. One of these, the Rood group, is discussed by Miss E. Coatsworth in Appendix III. The others, nos 22a, b, c, and 23, have been considered by some commentators to be Roman work and by others as work in Wilfrid's classicizing tradition (plate VII). 22, a, b, c, which were reconstructed by Collingwood into a single panel are considered by him to be Roman.[29]

The problem of the vinescroll panels is the most complex since first one should re-examine whether Collingwood was justified in his reconstruction. None of the fragments were found together and they appeared over a long period of time: c. was first drawn and mentioned in 1865 and was said by Greenwell to have been found on the site of the nave; b. was first drawn and mentioned in 1867, and there is no indication of its find-spot; a. was drawn and mentioned in 1888 and described by Hodges as having been found on Campy Hill north-east of the church. a. and c. are of the same thickness, but b. is 5 cm thicker. It also differs from the other two pieces in that the scene is enclosed within a single wide raised moulding whilst the inner mould-ing of the other two fragments is a double rounded type. On a. this is competently formed with a broad flat outer frame, but on c. the double moulding is bungled within a narrower recessed outer frame. Nevertheless despite these differences which could mean that the fragments are not part of single object, they are clearly part of the same scheme. There is little that is diagnostic in the sprawling plants of c. although it is not impossible to see them as of the same type with free curling tendrils as on the other pieces. There is no hint, however, as in Collingwood's drawing, that there is a trumpet binding on the right to account for the close packed stems. It would be more usual in classical work if this plant spilled from an urn, but the strands are noticeably more crowded than on the other fragments. On b. a small naked putto stands half turned, with feet braced on a plant scroll and is in the act of drawing a bow. The small curling tendrils of the vine and the widely spaced strands are the only clear characteristics of the plant form. Fragment a. is close packed with incident: at the top are the striding legs of a naked putto, at the bottom right the arm of a similar figure reaching up for a grape bunch, immediately above him is a cock, and on the bottom left the horned head of a goat reaches up towards a leaf. The vine tendrils in between these creatures are evenly spaced with large well shaped berry bunches and small naturalistic vine leaves. The curling tendrils are practically the only feature with which to compare this and the other scrolls. Despite these differences, it is possible to think of the three fragments as belonging to the same panel or perhaps two similar panels. It is unlikely that they were part of a free-standing screen since the backs are roughly finished and the pieces are of considerable thickness. Despite my earlier views I am now inclined to think that these pieces are Roman, since nowhere else in Anglo-Saxon art does one find naked putti, or this type of vine-scroll. If they were re-used in Wilfrid's church, instead of being built in as were so many other Roman carved pieces, they had no influence on the plant forms found on the crosses of the Hexham school.

The other panel, no. 23, which Taylor considered as part of a closure screen I have elsewhere[30] considered to be the work of continental craftsmen in the seventh century, but I now feel more inclined to see it also as a Roman piece. The panel is much mutilated but the high quality of the carving is not obliterated. It appears to have been originally framed by a triple moulding. Within this, a

double circular moulding frames a geometric rosette: the outline of
the thirteen outer petals is confidently inscribed, and the central
stamen and corona stand out in high relief. Panels with rosette ornament as part of the decoration of façades are known in seventh-
century Gaul[31] and the rosette motif remained popular in North
Italy and Gaul into the ninth century. Nevertheless, the complexity
of the centre of this panel is never found, and indeed it is difficult
to parallel it in Roman art in Britain. It is possible, however, that
this piece was re-used by Wilfrid's workmen since the rosette motif
is found on Hexham crosses which have survived—as for example on
no. 10.

Monumental Sculpture and the 'Hexham School' of Carving

The siting of the church and monastery on a marked eminence
within the loop of the river, is similar to other seventh-century
foundations in Northumbria, such as Bywell, Monkwearmouth and
Jarrow. At the two last cited there is some evidence for an early lay
cemetery, perhaps pre-dating the monastic foundation. At Hexham,
however, unless one considered that the small church to the east pre-
dated St Andrew's, there is no hint of a sequence from enclosed
cemetery through martyrium and cemetery to monastery.[32] Nevertheless there are a remarkable number of cist graves recorded,
particularly on the north side of the church and these could be an
earlier type than the wooden coffins which are found at Wearmouth/
Jarrow. The sole evidence for the siting of these graves is to be found
in Hodges' 1923 plan which was reproduced with explanatory numbering by the Taylors, 1960.[33] I follow their numbering. Two graves,
8 and 14, are probably disturbed by the north and south transepts of
the church, and therefore pre-date walls s and m3. With the exception of 3 and 9, which were sarcophogus burials, all the northern cist
burials could have been early although not necessarily earlier than
the Anglo-Saxon church. It may be significant that no inscriptions
were associated with these burials.

We have no clear archæological evidence for a division between lay
and monastic burial grounds on any Anglo-Saxon site, nor do we
know whether clergy graves would always be distinguishable. The
evidence from inscribed grave markers from Lindisfarne, Hartlepool

and Monkwearmouth, and plain inscribed crosses from Whitby seems to show that the graves might be distinguishable above ground. There is also evidence in Bede for the burial of clergy in solid stone sarcophogi, sometimes Roman ones re-used.[34]

Clustered round the small apse at the east of the Saxon church are a number of burials mostly of the sarcophagus type, one of which was covered by a lid, no. 17 (plate XVb), considered to be the tomb of Acca. This is a poor specimen to put alongside such inscribed grave covers of other priests such as the Hereberecht slab[35] from Monk-wearmouth. This cover and no. 15 (plate XVa), which has the same type of cross, seem more like the primitive grave markers of the tenth to eleventh centuries known for instance from Bothal or Wark-worth,[36] although the shaft type is unique. Nevertheless, the area between the east end of St Peter's and St Mary's which was clearly a confined space and included, according to some writers, an *atrium*,[37] was the area of some clergy burials. It was the burial place of Acca himself, if we can trust Symeon of Durham who says 'his body was buried on the outside of the wall, at the east end of the church of Hexham... Two stone crosses adorned with exquisite carvings were placed, the one at his head, the other at his feet. On the one that was at his head was an inscription stating that he was buried there.'[38] From that place three hundred years after his burial he was translated to a shrine within the church. Cross sockets still survive at the south-east of the apse.

The cross which since 1861 has been tentatively assigned to Acca, no. 1 (plates XVI, XVII and XVIIIa), was found in three different places (see p. 172), but the central section was found under the 1349 extensions of the choir, and the upper in digging warehouse foundations on the site of St Mary's church. The assumption that this is Acca's memorial rests today only on the fact that it is an 'exquisite carving', the inscription now being irrecoverable in its entirety (plate XVIIb). It certainly starts with an A, and, according to Greenwell at the end of the line there are some marks which may be resolved into Omega. 'The second line commences with SC, and nothing more can be made out until about the middle of the shaft when the words UNIGENITO FILIO DEI from the Nicene Creed can be read with absolute certainty'.[39] This cannot be read with cer-

tainty now and the SC could be SE but this does not contribute much
to our understanding of the lengthy inscription which this once was.
These suggestions are also accepted by M. J. Swanton.[40] He makes the
interesting point that the burial of Acca outside the church need not
have been a very honourable position since several of his successors
were buried inside. Certainly there are plenty of references in Bede to
the translation of abbots or priests from the exterior to the interior
of the church before the end of the eighth century. The fact that the
cross was broken up in the medieval period does not, however, necessarily contribute to the disassociation of the shaft from Acca. It seems
more reasonable to suppose that this was an epitaph rather than a
didactic inscription since there is a firm tradition of such epitaphs,
not the least important being that which was placed over Wilfrid's
tomb at Ripon.[41] This could have been in the form of an inscribed
plaque, of course, a tradition which survived as late as the late eighth-
century marble grave-stone of Pope Hadrian in which the lettering
is framed by a delicate vinescroll.[42]

It would indeed be valuable if one could assume, as Collingwood
did, that no. 1 was the Acca cross since it would provide a surer peg
for dating it and the monuments with related ornamental formulæ
than the feeble subjectivism of stylistic analysis and typology. It is
reasonable to assume that if monuments of the competence of no. 1
were produced at Hexham and if one can see the same schemes repeated on other monuments both there and in other Northumbrian
centres, then we can postulate a Hexham school of carvers. It seems
best, however, to review the evidence first.

Hexham 1 (plates XVI, XVII and XVIIIa) according to Greenwell[43] was made from two different blocks of stone, the upper from a
softer bed. Unfortunately the break would have come in the lost portion of the cross and so cannot now be checked. Each face is however
treated as a unit, surrounded by a fine double round moulding and
covered from the base to the top by a continuous plant scroll, save
for the eastern face which as we have seen is covered by an inscription. The base is enclosed by the same simple double moulding but
the top is elaborately capped by two framed bands of deep pellets
divided by a sunken moulding (plate XVIIa). This capping supports
the lower arm of the cross head which is a straight expanded type,

surrounded by pellets and inset with larger studs. This head type is not copied elsewhere at Hexham, nor anywhere else with this elaboration. It looks as if the carver were copying a metalwork prototype in which the head was inset with jewels and surrounded by filigree.[44] This and examples which survive on the continent from a later date give us some idea of the possible types. Interestingly, they all have the straight head.[45] The western face is covered by a fine wiry plant scroll which springs from two roots and bifurcates into two strands which cross forming oval medallions to enclose leaves and grape bunches (see plate XVIc). Within each medallion each group is differently organized; sometimes the bunches hang quite realistically, as in the lowest medallion, sometimes they coil and twist into impossible contortions for a naturalistic scroll. The berry bunches are triangular in form but not enclosed, and the leaves are small triangular fronds. Where the leaves and bunches leave the main stem there is slight thickening but nothing like the emphasis on the trumpet-like bindings one finds elsewhere in Northumbrian carvings, most pertinently on Hexham 2 and 3. The overwhelming impression of this face is of the flowing line of the double medallions unbroken by an overcomplexity in the crossings. Although the two narrow faces are also ornamented with the same formula, the smaller scale and the more elaborate contortions of the strands between each volute tend to break up the scheme into individual elements. The leaf and berry types are the same but they are less prominent than the spinning stems which in one place, the second volute from the base of the south face, turns the volute into an interlace motif of the same wiry springing type as the plant-scroll (plate XVId). The paired leaves at each crossing vary their organization above the two lowest volutes and so worn is the stone that it is difficult to be sure which are fruit and which are leaves. On this north face the medallions are markedly more rounded than on the others and at the top of the central section the plant seems to be moving towards the spiral form counterpointed scroll, which is found in other examples of the 'Hexham School' as first identified by Collingwood.

Two other crosses, nos 2 and 3, have been identified by some writers as the stone which stood at the foot of Acca's grave. No. 2 (plate XIX) which may have once been at Warden and then stood in the grounds of the Spital at Hexham was thought by Hodges[46] to have had this role and thus by implication to be of the same date as 1. Collingwood in his earlier discussion thought the Spital Cross looked earlier but in his later work decided that it 'need not be much later than Acca's death'.[47]

What remains of Hexham 2 seems to be the central portion of a shaft which has been broken at the bottom and has lost the upper section which was affixed to it by a dowel. The patterns both on the broad and narrow faces were obviously meant to continue. The edges are framed in simple roll mouldings with a light central groove. On one broad face a large crucifixion panel survives and this scene seems to have been divided from panels above and below by a broad flat band. This face is much worn but some detail survives. The figure of Christ and the lance bearer and sponge bearer encroach on the frame, in that Christ's arms, which are unnaturally short, extend to the edge of the frame as do the shoulders and arms of the subsidiary figures.[48] This may be because of the carver's ineptitude since the head of Christ appears unnaturally large and the subsidiary figures rather cramped. Christ's cross extends from the top to the bottom of the frame and stands on a stepped base which appears below the band, possibly once inscribed, on which the two attendant figures stand. This may be a further example of the carver's difficulty in getting the right proportions for his figures, since the band raises the figures. Christ stands erect with feet together, and head half turned to the right. He has a plain nimbus, long curling hair and wears a short tunic. The lance bearer on his right seems to be in the act of piercing his side and is shown in profile. The sponge bearer appears to be facing the spectator. The iconography of this scene and the Crucifixion plaque is discussed in Appendix III. It is sufficient to note at the moment that this panelled face distinguishes the cross from all others of the Hexham group, which cover all faces with plant scroll.

The other broad face shows a bold repetitive medallion scroll formed from a pair of heavy strands which swell into a trumpet with triple bindings towards the intersections and split into three tendrils, one continuing the scroll, one branching into a paired leaf and the other supporting a single heavy grape bunch. This formula is fol-

lowed for each of the four medallions which survive. The leaves are
spear-shaped and the berry bunches well shaped with a blunt triangular form. The narrow sides each show a single plant trail with
alternate facing volutes, few of which have survived. Each volute
swells into a trumpet shape with three bindings from which spring
leaves which cling to the upper and lower tendrils, which curl round
to end with a tightly packed blunt triangular berry bunch. These
bunches are flatter and less pointed in outline than on the Acca cross
and from each volute droops a paired leaf. On the other side (plate
XIXd) the trumpet opens out not into leaves but with a stiff stamen
with a bulbous end, a motif which is closely paralleled in Simonburn,
Northumberland, and Lancaster (see p. 134).

Hexham 3 is a large shaft which has been seen by Collingwood[49]
as possibly 'the cross seen by Symeon of Durham at the foot of Acca's
grave or—more likely—at the head of an adjacent grave, for it is not
usual to have two crosses to one interment and this is obviously not
a work of the same time and style as Acca's cross'. The stone had been
re-used as a step (see p. 172), and only one narrow and part of one
broad face survive (plate XVIIIb and c). It is possible to see that it
was less square in section than the Acca and Spital crosses, and this
may have a dating significance. The carving is deeper and coarser
than the two already discussed. The edge is a bold cable enclosing a
fine roll moulding. Inside this frame on the narrow face is a continuous undulating plant scroll with ten alternate facing volutes.
Each volute springs from a trumpet with three cross bindings and
coils once in a tight coil which closely encircles the rounded berry
bunches. From each volute drops a paired leaf with prominent
stylised veins and from the centre of the trumpet sprouts a similar
paired leaf on a stiff stalk. The prominently grooved leaves, the
relatively small rosette berry bunches, are organized in a close-
massed composition which altogether gives a very different effect
from 1 and 2. The section of the broad face which survives seems to
indicate a similarly close-packed scroll—a combination of the trumpet
and medallion scroll.[50] The remains of five volutes survive, of which
three have clear details. Each scroll swells into a trumpet with three
wavy bindings from which sprout three strands to form the central
motifs in the medallions below and above, and to support a stiff

paired leaf with a central stamen. The leaves are of the same general type as on the side scroll, but more angular in outline. The lowest medallion shows a composition of tendrils crossed into a split loop, the two above a composition of leaves and flower-like berry bunches, but it is impossible to reconstruct the whole with certainty. The cross from Stamfordham (plate XXc and d) has a similar composition of tangled scroll on one broad face and undulating scroll on the narrow. While on the other broad face is a medallion scroll of the type shown on Hexham 2. Possibly such a scroll could have ornamented the other broad face of Hexham 4.

One other fragment of vinescroll survives from Hexham—a base, and part of a shaft which Collingwood combines. The corner of the base which survives, Hexham 4, is not large enough for it to be certain that it fits the shaft (plate XXIa-c). The stone has been roughly hacked back at the base but the surviving upper part shows part of a horizontal undulating scroll enclosed in a broad outer and fine inner roll moulding. The solitary surviving volute springs from a trumpet and coils round to enclose tightly a rosette berry bunch of seven berries. The volute is framed by two heavy fronds and a single triangular leaf with incised centre. The only feature which might link this base to shaft 5 (plate XXId) is the feature which springs from the medallion, which could be like the triangular leaf flower found in the space filling of the volutes. The surviving heavy bunches on 4 and 5, however, are as similar to one another as each is to 3; for example, the way in which the stem penetrates the bunch and links with the central berry is the same on 5 and 3, but the plant trail of the narrow side of 3 is instructive in showing the varieties of berry type which can be found on one face.

The fragment of carving which remains on the other side of the base is a heart-shaped double strand and on the top a fragment of four stranded knot work, the earliest use of the interlace motif surviving on the crosses from Hexham. The cutting of the berried scroll is interesting because of the clear use of the punch for grooving out the design and similar marks are to be seen on the scrolls of 5. This technique, which could have a chronological significance, and is supported by a proximity in find-spot, perhaps links 4 and 5 more effectively than any similarities in the ornament of 3 and 4. 5 has survived in such a way as to afford no proof that it was a cross rather than a decorated jamb[51] or lintel, and there is not enough decoration to be certain of how the complete pattern of even one face was organized. The one and a half volutes which survive seem to be part of a trumpet medallion scroll of a very simplified type, crudely cut and with little feeling for the relative proportions of the various elements in the scroll.

Collingwood is the only writer who has attempted to assign a date to the Hexham vinescroll series, and to relate the work of the Hexham school of carvers to other monuments in Northumbria. We know practically nothing of the circumstances of production of Anglo-Saxon carving, but it does not seem unreasonable to think that the important monastic and cathedral centres such as Hexham and Ripon would have an influence on the monuments of their dependencies, or would loan their craftsmen further afield as Wearmouth or Jarrow craftsmen were loaned to the Picts.[52] Nevertheless, 'influences' which Collingwood saw are sometimes only one panel of plant scroll among other motifs, and one can only postulate for such resemblances a remote contact—or period fashion. We have seen on the vinescroll crosses the following similarities: the treatment of each face as a unit; the medallion scroll or the interlaced scroll on the broad faces, and the undulating scroll on the narrow faces. Moreover, none of these patterns is found on the fragments of architectural sculpture. They represent an independent ornamental tradition.

Collingwood's chronology was based on art historical criteria. 'At first, careful, elaborate and naturalistic, a style or school reaches its best result in the hands of some unusually capable craftsman; then his followers try to reproduce the standard results with less labour and thought, gradually debasing current motifs until some new influence arises to transform the tradition and renovate the style.'[53] Collingwood later calls this 'a law', but this is too strong a term, although the closer the contact between works of art in time and place the more relevant the statement becomes. But within the terms stated it is difficult to decide whether 2 represents the careful naturalistic beginnings and 1 the climax, or 1 the new brilliant touchstone for the new style and the rest an evolution. Collingwood's change of dates for 2, illustrates this problem well.

I am inclined to see the confident virtuosity of the cross 1 as the beginning of something new which was introduced, fully developed, into Northumbria and which set a fashion which ousted the earlier style of late Roman ornament at Hexham shown on the architectural sculpture, or the Germanic metalwork taste as found at the earlier foundation of Ripon on the interlace imposts (plate XId), or the very elaborately carved pillar which had been used as a step into the crypt[54] (plate XXIIIa and b). If one accepts that Hexham 1 could be the earliest of the vinescroll group one must be able to justify the appearance of such a style fully evolved. I think that it is possible to see that one model or group of models could have been used for all the plant scrolls both on Hexham 1 and 2 and the cross from Lowther in Westmorland, despite the different sculptural treatment (plate XXa and b). Ernst Kitzinger in his discussion of Anglo-Saxon vine-scroll[55] compared the undulating scroll with alternate facing berry bunches with late seventh-century mosaics from the Dome of the Rock, Jerusalem. Kitzinger's English parallel was a scroll from Aber-lady, but the scrolls on the narrow faces of Hexham 2 are identical with Kitzinger's example, even the leaves are of the same type and fill the space in the same way. Other mosaics from the Dome of the Rock octagonal arcade have split stems which curve off into side tendrils in the manner of Lowther 1, Heversham, or Lancaster. Also in the octagonal arcade one finds scrolls with paired leaves and two counter-pointed bunches in each volute in the manner of Lancaster 1.[56]

Remarkable as the mosaic scrolls are, there is even greater fantasy and variety in the repoussé bronze plates which cover the lintels and tie beams of the church. Here one finds medallion scrolls with spring-ing side tendrils, the grape bunches and leaves differently combined in each volute in the manner of Hexham 1.[57] There are also running scrolls with delicate and heavier tie bindings. The great variety of organization and indeed of details of leaf types in the Dome of the Rock is a salutory lesson in not attempting to inflate minute differ-ences which merely illustrate the experimentalism of the artists into an evolution of style. It should however be remarked that nowhere in this Middle Eastern series does one find anything but naturalistically shaped berry bunches.

One does not need to argue a direct contact between Hexham and the Middle East to explain the phenomenon of the Hexham plant scrolls, but these are so different from the stiff mechanical scrolls found elsewhere in western Europe in the seventh to eighth century that one must surely postulate either the importation of an artist, or of a notable model from that area on which several different types of vinescroll co-existed. The thin fine scrolls which are almost embossed on the surface of Hexham 1 could imply that such a model was of metalwork and I have earlier noted that the head type of this cross is reminiscent of metalwork. The translation of motifs from one medium to another—for example, from metalwork into book painting—is accepted for seventh/eighth-century art in England, and one could imagine a particularly remarkable golden cross serving as a model for this sculpture. It is possible that in the famous cross from Bischopshofen[58] which could be an Anglo-Saxon piece, the stylistic influence has gone the other way. The panels of interlace, the flowing plant scrolls and the head shape of the metal cross can all be paralleled, on stone crosses in Yorkshire of the late eighth to ninth centuries.

This fine metalwork style in sculpture need not have had a very long life; it is found most distinctively on Hexham 1, Lowther 1 (plate XXa and b) and Northallerton 1 (plate XXIIa and b). The more ponderous but nevertheless academic style of Hexham 2 and Stamfordham (plate XXc and d) need not necessarily be much later, but it is their more sculptural treatment which survives and produces plant scrolls which depart further from the vine by adding small flowers and changing the shape of the berry bunches. No. 5 could be as late as the ninth century and is linked with other ninth-century fragments in the West Riding of Yorkshire such as at Ilkley (see figure 1).

Only those Northumbrian crosses which carry the vinescroll on all four sides should be directly linked with the Hexham workshop (see figure 1), but the plant scrolls could be combined with other motifs which had been developed in other centres. It seems likely that Ripon, which began as a Celtic foundation, maintained for a period an interest in insular motifs, and later incorporated the medallion and spiral-form plant scroll into its repertoire. The perfect example of this is to be seen in the fragments of a magnificent cross from the

nearby site of Northallerton (plate XXIIa-e). Two faces of the shaft
are mutilated but one shows traces of a spiral form scroll. The other
side shows a tree-scroll with frond-like leaves and rosette berries
reminiscent of Falstone on the North Tyne. The other partially surviving face from Northallerton has a medallion vinescroll with
counterpointed berry bunches as at Lancaster, but framed in a zig-
zag moulding like the Ripon altar pillar. The form of the spine and
boss head is also probably derived from Ripon, and it is finished on
one face with a bossed edging, on the other with zig-zags. The centre-
piece of each side of the cross head is treated with five prominent
bosses like the base of a metal bowl.[59] On the edges of the arms, however, is a further repertoire of ornament in interlace leaf-scroll and
devolved balusters. One hesitates to decide between workshop and
period motifs, though, when one finds at Jarrow, a centre which otherwise has a different repertoire of sculptural ornament, a cross head
obviously copying a metal cross, with zig-zag ornament on the face
and balusters on the side arms[60] (plate XXIIf). It seems indeed as
though in the period of the greatest artistic activity of the monasteries
—the eighth century—there were common fashions and regular ex-
changes of models, but by the ninth century activity had lessened and
by the tenth century such centres were destroyed.

It may not be without significance, however, that in the West
Riding where the monastery at Ripon survived until the tenth
century, not only did the longnette, or spine and boss, cross head
perpetuate itself into the Viking period but the spiral form plant trail
also remained popular. Its later manifestations, for example, as combined with Scandinavian iconography on the Leeds shaft, are somewhat bizarre, but the situation is very different from that of Hexham
and the Tyne area. Here there seems to have been a complete break
with the old tradition of the plant scroll filling each face of the shaft.
Instead we find panels of interlace.

The earliest interlace at Hexham was perhaps to be found on the
lost fragment, 39 (see p. 124). It is also, as we have seen, combined
with the schematic vinescroll with sunken leaves and rosette berry
bunches on the cross base, 4, which can be dated on typological
grounds to the early ninth century. Not enough of the pattern on the
upper surface of the base (plate XXIc) survives to provide a complete

reconstruction of the type; but the strands are well cut and cross confidently, even though the carver has had some difficulty in turning the corner. Crosses 6, and 7, show increasing ineptitude and a new formula for Hexham shafts, whereby, as in the Lindisfarne manner, panels of interlace are the predominant or only ornamental motif. These crosses have the typical squat dimensions of later work, but on 6 the head is well shaped and enriched by a prominent roll moulding, and the cutting is quite deep and confident (plate XXIVd, e and f). Collingwood reconstructed face a of the head with the symbols of the evangelists because he saw there the feet of an eagle.[61] However, it is quite impossible to make anything certain out of the three little terminals which could be feet or leaves. Below enclosed by a flat outer frame and rounded inner frame is a panel of circular knot work, which is found at Alnmouth, on a grave cover in Durham and a cross from St Oswald's Church.[62]

I have discussed elsewhere this tradition of plaits which are found closely associated with the community of St Cuthbert in northern Northumbria.[63] The other side of the cross head is covered with close non-geometric plait, and the shaft shows a small panel of four strand interlace capping what may be an arch.

Number 7 (plate XXIVc), which has a similarly shaped head enriched by a small panel of interlace on the ends of the arms, also has plaits, Romilly Allen type 593, which can be paralleled on Durham crosses. The only broad face which can now be seen is framed by a plain flat outer moulding and inner roll moulding. These enclose a rambling spread of interlace, which Collingwood drew quite inaccurately; the small complete animal which he saw in the middle right of the shaft is clearly a reptilian head, but no other 'snakes' such as he saw at the top and bottom of the shaft are discernible. Nor can one make out the small quadruped which he saw on the cross head. Interlace with reptilian or animal heads is known elsewhere in Northumbria, at Lindisfarne and St Oswald's, Durham, and this reinforces the contact noted on 6. It seems reasonable therefore to see in these pieces the influence of the Lindisfarne school, perhaps when the community was at Chester-le-Street or Durham, but perhaps more likely after the move to Durham c. 1000 when the standard of workmanship of the sculpture revives elsewhere and when the community was in a stronger political position to exert influence in the Tyne valley.

At some stage, perhaps in the late tenth century, at the time when the Corbridge/Hexham area was the scene of decisive battles between the English and Scandinavian invaders, the churchyard seems to have been in use even though religious organization in the area must have been at a low ebb. This period is represented by a crude head, 12 (plate XXIVa and b), and part of a shaft, 8, and more interestingly by a 'hogback' with an interlace panel on the ridge (plate XVe). This type of monument, introduced into England by the Vikings, has been analysed by Mr J. T. Lang[64] who assigns it to the Brompton type and dates it to the late tenth century. It is a lonely outlier in Northumberland, but there is some evidence for Scandinavian place-names in Hexhamshire, and the hogback type continues in post-Conquest monuments at Hexham. It is possible, therefore, that we could see this as a new Scandinavian element in the permanent rather than transitory population of the area.

The sculpture which has survived from the church and cemeteries at Hexham provides a substantial memorial to the aspirations, contacts, and technical achievement of the people who occupied the site in the pre-Conquest period.

Notes

[1] Eddius, chapter XVII mentions the gospels as one of the treasures of Ripon. Recently an Oxford MS., Hatton 48, has been assigned to these foundations. See *supra*, p. 46.

[2] Eddius, chapter LV.

[3] Eddius, chapter XII.

[4] Raine, I, 12.
'Ipsos etiam et capitella columnarum quibus sustentantur, et arcum sanctuarii, historiis et imaginibus, et variis celaturarum figuris ex lapide prominentibus et picturarum et colorum grata varietate mirabilique decore decoravit.'

[5] 'Winchester New Minster and its Tenth Century Tower', *JBAA* 24 (1961), 41-8.

[6] R. J. Cramp, 'The Excavations at Monkwearmouth and Jarrow', *MA* 13 (1969), 39 and plate IV, B-C. A hand-list of Hexham stones is given as Appendix II.

[7] Abstract patterns are known from Wearmouth, *ibid.*, plate IV, D-E, and for figural painting see M. Biddle, 'Excavations at Winchester 1966', *Ant.J.*, 47 (1967), plate XXIII.

[8] J. Hubert, *Europe in the Dark Ages*, plate 99.

[9] J. Hubert, J. Porcher, W. F. Volbach, *L'Empire Carolingien* (Paris, 1968), fig. 43.

[10] Hubert, Porcher, Volbach, *L'Empire Carolingien*, fig. 43.

[11] Baldwin Brown, III, 259 and fig. 102.

[12] A similar fragment was found in excavations of the monastic buildings at Jarrow in 1971.

[13] C. C. Hodges, 'Simonburn Church, Northumberland', *AA* I (1925), 182, and fig. 21. This drawing is not accurate.

[14] R. J. Cramp, *Early Northumbrian Sculpture*, Jarrow Lecture 1965, 4 and plates 3 and 4.

[15] R. J. Cramp, *The Monastic Arts of Northumbria*, Arts Council (London, 1967), 22-3. This 'boar' I then considered to be a hound but further examination has convinced me that it has a hoof and that the 'tongue' is really a tusk.

[16] Such whitish, (?) gesso, bases, have been found on other sculpture from Northumbria, notably on pieces from Monkwearmouth.

[17] R. J. Cramp, *The Monastic Arts of Northumbria*, 24.

[18] Edward Gilbert, 'Early Northumbrian Architecture', *AA* 42 (1964), fig. 4. The last section of this frieze was taken down in the 1966 restoration of the tower, and now lies at the west end of the church. It is impossible to make out any detail on the stone today.

[19] Hubert, *Europe in the Dark Ages*, plates 68 and 70.

[20] No. 39 from Hexham, now lost, was of apparently very fine workmanship. It had a form of widely spaced knot, see p. 124 and plate XIe, which could represent an intermediate style of perhaps the late eighth century.

[21] W. G. Collingwood, 'Early Carved Stones', *AA* I (1925), 65-92 (pp. 69-70).

[22] Hubert, *Europe in the Dark Ages*, plate 99.

[23] H. M. and J. Taylor, 'The Seventh-century church at Hexham: a new appreciation', *AA* 39 (1961), 119, 129.

[24] F. J. Haverfield and W. Greenwell, *A Catalogue of the Sculptured and Inscribed Stones in the Cathedral Library, Durham* (Durham, 1899), 66, rightly pointed out eighth-century Italian parallels for this curlicue motif.

[25] Hodges and Gibson, 42.

[26] Carl Nordenfalk, *Early Medieval Painting* (Skira, 1957), 123, plate

[27] Savage and Hodges, plate 38.

[28] The interlace type is Romilly Allen's no. 619.

[29] Collingwood, 22-3, figure 28. Taylor, in *AA* 29 (1961), 119, considers these fragments and no. 23 as 'suitable for use in screen walls' in Wilfrid's church. Cramp, *The Monastic Arts of Northumbria* (1967), 21, calls 22a a 'decorative wall plaque' and 22b 'part of a decorative wall frieze' but considers they were part of the same scheme. I have recently discussed these pieces with Mr John Phillips of Sheffield University who is unwilling to accept them as Roman.

[30] R. J. Cramp, 'Early Northumbrian Sculpture', *Jarrow Lecture*, 1965, 4.

[31] Hubert, *Europe in the Dark Ages*, figure 48.

[32] This phenomenon has been discussed in detail by Charles Thomas, *The Early Christian Archæology of North Britain* (University of Glasgow, 1971), chapter 3. On the possibility of an earlier Christian structure at Hexham, however, see Edward Gilbert, *supra*, p. 81.

[33] Hodges' plan is now reproduced afresh by Dr Edward Gilbert, *supra*, p. 88, plan V.

[34] His description in *HE* IV, 11, of the burial of Sebbi, king of the East Saxons, mentions the preparation of his stone sarcophogus which proved to be too short. Having chipped away another two fingers from the stone to enlarge it the monks feared, before the miraculous shrinking of the corpse, that they would have to 'look for another'. Æthelthryth of Ely, who was buried at her own request in a wooden coffin, was reinterred at the time of her translation into the church, in a white marble sarcophogus which the Ely monks found on the Roman site of Grantchester when looking for blocks of stone to make a coffin. A stone coffin was apparently then a mark of distinction.

[35] Collingwood, figure 19.

[36] *ibid.*, figure 17.

[37] Prior Richard used the word in a context which Raine considers could mean cemetery, 'Atrium queque templi magnæ spiritudinis et fortidunis muro circumvallavit' (Raine, I, 13); and Ailred of Rievaulx says 'Est in civitate Hagulstaldensi ecclesia in honore Sanctæ Dei Genitricis extructa in orientali parte majori ecclesiæ, tanto intervallo divisa, ut et atrium intersit et via patens transeuntibus non desit' (Raine, I, 181).

[38] *Symeonis Monachi Opera Omnia* II, 33.

[39] Haverfield and Greenwell, *op. cit.*, 57.

[40] 'Bishop Acca and the Cross at Hexham', *AA* 48 (1970), 161.

[41] *HE* V, 19.

[42] *Karl der Grosse* III, ed. W. Braunfels and H. Schnitzler (Düsseldorf, 1965), 296, fig. 11.

[43] Haverfield and Greenwell, *op. cit.*, 58.

[44] Such elaborate metal crosses are described in Bede, as for example the cross which Paulinus brought with him to Northumbria and took back to Rochester (*HE* II, 20). An unpublished cross from Jarrow, plate XXIIf, is also obviously dependant on a metal prototype (see p. 136).

[45] Victor Elbern, 'Liturgisches berüt in edlen Materialen zur Zeit Karls des Grossen', *Karl der Grosse* III (Dusseldorf, 1966), 141, 144, 145.

[46] C. C. Hodges, 'The Pre-Conquest Churches of Northumbria', *Reliquary* 7 (1893), 11.

[47] W. G. Collingwood, 'The Ruthwell Cross in its Relation to other Monuments of the Early Christian Age', *Trans. Dumfr. Galloway Nat. Hist. Ant. Soc.* 5 (1916-18), 36, and 'A Pedigree of Anglian Crosses' *Antiquity* 6 (1932), 40.

[48] This feature can be paralleled on the Ruthwell Cross, as can Christ's hair type.

[49] 'Early Carved Stones', 78, and *Northumbrian Crosses*, 32, fig. 40.

[50] Collingwood, fig. 42. It is now impossible to check whether the cross head which Collingwood put on this shaft is a likely part, since it is now lost.

[51] Compare for example the jamb from Lastingham, W. G. Collingwood, 'Anglian and Anglo-Danish Sculpture in the North Riding of Yorkshire', *YAJ* 19 (1907), 358 and fig. p.

[52] *HE* V, 21.

[53] W. G. Collingwood, 'Early Carved Stones at Hexham', *AA* I (1925), 73-6.

[54] This piece has not hitherto been published. I have tentatively identified it as one of the corner posts of an altar. It bears a striking ornamental similarity to the famous altar from Cordoba; Thilo Ulbert, 'Skulptur in Spanien, 6-8 Jahrhundert', *Kolloqium über Spätantike and frühmittelalterliche skulptur* II (Mainz, 1970).

[55] 'Anglo-Saxon Vinescroll Ornament', *Antiquity* 10 (1936), 61-7 (67-8), plate 5.

[56] K. A. C. Cresswell, *Early Muslim Architecture* (2nd edition, Oxford, 1969), figures 153, 12c and 24b.

[57] *ibid.*, plate 3c.

[58] *Charlemagne*, Council of Europe Exhibition (Aix-la-Chapelle, 1965), 367, and plate 107.

[59] Collingwood was the first to point this out and to compare the Northallerton motif with the base of the Ormside bowl.

[60] This arm may perhaps be part of a cross head built into the north porch. It was discovered in excavations on the site in 1971, reused as part of a medieval drain.

[61] Collingwood, 154, and figure 180.

[62] Haverfield and Greenwell, *op. cit.*, 74 and 87. J. R. Allen, *The Early Christian Monuments of Scotland* (Edinburgh, 1903), pattern no. 696c.

[63] R. J. Cramp, 'A Cross from St. Oswald's Church, Durham, and its Stylistic Relationships', *Durham University Journal* 58 (1965-66), 119-24.

[64] 'Hogbacks in North East England', 81-3: unpublished M.A. thesis and projected publication. I am grateful to Mr Lang for his advice on this piece.

Chapter Six

THE ANGLO-SAXON METALWORK FROM HEXHAM

Richard N. Bailey

ONLY ONCE does it seem that a carefully planned excavation at Hexham yielded an example of Anglo-Saxon metalwork. That was in the eleventh century. Our record of it is preserved in an entry under the year 740 in the *Historia Regum*, a twelfth-century compilation attributed to Symeon of Durham.[1] This notes the death of Bishop Acca and his burial and goes on to describe the opening of his grave over three hundred years later. Among the relics found at this translation, which must date to after 1050, was an object shaped like an altar (*in modum altaris facta*) and made of two boards joined by silver nails. It carried an inscription reading ALMÆ TRINITATI. AGIÆ SOPHIÆ. SANCTÆ MARIÆ. In an important study Hunter Blair has shown that this passage is an interpolation by a Hexham propagandist, anxious to demonstrate the distinction of his church,[2] but there seems no reason to doubt that such an object was actually found. It has not survived but was presumably similar to the portable altar associated with St Cuthbert, perhaps with *brandea*, cloth or silk associated with the saint, between the boards.[3]

Today there are four pieces of metalwork from Hexham which can be assigned to the Anglo-Saxon period. All were found in a short period of thirty years between 1830 and 1860, but, since there is little else to link them together, they are best treated separately.

The Bucket

William Errington, a common carrier operating between Hexham and Newcastle, died on 13 October 1832. Two days later, the abbey's sexton and his assistant were preparing his grave when they unearthed a bronze bucket containing several thousand Anglo-Saxon coins. The coins are discussed by H. E. Pagan in Appendix IV: our concern here is with the archæological context of the discovery and with the bucket itself.

The first account of the sexton's find appeared in the *Newcastle Chronicle* on 20 October. It is clear that the writer had no direct knowledge of the event but his claim that the 'metal container or safe' had been found amongst the remains of a stone coffin, in association with a helmeted skull, was to be repeated in various nineteenth-century local histories.[4] A week later, on 27 October, the *Newcastle Chronicle* issued a corrected version of the discovery which denied the existence of associated finds.[5] From this account and from the scholarly publication by the Newcastle lawyer-antiquary John Adamson,[6] it is possible to reconstruct the place and circumstances of the bucket's recovery.

Errington's grave was dug some three yards from the west wall of the north transept in an area known as Campy Hill. Its precise position on this line cannot be fixed with certainty but is likely to have been nearer the north, rather than the south, corner. This would best fit Joseph Ridley's description of the grave, contained in an article describing Campy Hill in the middle years of the nineteenth century, as 'just opposite the gate, and very near the entrance to the ground'.[7] There is a (now recumbent) slab recording the names of several members of the Errington family lying opposite the buttress on the north side of the central window of the transept: this may well mark the site of the Errington graves though disturbance to memorials in this area during the 1899-1908 restorations and the 1953 landscaping do not allow it to be used as convincing evidence for location. It is, nevertheless, intriguing to notice that the present site of the memorial slab marks the north-west corner of a possible pre-Norman transept or linking-structure which can be reconstructed on the basis of Hodges' observations of Anglo-Saxon walling. If the grave of William Errington was on a line with this slab and three yards from the present transept wall it would lie just clear of the north wall of this earlier structure.[8]

Despite the fact that the sexton and his assistant had laboured down through some seven or eight feet in digging the grave there is no reason to infer that the bucket was originally buried at such a depth. The evidence of writers, plans and photographs of the nineteenth century show that successive burials and the debris of the ruined nave had combined to raise the surface of this part of the graveyard to a height at least six feet above the apparent Anglo-Saxon flooring in the present building. It follows that the bucket and the coins were placed just below ground level, possibly against the church wall. Such a site could easily be re-located for the recovery which was planned but, for some reason, never took place.

Late in December 1841 William Errington's grave was re-opened for the burial of his nephew, and the local historian J(oseph) R(idley) supplied an appropriately dramatic account of the event to the *Gateshead Observer* for 31 December.[9] The sight was both 'gratifying and repulsive' to him. The repulsion was part of his campaign against the continuation of burial in crowded urban cemeteries which he saw as both detrimental to general health and offensive to those who, like Ridley himself, had seen 'the bones of my kindred kicked by the unhallowed hoof of a ruthless sexton'. The gratification lay in the recovery of some fifty coins which had not been collected in 1832. His account leaves no doubt that this find was part of the same hoard.

During the nineteenth century there were parts of the bucket in at least three different places. In 1833 the British Museum received most of what had survived from the incumbent and the Lord of the Manor of Hexham, the Reverend W. Airey and Mr Beaumont.[10] But other pieces seem to have been dispersed, along with hundreds of the coins, into the Hexham neighbourhood. One small fragment is now in the Northumbrian cabinet of the Heberden coin room of the Ashmolean Museum.[11] A third, and more important, set of fragments were presented to the British Museum in 1884 by Dr W. D. Fairless and these presumably came from the collection of his father, Joseph Fairless (1789-1873), a Hexham painter and decorator who was an assiduous collector.[12] Unfortunately it is not possible to establish whether the Fairless fragments came from the 1832 find, at a time when he was churchwarden, or the re-opening of 1841 when the *Gateshead Observer* account shows that he was present.[13] The importance of this Fairless donation will be noticed later in this discussion.

It would be neither appropriate nor possible within the compass of this chapter to give a detailed description of the bucket: this must await the relevant volume of the *Catalogue of Antiquities of the Later*

Saxon Period. What follows is therefore confined to a general account of the condition, dimensions and decoration of the vessel, drawing attention to important elements which have not previously been noticed.

The bucket (plate XXV) is in a very fragmentary state and large areas have required heavy restoration. Even those parts which have survived are riddled with corrosion. Standing to a total height, excluding the handle, of 26.3 cm, it tapers from an external base diameter of 25.6 cm to one of 17.5 at the lip. Three pairs of raised bands ornament the body whilst, on the base, a circle has been hammered up to appear as a raised ring within the bucket (plate XXVIIa). The edges of this base have been bent down and riveted to the sides of the bucket, the join being concealed by a tubular binding which is similarly fixed with rivets. At the top of the bucket (plates XXV-VI) the lip has been bent into a shape resembling a crochet hook and a tubular binding squeezed around it. This split tube held in place the open ends of twelve V-shaped sheaths whose apexes were riveted to the sides of the bucket. The sheaths framed and held triangular vandykes of sheet bronze *pressblech* decorated with double contoured interlace. Only six sheaths and vandykes now survive, many only in fragments. Apart from a raised border the handle is flat, expanding at the middle and ends. There are difficulties in establishing the exact details of the handle attachments but the basic system is clear enough: the handle end is riveted between the upper ends of two plates whose lower sections are riveted to each other through the bucket. Cross-plates held these larger plates in position.

The two attachment plates fixed on the outside of the bucket carry elaborate decoration which has been hilariously misunderstood in the past (plate XXVI). At the top is a flat-headed human mask with large eyes, the handle rivet visible on the brow. It is the ornament below this which has caused confusion.[14] Adamson saw the two heads as having pendant draperies whilst in 1910 Gustafson referred to 'the peculiar shape lower down'. With less reticence Hodges and Gibson spoke of 'demi-female figures in bold relief' but it was left to Smith in 1923 to openly declare that the entire decoration was one of 'plates bearing female busts'. From that date this identification of naked females has been widely repeated, at its most engaging when Lethbridge invoked the figure of the Earth Mother Goddess to explain their presence.

Sadly, the naked females do not in fact exist. When the bucket was on exhibition in 1967 at Hexham both Professor Charles Thomas and I independently noticed that the standard interpretation was false. Indeed, the careful drawings prepared for Adamson show what is concealed in the better-known illustration in the British Museum *Guide* —that the 'female breasts' are the two ears, and the 'belly' the forehead, of a small crouching quadruped with backward turned head, modelled haunches, tapering tummy and little tail flung over his back.

The present appearance of the bucket owes much to nineteenth-century restoration. Current re-treatment in the Research Laboratory at the British Museum has revealed the full extent of this modern work and shows that some of the more intriguing aspects of the vessel are less than a century old.[15] This early restoration had united the 1832 remains, illustrated by Adamson, with the pieces from the Fairless collection. The various fragments were soldered together and the lacunæ filled with brown paper which had been stiffened with glue: the silver patches which are now on the sides of the bucket are not traces of original tinning but drops of solder attributable to either this restoration or to Fairless. In order to strengthen the object for exhibition it had been mounted on a wooden frame to which it was attached by nails hammered through the bronze sheet. It is this attachment which explains the holes in the base ring and accounts for their absence from the Adamson illustration. Three lines of holes on the sides of the bucket have a similar explanation: one runs round the base at a height of *c.* 2 cm from the bottom, a second can be seen around the rim and a third runs vertically below vandyke 4 (numbering from the spectator's left). Other holes, such as the one behind vandyke 5 and those within the frame of vandyke 1, are also of relatively modern origin.[16] Only the perforations flanking the upper part of the handle attachments are original since they are visible in Adamson's engraving and carried cross-plates whose vestigial remains can be seen on the inside of the bucket. There is thus no evidence for the attachment of decorative strips or pendant ornaments such as occur on some pagan buckets and on certain hanging bowls.[17]

One related point should be recorded before proceeding to a discussion of the date, function and ultimate origin of the bucket. The placing of the frames and vandykes is a conventional one which dates only from the nineteenth-century restoration. The material presented by Fairless included, according to the Museum's register and the accompanying sketches, at least three frames and four vandyke fragments. Comparison with Adamson's drawings, showing the 1832 situation, allows identification of some of the Fairless pieces but the relevant point for the present discussion is that all of the Fairless material has been placed on the same side of the bucket. There can be no certainty that this was their original side nor, even if it were, that they are now in the exact position which they occupied before the 1832 disinterment.

The bucket has been strangely neglected by scholars. It is not, perhaps, unreasonable to attribute this neglect to the fact that Baldwin Brown did not live to write his projected account.[18] Clearly, however, it warrants attention both as an example of a metalwork find from an area where such items are scarce and as an example of a piece associated with a coin hoard dating to the mid-ninth century.

Discussion is hampered by two factors. The first is the lack of a *corpus* of insular buckets. The second is that the Christian conversion of Anglo-Saxon England had a disastrous effect on the survival of material for archæological analysis. Grave goods deposited with the pagan dead are a major source for our knowledge of their life but Christian teaching that man takes nothing from this world has the unfortunate result of leaving little within it for modern study. Consequently, while pre-seventh-century metalwork has survived in some quantity, comparable material from the Christian period is rare. It is thus a sobering exercise to contrast the few vessels and containers, dating between the seventh and eleventh centuries, which have survived in Britain with those known from contemporary, but pagan, Scandinavia.[19] It is indeed only the fortunate fact that Viking raiders and traders were pagans which accounts for the present existence of any quantity of insular Christian metalwork because, ironically, it is in the graves of ninth- and tenth-century Scandinavians that Christian metalwork from Britain was best preserved.[20]

Among the surviving buckets the Hexham example is a rarity in being completely of bronze and not, like so many Anglo-Saxon, Celtic and continental buckets, of wood bound in bronze. Such a vessel cannot, however, have been beyond the technical skill of insular metalworkers in the post-Roman period for they could produce bronze hanging bowls and workboxes, elaborate bronze bindings and the bronze vessels (*æreos caucos*) which the seventh-century King Edwin had made for the use of travellers within his kingdom.[21]

Recognizing, then, the extreme rarity of the bucket's make-up, it is perhaps best to begin an analysis with the vandykes. The background for this ornament is certainly Anglo-Saxon and probably ultimately Frankish. Buckets from the Frankish Rhineland in the sixth and seventh centuries frequently use this type of decoration[22] and it is not uncommon among the numerous Anglo-Saxon buckets of the pagan period.[23] In both areas the buckets concerned are bronze-bound wooden vessels and this triangular system may well originally have had a functional rôle in the construction of this particular type of container, the triangles being cut in one piece with the binding strip and thus serving to attach it more firmly to the wooden staves. Residual traces of this unitary type can be found on English pagan buckets but on both sides of the English Channel, well before the seventh century, there are buckets with the vandykes attached in the same manner as those at Hexham with their upper parts held beneath a binding strip and the lower apex pierced by a single rivet.[24]

It may seem dangerous to ignore the possible existence of this type of bucket decoration in Ireland since the early conversion of Celtic areas may have deprived us of similar material. Ireland certainly does have bronze buckets but none has pendant vandykes like the English or Frankish containers.[25] If, to this fact, we add Wilson's comment that *pressblech* (of the Hexham type) is 'more commonly found in England than in the Celtic lands',[26] then the Anglo-Saxon nature of this part of the bucket's decoration seems entirely convincing.

The fact that comparable buckets all belong to the pagan period does not imply that the Hexham bucket has to be placed into a similar context. In this respect it is useful to have a close parallel for the vandykes and their frames in the book binding of the Codex Victor, a Fulda manuscript associated with St Boniface.[27] Wilson's examination of the binding conclusively demonstrates that it is of

Northumbrian origin and can be dated to the late seventh or eighth centuries. Its relevance here is that the binding ornament is partly made up of vandykes of bronze *pressblech* held beneath triangular frames. The parallel with Hexham's bucket decoration is a striking one, and opens the possibility of a Christian context for this object.

When we turn to the handle attachments we are provided with a firmer indication of a dating to the Christian period. We are also faced with analogues amongst material for which some type of Celtic origin has long been assumed. The presence of a human head at the point of handle attachment seems to have a long history and a widespread distribution[28] but the most relevant parallels for this modelled feature are to be found amongst insular buckets and hanging bowls which ultimately found a resting place in ninth- and tenth-century Viking graves in Scandinavia.

The most impressive parallel, not least because the entire object is of the same shape as the Hexham container, is the so-called Buddha bucket from the Oseberg ship burial (plate XXV).[29] Here on the handle attachment is the same type of broad face, the same stress on the eyes and the same flat head. Despite difference in expression, and in the presence of an enamelled body, the Hexham and Oseberg heads clearly belong to the same art world. Alongside Oseberg can be ranged a series of escutcheons from hanging bowls which, although they do not fulfil precisely the same function as a handle attachment,[30] were placed at the points where a cord or chain was fastened for suspension. The most important of these are the ones from Løland and the River Maas, which have two heads with broad faces, flat foreheads and mouths very like those from Hexham, opposed across a rectangle.[31] From Myklebostad comes another hanging bowl with anthropomorphic escutcheons which can also be grouped with this set.[32]

Before drawing deductions from these parallels it would be opportune to draw attention to the existence of an animal similar to the newly recognized Hexham beast on yet another hanging bowl found at the Norwegian site of Gausel and now in the University Museum in Bergen (plate XXVI).[33] Here again is a crouching quadruped with backward turned head and tail flung over his back; wryly one notices that his front view resembles a female torso even more closely than does that from Hexham.

The most useful function of these parallels is that they help to tie down the date of the Hexham bucket since they have been found in Viking graves which belong, at earliest, to the ninth century. There is general agreement that they represent loot or trade from the British Isles and that the chronological horizon for this material is the eighth or early ninth century. An eighth-century dating for the bucket would be consonant with that indicated by the Fulda book binding and the Scandinavian finds: this would also agree with its concealment, as Mr Pagan's study shows, with coins belonging to the middle years of the ninth century.

Given the Anglo-Saxon background for the vandykes, Northumbria would seem an appropriate area for the manufacture of the bucket. Yet both the Oseberg bucket and the hanging bowls have been claimed as Irish products.[34] This view is no longer universally accepted but, even if it were, it does not follow that the Hexham bucket must be similarly assigned to Ireland. Contacts between Ireland and Christian Northumbria both before and after the council of Whitby are well documented and show the means by which Irish-derived elements could enter the art of Northumbria.[35] That such elements were present in the late seventh and eighth centuries is now a commonplace of art history and can be exemplified by material as various as the Lindisfarne Gospels and the millifiore glasswork found at Monkwearmouth and Jarrow.[36] It is now widely recognized that there was a high degree of penetration of artistic techniques and motifs between Northumbria, Pictland and Ireland:[37] the term 'Hiberno-Saxon' which has been coined to describe this fused art is an appropriate one for the Hexham bucket.

Since this is the first occasion on which the Hexham bucket and the Gausel bowl have been linked together, it seems worth suggesting that the Norwegian find may also be a Northumbrian product. The naturalistic modelled animals are not the most likely beasts to find in insular art but they can be grouped with the little lion in the base of the lost bowl from the River Witham[38] and, less closely, with the beast on the escutcheon of the bowl from St Ninian's Isle.[39] Since both of these bowls have been claimed, on other grounds, as Northumbrian and since the Hexham bucket was found in Northumbria and uses vandykes of an Anglo-Saxon type, it seems reasonable to suggest that the possibility of a similar origin for the Gausel bowl ought now to be entertained.

The original function of the Hexham bucket is a mystery. It could have been a container used within the monastery, its broad base giving it stability and its narrow lip preventing spilling. This narrow lip presumably rules out the possibility that it was used to contain ink, like the bronze bucket known from St Denis.[40] Its unique make-up and its relatively elaborate decoration might suggest that it had a less utilitarian purpose. Its use as a liturgical bucket is a possibility: these are often mentioned in lists of church possessions[41] and can be seen in use by the diminutive figures who cram the delightful depictions of sacramentary acts on the book-cover of the ninth-century Drogo Sacramentary.[42] But most of the known liturgical buckets, such as the famous lead examples from North Africa,[43] do not have a narrow mouth. In any case if it were used for liquid it would require careful caulking. It is not, of course, impossible that it was used as a store for the monastery's coinage and that it was not entirely misused when hidden on the site of what was to be the grave of one of Hexham's later citizens.

The Chalice

The chalice, now kept in a display safe in the south aisle of the abbey choir, is the only example of Hexham's Anglo-Saxon metalwork which remains in the town where it was found (plate XXIX).

Made of a copper-based alloy it was once heavily gilded. As the result of a slight distortion of the foot its height now varies between 6.2 and 6.7 cm. The chalice was originally made in three separate parts: the foot with its integral base ring, the hollow knot and the shallow broad bowl. These were joined together by a rivet passing through all three sections and the end of the rivet, hammered flat, can be seen inside the foot and bowl.

The chalice was found in 1860, in circumstances which will be examined below, and was acquired by Dr Edward Charlton, a major figure in Newcastle's medical, scientific, literary and antiquarian activities. As one of the secretaries of the Newcastle Society of Antiquaries he exhibited it to the society at its meeting on 5 December 1860.[44] When he died in 1874 the chalice was bought by the Reverend Walker Featherstonhaugh who was Rector of Edmondbyers from 1856 until his death in 1904.[45] Featherstonhaugh contributed a short note on it to *The Antiquary* in 1881[46] and in October 1890 it was once more exhibited to the Newcastle Society of Antiquaries. The published account of that meeting includes the earliest illustration of the object and also records Featherstonhaugh's intention of placing the chalice in the Society's Black Gate Museum.[45] The Museum's register, however, shows no trace of its accession and two years later, when Cripps and Hodges published a fuller description of the chalice, it is still recorded as belonging to Featherstonhaugh.[47] With that publication it mysteriously disappeared for half a century.

Its re-emergence, equally mysterious, is documented in the minute book of the abbey's Parochial Church Council which records that, at their February meeting in 1957, members were shown the chalice which had been presented by 'an anonymous donor'. The date of this presentation must lie late in 1956 or in the early weeks of 1957. Despite extensive enquiries, and the help of the Abbey staff who were most closely involved, it has not proved possible to recover details of this presentation, still less the identity of the donor. The only relevant account is given in the unlikely source of *A Children's Guide to the Abbey* where it is said to have been handed in by a visitor. It is probable that the donor was a member of the Featherstonhaugh family but attempts to trace its ownership through the Reverend Walker's will (in which it is not specifically itemized) have so far proved unsuccessful. Since its re-discovery it has been published on several occasions.[48]

If it is difficult to reconstruct an event which occurred but fifteen years ago it has proved even more frustrating to disentangle the circumstances surrounding the original discovery. This took place during that restoration of the Abbey in 1858-60 which Hodges labelled 'a permanent disgrace to Hexham'.[49] When he exhibited the chalice in 1860 Charlton said that it had been found 'recently in the transept of Hexham Abbey, while digging a deep trench there for a warming apparatus'. There is no evidence that Charlton was present when it was found: he presumably acquired it from the contractor who is known to have disposed of material which, by some chance, remained surplus to his destructive and acquisitive activities.[50]

In contrast to Charlton's account Featherstonhaugh is much more specific, asserting that it was found 'on the breast of, no doubt, a priest buried in a stone coffin in the north transept'.[51] How reliable is this statement, written some twenty years after the discovery? Featherstonhaugh's account could have come from Charlton in 1860 since the minute book of the Newcastle Society of Antiquaries shows that Featherstonhaugh was one of twelve members present when the chalice was originally exhibited. Yet, if the find-spot was known in such detail in 1860, it seems strange that neither the published account nor the minute book carry any record of it. It is much more likely that Featherstonhaugh was either building on Charlton's comments on the usual context of chalice finds or was echoing local tradition such as that which had associated a coffin and helmet with the 1832 bucket find. His location in the north transept is equally suspicious and may be based on inference from the well-known account of Hexham's 1860 heating installation which is quoted below.[52]

Attempts to establish the lines of the deep trench mentioned by Charlton have met with only limited success since contemporary descriptions of the 1860 heating system are inconsistent. A writer in the *Builder*, for example, seems to point to the existence of a deep trench in the north transept as well as giving a valuable insight into the style of the 1860 restoration:[53]

'On the day we visited the church they were forming a large warm-air drain, six feet wide and six feet deep, and one hundred and twenty feet long, through the length of the north transept; that is to say making a cutting through layer upon layer of coffins and skeletons—the burials of generations, the fragments of which were being wheeled out openly to the churchyard.'

This would seem to fit neatly with Featherstonhaugh's claim for a north transept location if it were not for the fact that the *entire* transepts only measure 135 feet. There are similar problems in interpreting the information supplied in the *Ecclesiologist* where the writer seems to have confused north with south.[54] In fact the most likely candidate for Charlton's 'deep trench' is the one which now runs north from the south transept door as far as the southernmost bay of the north transept aisle: it is clear from a conflation of various sources that this must belong to the 1860 system and that it is of considerable dimensions. There were, however, undoubtedly other trenches and, short of removing all the paving in the transepts to distinguish the sequence of nineteenth-century systems, it would be hazardous to locate the chalice's find-spot more precisely than Charlton's 'the transept of Hexham Abbey'.[55]

We are, then, left with the problem of dating the chalice without any firm information about its archæological context. There is no doubt that Cripps was correct in assigning it to a period before the thirteenth century:[56] the lack of stem and the dominance of the knot are but two of the features which distinguish this chalice from the thirteenth-century types classified by Oman.[57] Twelfth-century chalices, such as that of Hubert Walter of Canterbury,[58] share some of these characteristics but it is only in the period before the early twelfth century that a satisfactory set of parallels can be found.

There are serious difficulties in the typological and chronological ordering of western European chalices in this period. The literary evidence shows that there were large numbers[59] and that they fulfilled a great variety of functions, many of which demanded differing shapes and dimensions of chalice. There was the votive chalice, the *calix ministerialis* used for the administration of the Eucharist to the faithful, the *calix minor* used for private celebration, the *calix offerendarius* used for offering wine, the *calix viaticus* used when travelling and the *calix baptismalis* from which mixed milk and honey was given to the newly baptized. Such a list does not exhaust the range of possibilities but sufficiently indicates both the variety and numbers of what once existed.

Surviving chalices, by comparison, are few. Elbern's invaluable study[60] lists a total of less than forty for the whole of western Europe. From the British Isles there are, at most, only five examples including that from Hexham. The other four have little in common, varying greatly in size, splendour and date. The magnificent handled chalice from Ardagh, for example, has few links with the lead funerary chalice from Hazleton in Gloucestershire and nearly three centuries must separate their dates of production. There have been doubts as to whether the silver cup found with a late ninth-century hoard at Trewhiddle in Cornwall can be identified as a chalice and similar doubts have, more justifiably, been cast on the identity of a bronze cup found with the Ardagh chalice.[61] It will be apparent from this summary that the insular chalices do not form an adequate *corpus* for comparison with Hexham.

The continental European material listed by Elbern provides a better group for comparative study, even though the total number amounts to only thirty-two. Unfortunately these are not evenly distributed either chronologically or geographically. A high proportion come from Germany and from the graves of high-ranking ecclesiastics of the tenth and eleventh centuries. Even with the aid of contemporary illustrations (evidence which must be handled with caution) a satisfactory typology for the various types of chalice is therefore not now recoverable. As a result the suggested datings for the Hexham chalice have covered the entire Christian Anglo-Saxon period.[62]

The best starting point for an analysis is with its three-part composite structure because this does not seem to be found on the continent where the knot and foot are a unitary feature. Since the Trewhiddle chalice has a similar three-part composition and so too, in a differing way, does the large Ardagh chalice, it seems likely that the Hexham structure is an insular one. The arched foot has also been claimed by Elbern as an insular characteristic; this again is found on the Trewhiddle and large Ardagh chalices and Elbern has explained its occasional occurrence on the continent, notably on the Silos chalice, as a sign of British influence.[63] At very least it is clear that the Hexham chalice would not be out of place as an insular product.

None of the insular chalices have a pearled ring between knot and bowl like Hexham, though Wilson's reconstruction of the damaged Trewhiddle chalice posits one placed between the foot and knot.[64] Equivalent rings are, however, found frequently amongst the pre-twelfth-century material on the continent: eighth-century examples are provided by the Tassilo[65] and Petöhaza chalices whilst, at the other end of the chronological scale, there are examples on the grave chalices of the eleventh-century ecclesiastics, Hezilo at Hildesheim and Udo and Poppo at Trier (plate XXIX).[66]

While recognizing that the Hexham chalice has links in its pearled ring with pre-twelfth-century European chalices and, in its three-part structure and arched foot, shows features which seem to be insular, is it possible to give it a closer dating?

Elbern's dating to the eleventh century seems the most convincing of those so far put forward. There are such close parallels between the Hexham chalice and those from the graves of eleventh-century continental ecclesiastics (plate XXIX)[67] that it would be difficult to deny the possibility of a late date within the Anglo-Saxon period. Such a date is also indicated by the broad and shallow nature of the Hexham bowl which has a great deal in common with those found on Romanesque chalices. The comparison which Elbern has drawn with the chalice held by Ecclesia on a tenth-century Fulda illumination[68] is a further indication of a late Saxon date. Only sentiment can justify placing the Hexham chalice before the tenth century.

The find-spot, even if we disregard Featherstonhaugh's 'coffin', would suggest that the Hexham chalice ended its useful life as a grave-chalice. In size it can be compared with at least fifteen of the continental grave-chalices listed by Elbern.[69] All of these, however, are made of precious metal and were presumably in use as portable chalices before they were placed in the grave. It is likely that the gilding on the Hexham chalice was intended to make it appear similarly impressive:[70] it, too, was probably once a portable chalice. It is certainly of a size appropriate for use with the few pre-Norman portable altars known in Britain.[71]

The Silver Plaque

One of the engravings illustrating Raine's collection of Hexham documents, published in 1864, shows a small silver plate 'found in Hexham church'.[72] The same block was used by Hodges in 1889 and given a similar caption.[73] Yet its first owner gave a very different account of its origin when he exhibited the object to the Society of Antiquaries of London in May 1858. He was the Reverend Frederick Lee, a notable scholar and church dignitary, who reported that he had 'purchased this curious object in Yorkshire of a travelling collector of old gold and silver, who informed him that it was found in the garden or in the ruins of an old house in Hexham'.[74] The travelling collector may have been anxious to conceal the fact that the source of the plaque was the church or the reference to ruins may be an allusion either to the site of the original nave or to the buildings at the eastern end of the church which were then being demolished. Whatever the explanation, Raine's statement that the plaque came from the church must be treated with caution.

The plaque (plate XXVII) was presented to the British Museum by Lee.[75] It measures 7.5 by 10 cm and the decoration has been incised on the thin silver sheet from both sides. Its present condition differs little from that shown in Raine's engraving, the drawing in the *Guide to Anglo-Saxon Antiquities* showing a restored version.[76] The dominant impression made by this object is one of crude and careless execution. The outer frame is formed by hachured lines which over-run their inside border in the same way as the lines of the inner frame over-run each other. In the (spectator's) lower right corner the inner frame has been drawn twice. Some of the lines of the half-length figure cross the frame whilst others, like the halo to the right of the neck, are not properly completed. The contrast between the incompetent nature of the workmanship and the value of the metal is very striking.

The figure's face is suggested by a simple dot eye, placed beneath eyebrows which, to the left, are connected to the line of an L-shaped nose. Two parallel lines render the mouth and a small lunate shape below this represents the chin. There is a strongly marked neck-line; the clothing requires further discussion below but, like the facial features, is rendered by the same technique of incising from both sides of the sheet. Round the head is what is presumably intended as a halo (rather than hood or hair) though the problem of the interpretation of this type of surround is one that is familiar in other media, notably sculpture, in the pre-Norman period.

The clothing has evoked surprisingly little comment but is, in fact, very puzzling. The problem lies in the apparent cross-marked strip. Lee suggested that this was a kind of pallium, the symbol of archepiscopal office which was the gift of the Pope. This interpretation has been accepted by both Smith and Cramp[77] but is not, I believe, possible. Both in illustrations and in surviving examples, such as those recently discovered at York,[78] the pallium is always a cross-decorated strip which hangs down at both front and back, usually from a loop encircling the neck or shoulder line. There are differences in methods of folding and pinning but no pallium resembles the Hexham strip is terminating some distance short of the neck-line.

There are three possible interpretations of this strip and the accompanying drapery. The first is that the figure is wearing some kind of cloak or bratt, pinned at the chest and arranged to show a facing panel sewn on to the under-garment. It would, however, be unusual for such a strip not to be carried up to the neck-line. The other two interpretations depend on the fact that the strip is not a single feature but that the upper part, with a single incised cross, is intended to be book-shaped. Careful examination shows that there is a distinct lower edge to this object, particularly well marked at the left hand corner, which cannot be confused with the sweep of the garment. This edge and corner have, importantly, been emphasized by lines incised from both sides of the sheet. Against this lower edge is what can only be described as a squashed semicircular incision. This rectangular shape could be interpreted as some type of book-satchel or portable reliquary, the cross and semicircle suggesting its decoration and hasp.[79] Alternatively the artist may have envisaged the object as a sacred book held in garment covered hands—a sketched version of a pose known elsewhere in medieval art.[80] In either case the strip below, with its two crosses, must be seen as decoration sewn on to an under-garment or, more likely, on to a cloak or low-slung chasuble.

This type of crude linear drawing is difficult to date but it is a style which did exist in Anglo-Saxon England and is best represented by the ornament of St Cuthbert's seventh-century coffin-reliquary.[81] The detail on the Hexham face in which the eyebrow is continued into the nose line, as though seen in half-profile, is, indeed, one found on the coffin. The art of the coffin has long been linked to that of Merovingian Gaul and it is there, in work of the sixth to eighth centuries, that we find the best parallels for the schematic linear style of the Hexham silver sheet.[82] The most striking comparison is one with the reliquary casket of St Mumma at Saint-Benoit-sur-Loire which belongs to the seventh or eighth centuries.[83] Here the drapery is equally schematic and the facial features as crude while the figures are surrounded by a hachured border like Hexham. A seventh-century date for the silver plaque would not, therefore, be inappropriate and, if it is not a Merovingian piece, then it certainly seems to bear the marks of stylistic influence from that area.

Several functions for the plaque can be suggested though for most it must be assumed that the damaged areas once contained nail holes or that the whole sheet was stuck down with a mastic similar to that known on the Cuthbert portable altar.[84] Though it is much smaller than the rectangular plates which cover Cuthbert's portable altar the Hexham plaque could have fulfilled the same purpose, even though the workmanship is much less accomplished. Equally it could have formed part of the wall or roof of a house-shaped shrine, been part of a book cover or even acted as an altar mount.[85] This plethora of possibilities reflects a general puzzlement about this object.

The Gold Ring

The gold ring, shown in plate XXVIII, is now in the collection of His Grace the Duke of Northumberland at Alnwick Castle. It was presented to the fourth Duke by Joseph Fairless and the letter, dated 6 November 1858, which accompanied this donation is preserved in the ring cabinet. A drawing and facsimile of the ring were exhibited by Fairless to the Archæological Institute in November of 1853 and the report describes it as having been found 'about August last in a field near Hexham'.[86]

We have seen that Fairless was a collector and numismatist and, it would appear, one of the few citizens of Hexham in the second quarter of the nineteenth century who had a scholarly interest in the Abbey and its past. Through this interest he came into contact with Albert Way, sometime Director of the London Society of Antiquaries, founder of what became the Royal Archæological Institute and a leading figure in British archæology in the nineteenth century. Fairless's letter to the Duke mentions that Way had seen the ring and it was doubtless through his influence that the donation took place for, during this period, Way was acting as adviser to the Duke on archæological matters and was engaged in acquiring material for the growing Alnwick collection. To Way fell the task of preparing a catalogue of this archæological material and it is presumably as a result of preparatory work that we have his manuscript catalogue of the ring collection, dated 1 May 1867, which is now kept in the Alnwick ring cabinet. The entry on page ten describes the ring presented by Fairless, giving it a weight of 168 grains, and reports that it was found 'about August 1853, by a woman engaged in field-work near Hexham'.

It appears that Way habitually prepared engravings before he had completed the catalogue of which they were to form a part, and it is this practice which explains the existence of two unpublished engravings of the Fairless ring. One, showing the panels labelled 6 and 7 on plate XXVIII, is stuck into the Alnwick manuscript whilst an extended drawing is preserved in a portfolio of engravings now in the Department of Medieval and Later Antiquities in the British Museum. In the event Way did not live to finish his publication and the work was eventually completed by J. Collingwood Bruce in 1880.[87] For some reason this ring, with others, does not figure in the published catalogue and, as a result, the ring's existence was forgotten by all but a few local historians.[88] It was not until 1956 that it was noticed in a scholarly publication[89] and another eight years passed before the publication of a line drawing and a description achieved what Way had planned nearly a century before.[90]

We have already seen that Fairless and Way dated the discovery to August 1853. They also locate the discovery near Hexham. Further information about the find is available from Raine's collection of early Hexham documents.[91] In an appendix to his 1865 volume Raine acknowledged additional details furnished by Fairless about the Ogle shrine. There then follows a paragraph set in quotation marks, beginning 'Mr. Fairless had in his possession a massive gold ring, weighing 168 grains, which was found in a field near Corbridge ...'. The passage appears to be a re-working of the report of Fairless's exhibition of the ring to the Archæological Institute in 1853 but there has been a deliberate change of Hexham in favour of Corbridge. In view of his contact with Fairless I am inclined to give this contribution more weight than has been accorded to Raine's other statements about the sources of Hexham metalwork. It would seem that this object is best designated as the Hexham/Corbridge ring and that the find-spot lay between the two towns.

The ring (plate XXVIII) is of gold, 0.15-0.2 cm thick and with an inside diameter of 2.05 cm. The hoop is between 0.6 and 0.65 cm broad and has a beaded border running round either edge. Within this border are eight rectangular fields containing carved ornament. For convenience of reference these will be numbered as in Wilson's drawing. Panel 1 contains two loops whose strands merge with the frame. Panel 2 has a semi-zoomorphic ornament: the beast's body is bound by two incised lines across the middle and terminates at both ends in a haunch and leg. The haunches and the lower part of the body have nicked outlines. Panel 3 resembles panel 1 though, in place of a right hand loop, there are two lobed ends. Panel 4 contained zoomorphic ornament but this has been obliterated by a large hole which is also shown in Way's engraving. Since the hole was not a part of the original scheme it must have formed the setting for a jewel at some date after the ring's manufacture, possibly even in the nineteenth century. Panel 5 carries an animal resembling a sea horse set on its side. The tail is foliate, an incised line crosses the neck and the outline of the body has a double nick. The drilled eye is well marked. Panel 6 is filled by two St Andrew's crosses. Panel 7 resembles panel 2 and has similar binding and nicking. Panel 8 contains the most recognizable animal, crouching and with its head upturned. The single back leg has a well-shaped haunch and two nicks in its rear profile and the body has similar nicks on both back and belly. There is a single incision for the collar, a bump above the drilled eye, and a slightly beaked mouth. Above the front paw and over the back are detached billets of ornament.

This last panel offers the best starting point for fixing the date of the Hexham/Corbridge ring. The treatment of the animal is entirely characteristic of the ninth-century phase of Anglo-Saxon art which art-historians have labelled as Trewhiddle.[92] The nicks in the outline and the bump over the eye recur so frequently across the Trewhiddle corpus that a catalogue of parallels would be tedious. The slightly beaked mouth can be seen on the Strickland and Beeston Tor animals and the same two brooches provide parallels for the collars. The 'sea-horse' belongs to the same art world: there are good parallels for animals which dissolve into foliate forms on the swords from Grøn-neberg and Fiskerton[93] and on the strap-end from Stratton. The two semi-zoomorphic S-shapes have analogies on the Grønneberg and

Ingleton swords. The Ingleton sword, together with that from Abingdon and a strap-end from Hauxton Mill[94] have the Hexham/Corbridge binding across the animal's tummy whilst swords from Hegge, Fiskerton and Dolven[95] are decorated with quatrefoils which are very like the St Andrew's crosses on the Fairless ring. The loops with infilling occur among the material already listed and the free lobed ends and use of the framing panel can be seen on the sword from Hoven.[96] Finally, the use of beaded borders is a hallmark of this phase of Anglo-Saxon metalwork.

The Hexham/Corbridge ring thus fits happily into a ninth-century context, its animal art being of a type known all over Anglo-Saxon England. In view of the geographical spread of objects decorated in the Trewhiddle style it is no surprise to find that the ring which most closely resembles this Northumbrian example comes from Poslingford in Suffolk.[97] This also is a gold ring with eight rectangular frames set within beaded borders. It is the only other Trewhiddle-style ring to have the rare rectangular framing of this type of animal.[98]

If a ninth-century date is accepted then there is a problem posed by a part of Way's manuscript description. He noted that in one of the panels 'traces of blue colour appeared; it is probable that the field in each of them may have been decorated with enamel'. The closest apparent parallel for this at the date is the 'dark blue vitreous paste' remarked by Petersen in his description of the English ring found in the great Norwegian hoard at Hon.[99] I am grateful to Ellen-Karine Hougen, of the Universitets Oldsaksamling Oslo, for the information that this paste has been identified as blue glass. Without this example from Hon it is doubtful if it can be shown that any ninth-century ring carried blue champlevé enamel and it seems much more likely that Way's traces were of niello. This inlay is found in Trewhiddle art elsewhere and would make an effective colour contrast to the gold of this attractive ring.[100]

Four objects, however unique and interesting, are a poor haul from a major site and it is perhaps ironic that, in a volume concerned with Wilfrid and Hexham, this chapter has removed the chalice to a date at least three centuries after the saint and suggested that Corbridge has as much claim to the ring as Hexham. But Bede and Eddius remind us of what has disappeared. Eddius, well trained in the methods of medieval rhetoric, was suitably overcome at the ornaments of gold, silver and precious stones which Acca gave to Hexham.[101] It is Bede, however, who brings us closer to the subject of this book when he reproduces the epitaph placed over Wilfrid's tomb at Ripon:

'He set high in gleaming ore the trophy of the cross; golden the gospels four he made for it, lodged in a shrine of gold as is their due.'[102]

It is appropriate for the present chapter that this memorial shows that part of the saint's impact on his contemporaries could be measured in metallic splendour.

Acknowledgments
For permission to examine and publish material in their collections I am indebted to the following individuals and institutions: His Grace the Duke of Northumberland, K.G.; the Rector and Churchwardens of Hexham; the Trustees of the British Museum and Dr R. L. S. Bruce-Mitford, Keeper of the Department of Medieval and Later Antiquities; the Northumberland County Record Office. Apart from information and illustrations which are specifically acknowledged in the text and captions I am grateful for generous help and advice from Mrs Leslie Webster, Mr and Mrs J. T. Lang, Mr R. Miket, Professor Charles Thomas, Mr G. W. Trayhurn and Professor G. Zarnecki. My wife undertook the initial search of local newspapers: for this and her subsequent help and forbearance I am deeply grateful. Finally I acknowledge with gratitude a grant from the research fund of the University of Newcastle upon Tyne which enabled me to examine the Hexham bucket in London.

Notes

[1] *Symeonis Monachi Omnia* II, 33.
[2] P. Hunter Blair, 'Observations on the *Historia Regum*', *Celt and Saxon: Studies in the Early British Border*, ed. N. K. Chadwick (Cambridge, 1964), 70-1, 87-90: cf. H. S. Offler, 'Hexham and the *Historia Regum*', *DN* 2 (1970), 51-62.

[3] For the Cuthbert altar see C. A. R. Radford, 'The portable altar', *The Relics of St. Cuthbert*, ed. C. F. Battiscombe (Oxford, 1956), 326-35. For a commentary on these and other British altars see C. Thomas, *The Early Christian Archæology of North Britain* (London, 1971), 190-8.

[4] *e.g.* M. A. Richardson, *The Local Historian's Table Book* 4 (Newcastle, 1844), 139.

[5] A similar account can be found in the *Newcastle Courant* for 27 October and the *Tyne Mercury* for 30 October.

[6] J. Adamson, 'An account of the discovery at Hexham, in Northumberland, of a brass vessel, containing a large number of the Anglo-Saxon coins called stycas', *Archæologia* 25 (1834), 279-310, reprinted in *AA* 3 (1844), 77-108.

[7] J. Ridley, *The Hexham Chronicle: The Thirty-Nine Articles Contributed to the Local Historian's Table Book* (Hexham, 1862), 62. The gate can be seen near the north-west angle of the north transept in Hodges, plate 53.

[8] H. M. and J. Taylor, 'The seventh-century church at Hexham: a new appreciation', *AA* 39 (1961), figure I reproduces Hodges' plan (for this plan, see now *supra*, p. 88). A transept (so Baldwin-Brown) or linking structure (so Taylors) would have a north-west angle at the Errington slab if wall m_2 were projected to a position equivalent to the junction of walls n_2 and o_2.

[9] His letter is dated to the 27th and he describes the events as occurring on that day. In his *The Hexham Chronicle*, 59, he ascribes the discovery to the 23rd.

[10] Registration number 33, 7-1, 1. The record shows that Adamson was also involved.

[11] I am grateful to Dr D. M. Metcalf and Mr D. Hinton for confirmation of the existence of this fragment noted by J. D. A. Thompson, *An Inventory of British Coin Hoards* (London, 1956), no. 188. There is, however, doubt about the donor's identity.

[12] Registration number 84, 3-10, 1. It is clear from Hodges that Dr Fairless had inherited his father's notes, sketches and archæological collection.

[13] Since he was present in 1841 his own account of the site of the 1832 discovery is welcome confirmation of Adamson's information about location, J. Fairless, *Guide to the Abbey Church at Hexham* (Hexham, 1853), 17. His collection of coins from the hoard, numbering nearly 700, must have come from the first discovery.

[14] For the material in this paragraph see: Adamson, 'An account of the discovery', 282: G. Gustafson, 'Notes on a decorated bucket from the Oseberg find', *Saga Book* 5 (1910), 304: Hodges and Gibson, 86: R. A. Smith, *Guide to Anglo-Saxon Antiquities* (British Museum, 1923), 105: S. Grieg, *Osebergfundet* II (Oslo, 1928), 76: T. C. Lethbridge, 'Christian saints or pagan gods?', *Jour. Royal Anthrop. Inst.*, 83 (1955), 177: R. J. Cramp, *The Monastic Arts of Northumbria* (Arts Council, 1967), 18: P. Rahtz, 'Excavations on Glastonbury Tor...', *Arch. Jour.*, 127 (1971), 54.

[15] I am very grateful to the Laboratory for a report on this work, communicated by Mrs Leslie Webster, which forms the basis for this paragraph.

[16] Plate XXVIb shows vandyke 1 without its triangular sheet since the photograph was taken during restoration work.

[17] *e.g.* A. R. Cotton, 'Saxon discoveries at Fetcham', *Ant. Jour.*, 13 (1933), fig. 2, and F. Henry, 'Hanging bowls', *JRSAI* 66 (1936), 209-46.

[18] Baldwin-Brown, IV, 467.

[19] See H. Arbman, *Birka I: Die Gräber* (Stockholm, 1940), plates 197-211 or J. Petersen, *Vikingetidens Redskaper* (Oslo, 1951), 369-96, 419-21. Consider also the implications of the discovery of a pail described in P. H. Rahtz *et al.*, 'Three post-Roman finds from the Temple Well at Pagan's Hill, Somerset', *MA* 2 (1958), 108-11.

[20] See *Viking Antiquities in Great Britain and Ireland*, part V: *British Antiquities ... Found in Norway*, ed. H. Shetelig (Oslo, 1940), and E. Bakka, 'Some English decorated metal objects found in Norwegian Viking graves', *Årbok for Universitet i Bergen* (1963).

[21] For Edwin see *HE* II, 16. The archæological material can be seen in the works listed in notes 17 and 20 above. For imported bronze containers in the pagan period see F. H. Thompson, 'Anglo-Saxon sites in Lincolnshire', *Ant. Jour.*, 36 (1956), 194-9, and Baldwin-Brown, IV, plate 114.

[22] The fullest discussion of the material is J. B. Cochet, *Sépultures Gauloises, Romaines, Franques et Normandes* (Paris, 1857), 279-301. More accessible are illustrations in *Dictionaire d'Archéologie Chrétienne et de Liturgie*, ed. F. Cabrol and H. Leclercq (Paris, 1903-) s.n. *seau*. For recently discovered examples from Waldwisse, Cologne and Krefeld-Gellep see: E. M. Delort's report in *Gallia* 11 (1953), 144, fig. 6: O. Doppelfeld, 'Das fränkische Knabengrab unter dem Chor des Kölner Domes', *Germania* 42 (1964), 178 and plate 42: E. Pirling, 'Ein fränkisches Fürstengrab aus Krefeld-Gellep', *ibid.*, 206-7, 215 and plate 15.

[23] Representative examples are those from Loveden Hill, Roundway, Fetcham and Bidford-on-Avon: K. R. Fennell, 'The Loveden man', *Frühmittelalterliche Studien* 3 (1969), 211-15: M. E. Cunnington and E. H. Goddard, *Catalogue of the Antiquities in the Museum ... at Devizes* 2 (Devizes, 1911), plate 54: Cotton, 'Some discoveries at Fetcham', fig. 2: J. Humphreys *et al.*, 'An Anglo-Saxon cemetery at Bidford-on-Avon, Warwickshire', *Arch.*, 73 (1922-3), 100.

[24] All of the examples quoted in note 23 are of this type and so is that from Cologne noted in note 22. A similar type of binding of pendant vandykes is found on the Sutton Hoo horns and maplewood bowls, R. L. S. Bruce-Mitford, *The Sutton Hoo Ship Burial: A Handbook*, 2nd ed. (London, 1972), plates H and 19, and figures 6, 11 and 12.

[25] I am grateful to Dr J. Raftery for confirmation of this.

[26] D. M. Wilson, *Some Reflections on the St. Ninian's Isle Treasure* (Jarrow Lecture, 1969), 13.

[27] D. M. Wilson, 'An Anglo-Saxon book binding at Fulda', *Ant. Jour.*, 41 (1961), 199-217.

[28] See the late Iron Age material discussed in I. M. Stead, 'The reconstruction of Iron Age buckets from Aylesford and Baldock', *BMQ* 35 (1971), 250-82. For a pagan Saxon example see Fetcham (note 17) and for Ottonian situlæ, J. Beckwith, *Early Medieval Art* (London, 1964), plates 111 and 119.

[29] Grieg, *Osebergfundet*, 72 ff. The parallel with Hexham was first noted by Gustafson, 'Notes on a decorated bucket', 304.

[30] E. Fowler, 'Hanging bowls', *Studies in Ancient Europe*, ed. J. M. Coles and D. D. A. Simpson (Leicester, 1968), 288-90.

[31] Henry, 'Hanging bowls', plate 36(6): F. Henry, 'Miscellanea: Hanging bowls', *JRSAI* 67 (1937), 131 and plate 13. cf., the Hommersåk escutcheon in Shetelig, *Viking Antiquities*, fig. 101.

[32] Henry, 'Hanging bowls', plate 38(2).

[33] Registration number B.4233u: Shetelig, *Viking Antiquities*, 92-3.

[34] This view has long been maintained by F. Henry, particularly in her analysis of enamelling and millifiore techniques: see her *Irish Art in the Early Christian Period to A.D. 800* (London, 1965), and *Irish Art during the Viking Invasions 800–1020* (London, 1967), together with her earlier paper, 'Irish enamels of the Dark Ages', *Dark-Age Britain*, ed. D. B. Harden (London, 1956), 71-88.

[35] For a recent summary of the later period see K. Hughes, 'Evidence for contacts between the churches of the Irish and English from the Synod of Whitby to the Viking Age', *England Before the Conquest*, ed. P. Clemoes and K. Hughes (Cambridge 1971), 49-67.

[36] For Lindisfarne compare the views of F. Henry, *Irish Art to A.D. 800*, 192 ff., or in 'The Lindisfarne Gospels', *Antiquity* 37 (1963), 100-10 with those of R. L. S. Bruce-Mitford in *Evangeliorum Quattuor Codex Lindisfarnensis*, II, ed. T. D. Kendrick *et al.* (Olten Lausanne, 1966), 109-15 and 251-2. For Jarrow and Monkwear-

mouth, see R. J. Cramp, 'Decorated window glass and millifiore from Monk-wearmouth', *Ant. Jour.*, 50 (1970), 330-3.

37 Exemplification would involve listing most recent papers on insular art. For Anglo-Saxon influence on the art of Pictland and Ireland see D. M. Wilson, *Reflections on the St. Ninian's Isle Treasure*, and F. Henry, 'On some early Christian objects in the Ulster Museum', *JRSAI* 95 (1965), 51-63.

38 T. D. Kendrick, 'A late Saxon hanging bowl', *Ant. Jour.*, 21 (1941), 161-2.

39 A. C. O'Dell *et al.*, 'The St. Ninian's Isle silver hoard', *Antiquity* 33 (1959), plate 30, and Wilson, *Reflections on the St. Ninian's Isle Treasure*, 13-15.

40 M. Conway, 'The Abbey of St. Denis', *Arch.*, 66 (1915), 122 and plate 7.

41 *e.g.* C. Davis-Weyer, *Early Medieval Art 300–1150* (New York, 1971), 95-6; A. J. Robertson, *Anglo-Saxon Charters* (Cambridge, 1939), 72; *Liber Eliensis*, ed. E. O. Blake (London, 1962), 194.

42 J. Hubert *et al.*, *Carolingian Art* (London, 1970), plates 214-15.

43 Cabrol and Leclercq, *Dictionnaire*, figs 116 and 169.

44 *AA* 5 (1861), 170-1.

45 *PSAN* 4 (1889-1890), 278.

46 *The Antiquary* 4 (1881), 37.

47 W. Cripps, 'A bronze grave-chalice from Hexham Priory Church' (with appendix by C. C. Hodges), *AA* 15 (1892), 192-3. The accompanying note in *PSAN* 5 (1893), 28, shows the ownership. The account given in *A History of Northumberland*, III(i) (Newcastle, 1896), 175-6, is entirely erroneous.

48 A. G. Hardie, 'A copper-gilt chalice from Hexham Abbey', *AA* 35 (1957), 284-5: D. M. Wilson, 'The Trewhiddle hoard', *Arch.*, 98 (1961), 90-2: D. M. Wilson, *Anglo-Saxon Ornamental Metalwork 700–1100* (London, 1964), 54: V. H. Elbern, 'Der eucharistische Kelch im frühen Mittelalter', *Zeitschrift des Deutschen Vereins für Kunstwissenschaft* 17 (1963), 48 and 69: V. H. Elbern, 'Eine Gruppe insularer Kelche des frühen Mittelalters', *Festschrift für Peter Metz* (Berlin, 1965), 119 ff. It has also received passing mention and illustration in other publications.

49 Hodges, 49.

50 This aspect of the work was adversely commented on at the time. See the anonymous 'Renovations and spoliations in Hexham Abbey Church', *Ecclesiologist* 21 (1860), 347-8, and F. R. Wilson, 'On Hexham Abbey Church', *DN* I (1870), 19 and 27.

51 *The Antiquary* 4 (1881), 37.

52 I know of no evidence for the (ambiguous) location of the find in the choir which is given by the architectural contributor to Raine, II, lxxvii. Hodges always followed Charlton's location in 'the transept', even suggesting the possibility of the southern area (*AA* 15 (1892), 193), until a late collaborative publication in which he incomprehensibly dated the discovery to 'about 1850' and placed it in the north transept 'in making a grave' (Hodges and Gibson, 85).

53 *Builder* 18, no. 925 (1860), 681.

54 'Renovations and spoliations', 347.

55 I am grateful to R. W. Gregory and Partners, the Abbey's heating engineers, for generously making available their plans of the trenches re-used in the twentieth-century systems. The minute book of the 1860 restoration committee survives in the Northumberland County Record Office but only gives details of a heating system which was eventually rejected.

56 Cripps, 'A bronze grave-chalice', 192-3.

57 C. Oman, *English Church Plate 597–1830* (London, 1957), 41-2.

58 *ibid.*, plate 2. See also the material listed by Wilson, 'The Trewhiddle hoard', 91.

59 *e.g.* Elbern, 'Der eucharistische Kelch', 57-8: Davis-Weyer, *Early Medieval Art*, 96: Robertson, *Anglo-Saxon Charters*, 72 and 226: *Liber Eliensis*, 196.

60 Elbern, 'Der eucharistische Kelch', 1-76 and 117-88, with a catalogue on pp. 67-76.

[61] All examples in this paragraph are illustrated in Elbern, 'Der eucharistische Kelch' and Elbern, 'Eine Gruppe insularer Kelche'. For fuller illustration and description of the Trewhiddle and large Ardagh chalice see Wilson, 'The Trewhiddle hoard', 88-92, and Henry, *Irish Art to A.D. 800*, 107 ff. Possible chalice fragments, such as the Steeple Bumpstead boss, have been excluded from this discussion.

[62] *e.g.* Thomas, *Early Christian Archæology*, 198 ('could be ... seventh century'): Cramp, *Monastic Arts*, 16 (eighth or ninth century): Elbern, 'Der eucharistische Kelch', 119 (eleventh century).

[63] This argument is best stated in Elbern, 'Eine Gruppe insularer Kelche'.

[64] Wilson, 'The Trewhiddle hoard', fig. 3.

[65] G. Haseloff, *Der Tassilokelch* (Munich, 1951), is the classic publication of this insular-influenced chalice.

[66] Elbern, 'Der eucharistische Kelch', nos 13, 17, 30, 32 and 33. See also nos 2 and 21. I am grateful to Professor Elbern and to Dr F. Ronig for assistance in obtaining photographs of the Trier and Hildersheim chalices.

[67] See Elbern, 'Der eucharistische Kelch', plates 55, 56 and 60.

[68] *ibid.*, plate 100.

[69] *ibid.*, nos 1, 2, 3, 5, 12, 13, 14, 15, 16, 21, 25, 28, 32, 33 and 34.

[70] Elbern lists five copper gilt chalices. Except for one from Stuttgart they are all more elaborate than Hexham.

[71] J. Braun, *Der Christliche Altar* (Munich, 1924), I, 434 ff: Oman, *English Church Plate*, 63-4: Thomas, *Early Christian Archæology*, 191-8.

[72] Raine, I, clxxxii and cxci.

[73] C. C. Hodges, *A Guide to Hexham* (Hexham, 1889), 31.

[74] *PSAL* 4 (1857-9), 202. A similar account is given in the report in *The Gentleman's Magazine* 49 (1858), 647.

[75] Registration number 58, 8-14, I. The number on the photograph is incorrect.

[76] Figure 128.

[77] Smith, *Guide to Anglo-Saxon Antiquities*, 105: Cramp, *Monastic Arts*, 17.

[78] H. G. Ramm *et al.*, 'The tombs of the Archbishops ... in York Minster and their contents', *Arch.*, 103 (1971), plate 60. The fundamental discussion of the pallium is that in J. Braun, *Die Liturgische Gewandung im Occident und Orient* (Freiburg, 1907).

[79] For a discussion of portable reliquaries and book-satchels see J. Raftery, *Christian Art in Ancient Ireland* (Dublin, 1941), 51 ff. Crosses of the Viking period at Nunburnholme, Stonegrave and York show such rectangular reliquaries suspended from the neck.

[80] For a figure holding a book with cruciform cover decoration see J. Beckwith, *Early Christian and Byzantine Art* (London, 1970), plate 141. Northumbrian sculpture shows several figures holding books with their hands covered; W. G. Collingwood, *Northumbrian Crosses* (London, 1927) figures 63 and 98.

[81] E. Kitzinger, 'The coffin-reliquary', *The Relics of St. Cuthbert*, ed. C. F. Battiscombe, especially 289-92.

[82] See E. Salin, *La Civilisation Mérovingienne*, IV (Paris, 1959), 255 ff., and J. Hubert *et al.*, *Europe in the Dark Ages* (London, 1969), especially plates 26, 297 and 305.

[83] Hubert, *Europe in the Dark Ages*, plate 311. For dating see W. Braunfels, *L'Exposition Charlemagne, Oeuvre, Rayonnement et Survivance* (Aix la Chapelle, 1965), 131.

[84] Radford, 'The portable altar', 329.

[85] I am indebted to Mrs L. Webster for drawing my attention to the description of (apparently repoussé) decorated silver sheets on altars described in *Æthelwulf: De Abbatibus*, ed. A. Campbell (Oxford, 1967), lines 643-5.

[86] *Arch. Jour.*, 10 (1854), 367-8. A similar location was given when Fairless exhibited the ring at Newcastle in March 1858, *AA* 3 (1859), 45.

[87] J. Collingwood Bruce, *A Descriptive Catalogue of Antiquities, Chiefly British, at Alnwick Castle* (Newcastle, 1880). An account of Way's involvement will be found on pp. viii-x. I am grateful to Mrs Webster for information about Way's methods of work.

[88] *e.g.* Hodges, 21.

[89] D. M. Wilson, 'The Poslingford ring', *BMQ* 20 (1956), 91.

[90] Wilson, *Anglo-Saxon Ornamental Metalwork 700—1100* (London, 1964), figure 4.

[91] Raine, II, 202. See also I, clxxx.

[92] Wilson, 'The Trewhiddle hoard', 99-108, and Wilson, *Anglo-Saxon Ornamental Metalwork*, 21-34. Unless otherwise stated all parallels quoted below will be found illustrated in the latter publication.

[93] R. L. S. Bruce-Mitford, 'Late Saxon disc brooches', *Dark Age Britain*, ed. D. B. Harden (London, 1956), plate 23A. D. M. Wilson, 'Some neglected late Anglo-Saxon swords', *MA* 9 (1965), plate 2C.

[94] For Hauxton Mill see *Victoria County History of Cambridge*, I (1938), plate II (H).

[95] Wilson, 'Some neglected swords', plate 3A, and Bruce-Mitford, 'Late Saxon disc brooches', plates 23C and D.

[96] Bruce-Mitford, *op. cit.*, plate 21A.

[97] See note 89.

[98] J. Graham-Campbell, 'An Anglo-Saxon ornamented silver strip from the Cuerdale hoard', *MA* 14 (1970), 152-3, publishes the only other known example in the entire Trewhiddle corpus.

[99] Shetelig, *Viking Antiquities*, 177. See also A. W. Brøgger, 'Rolvsøyætten', *Bergens Museums Aarbok*, 1920-1, 18.

[100] I am grateful to Professor D. M. Wilson for advice on these inlays.

[101] Eddius, chapter XXII.

[102] *HE* V, 19. The translation is taken, by permission of the Clarendon Press, Oxford, from *Bede's Ecclesiastical History*, ed. B. Colgrave and R. A. B. Mynors (Oxford, 1969).

THE DONATION OF HEXHAM

Michael Roper

The details of the donation of Hexham to Wilfrid are very largely un-recorded. Eddius merely states that he built a church there to the glory of God and the honour of St Andrew on land given to him by the saintly Queen Æthelthryth, and Richard of Hexham, the mid-twelfth-century prior of the Augustinian house at Hexham, adds very little.[1]

Eddius does not date the donation, but from the place which it occupies in his text it must have occurred within the period 669 to 678. Richard attempted to be more specific and suggested that it was *circa Dominicæ Incarnationis annum DCLXXIIIIm.*[2] Another source of uncertain proven-ance and authority, *a liber incerti autoris de episcopis Lindisfarnensibus*, dated the foundation of Hexham to 673.[3] An alternative way of arriving at a date is to consider the career of the donor, Æthelthryth. It has been assumed that she made the grant before her entry upon the monastic life at Coldingham, when she would have had to take the normal monastic vow of personal poverty. On the other hand, Eddius calls her *Deo dicata*, which seems to indicate that she had already taken the veil at the time of the donation, although it need not rule out a simultaneous transaction.[4] It seems unlikely that the grant was later than her departure for Ely. Un-fortunately the date of Æthelthryth's entry into Coldingham is in doubt. Bede dates the event twelve years after her marriage to Ecgfrith, which Florence of Worcester places in 660. This would date her entry into Cold-ingham to 672 and her departure for Ely in the following year 673. On the other hand there are reasonable grounds for supposing that she died in 679, and Bede says that she had been an abbess for seven years, which places the foundation of Ely in 672 and her entry into Coldingham in 671:[5] unless she actually died in her seventh year as abbess which brings the dates back to 672 and 673. The *Liber Eliensis* gives 673 as the date of her coming to Ely.[6] Thus it is difficult to date the donation precisely and it becomes a matter of personal preference which year between 671 and 673 is chosen. The building of the church at Hexham was probably begun at the time of the donation, but it is unlikely that it was completed before 674.

Neither Eddius nor Richard records the extent of the donation. For Eddius it constituted a *regio;* Richard calls it a *villa cum circumiacente regione.*[7] No other sources shed any direct light on the matter and we are compelled, therefore, to work back from evidence of a later date. The Liberty or Regality of Hexham or Hexhamshire seems to have existed as a separate administrative unit with its own reeve (*præpositus*) from at least the late tenth century, when it was part of the estates of the bishops of Durham, into whose hands it had passed in the middle of the ninth century, after a vacancy of the see of Hexham which had lasted from the first half of the ninth century.[8] It seems not unreasonable to assume that the Liberty corresponded to the estates of the bishops of Hexham in the early ninth century. Whether it also corresponded to the *regio* granted to Wilfrid is less certain, although there must have been some connexion. This seems to be confirmed by the claim to the Liberty by the archbishops of York, a claim *a primitiva ius fundatione*, presumably based on the fact that Wilfrid was bishop of York at the time of the donation.[9] The right of the bishops of Durham appears to have been first questioned by Archbishop Ælfric, probably soon after his consecration in 1023, but the Liberty was not finally obtained by the archbishops until 1070-1, during the vacancy of the see of Durham, and the church of Hexham not until 1083, when Eilaf I, hereditary priest of Hexham and treasurer of Durham, refused to become a monk under the new constitution of Bishop William of St Calais.[10] When Archbishop Thomas II founded an Augustinian priory at Hexham in 1113, he retained the Liberty for the archbishops.

By 1295 and probably earlier the Liberty of Hexhamshire comprised the modern parishes of Hexham, Allendale, Whitley and St John Lee with the chapelry of St Oswald, a territory extending some twenty-four miles north to south and varying in breadth from half a mile at its narrowest to eleven at its broadest and with a total area of about ninety-two square miles.[11] Even if Wilfrid's estate comprised only the township of Hexham and the four Quarters of Hexhamshire, the modern parishes of Hexham and Whitley, this would represent a substantial estate of about thirty square miles.[12] The church of St John Lee or *Erneshow*, however, belonged to the church of Hexham in the twelfth century; even earlier it had been frequented by John of Beverley, and Richard of Hexham says that Wilfrid himself dedicated an oratory there to St Michael.[13] It is possible, therefore, that the donation of Æthelthryth was the whole, or at least a substantial part, of the Liberty of Hexhamshire as it existed in the thirteenth century.

Notes

[1] Eddius, chapter XXII; Raine I, 8-9.

[2] J. Raine I, 9, 10, 23.

[3] J. Leland, *Collectanea*, ed. T. Hearne (Oxford, 1715) I (ii), 368.

[4] C. E. Whiting, 'The Anglian Bishops of Hexham', *AA* 24 (1946), 121; Plummer II 318.

[5] *HE* IV, 19; *Chronicon ex Chronicis* I, 24; Plummer II, 239.

[6] *Liber Eliensis*, ed. E. O. Blake (Camden Third Series, XCII; London, 1962), 33.

[7] Raine I, 9, 23.

[8] Raine I, l-li & App. iv; *A History of Northumberland* III, ed. A. B. Hinds (London & Newcastle, 1896), 20-2; H. E. Craster, 'The Red Book of Durham', *EHR* 40

(1925), 524; H. S. Offler, 'A Note on the last Medieval Bishops of Hexham', *AA* 40 (1962), 163.

⁹ *Papers and Letters from the Northern Registers*, ed. J. Raine (Rolls Series: London, 1873), 240; cf., *The Register of Archbishop Greenfield* II, ed. W. Brown and A. H. Thompson, Surtees Soc. CXLIX (1934), 201.

¹⁰ Leland, *op. cit.*, 378; Raine I, 191 & App. iv; *Durham Episcopal Charters* 1071-1152, ed. H. S. Offler, Surtees Soc. CLXXIX (1968), 22-3, 122. The charter by which Archbishop Thomas I is said to have confirmed the church and *parrochia* of Hexham to Durham about 1083 is unquestionably spurious: *Historia Dunelmensis Scriptores Tres*, ed. J. Raine, Surtees Soc. IX (1839), App. v; *Feodarium Prioratus Dunelmensis*, ed. W. Greenfield, Surtees Soc. LVIII (1872), lxxvi-lxxix; W. Farrer, *Early Yorkshire Charters* II (Edinburgh, 1915), 262-4. A late source assigns the loss of Hexham by Durham to the episcopate of Ranulf Flambard (1099-1128): Raine I, lviii, 220. For the questioning by Ælfric of Durham's right to Hexham (Leland, *loc. cit.*), see also the incomplete passage at the end of *Liber de Monasterii de Hyda* (Rolls Series: London, 1866), 279. The last word in the latter (*Hangus*) should read *Haugus* ... (ie., *Haugustaldesham*). The passage is misinterpreted in J. M. Cooper, *The Last Four Anglo-Saxon Archbishops of York* (Borthwick Papers No. 38: York, 1970), 17.

¹¹ *Hist. of Northumberland* III, 1, 31-4. Hexhamshire is mentioned by name in 1226: Raine II, 93.

¹² Raine I, xiv, and Whiting, *loc. cit.*, take this smaller area to represent Æthelthryth's donation. If the three portions of Hexham Common are included, the area becomes thirty-eight square miles. However, these appear to have remained unenclosed until 1800. Cf., *Hist. of Northumberland* IV, ed. J. C. Hodgson (1897), 1-73.

¹³ Raine I, 15-16, 18, 80; *HE* V, 2; Folcard, *Vita S. Johannis ep. Ebor.*, in *HCY* I, 246; Plummer II, 274. Errington in St John Lee was in the *parrochia* of Hexham before the middle of the twelfth century (Raine I, 95); Anick, also in St John Lee, was held by the archbishops of York before 1226 (Raine II, 91).

HEXHAM ANGLO-SAXON SCULPTURE
(A hand-list)

Rosemary Cramp

1. Cross shaft in four pieces (Acca's cross)
   Present location: In the south transept of Hexham abbey.
   Evidence for discovery:
   (a) Lowest part used as lintel of cottage at Dilston. Removed to Durham before 1888.
   (b) Large inscribed fragment near east end of the abbey church in 1858.
   (c) Top of shaft (two pieces) found in 1870 in foundation of a warehouse near St Mary's church.
   Dimensions: HEIGHT: 357.5 cm. WIDTH: 36 cm.>27 cm. DEPTH: 25 cm.>18.5 cm.

2. Cross shaft (Spital Cross)
   Present location: In the south transept of Hexham abbey.
   Evidence for discovery: First mentioned in the grounds of the Spital, near Hexham, in 1861. Footnote suggests it may originally have come from Warden.
   Dimensions: HEIGHT: 104.2 cm. WIDTH: 33 cm.>27 cm. DEPTH: 25.5 cm.>21 cm.

3. Cross shaft in two pieces
   Present location: In the Chapter Library, Durham. Catalogue no. IV.
   Evidence for discovery: Found in 1854 used as a step in Bell's Chemist's shop in the Market Place, Hexham, next to St Mary's church.
   Dimensions: HEIGHT: 87 cm. top, 92 cm. bottom. WIDTH: max. 29 cm. DEPTH: *c.* 17 cm. (incomplete).

4. Cross base
   Present location: In niche in north wall of modern nave of Hexham abbey.
   Evidence for discovery: Found in 1864 in the garden of Abbey Gate House, which adjoins the churchyard. Presented to the church by Dr C. R. Kendal in 1907.
   Dimensions: HEIGHT: 31.1 cm. WIDTH: 30.7 cm. DEPTH: 15.2 cm.

5. Shaft fragment or string course
   Present location: In the Chapter Library, Durham. Catalogue no. V.

Evidence for discovery: Found in 1890 in taking down an old house in Market Street, Hexham.
Dimensions: HEIGHT: 22.3 cm. WIDTH: 14 cm. DEPTH: 14 cm.

6. Cross shaft
Present location: In niche in north wall of modern nave of Hexham abbey.
Evidence for discovery: Found May 1908 in the foundation of the apse of the Norman Choir.
Dimensions: HEIGHT: 37.1 cm. WIDTH: 26 cm. DEPTH: 14 cm.

7. Cross shaft
Present location: Built into niche in north wall of modern nave of Hexham abbey.
Evidence for discovery: Found in 1870 on the site of the Canon's Day Room.
Dimensions: HEIGHT: 78.2 cm. WIDTH: 35.5 cm.>30.5 cm. DEPTH: 14 cm.

8. Fragment of cross shaft
Present location: In the Chapter Library, Durham. Catalogue no. VII.
Evidence for discovery: No record of discovery but referred to as in the possession of Mr Fairless of Hexham in 1865 and probably also in 1861.
Dimensions: HEIGHT: 37 cm. WIDTH: 17.5 cm. (broken). DEPTH: 11.5 cm. (broken).

9. Centre of a cross head
Present location: Lost.
Evidence for discovery: First mentioned in 1921 as in the possession of H. F. Lockhart, Esq., of Hexham. Found about thirty years before in repairing a kitchen fireplace in a cottage next to Lockhart's house.
Dimensions: unknown.

10. Cross head
Present location: The Chapter Library, Durham. Catalogue no. VI.
Evidence for discovery: First mentioned in 1888. One of the stones bought from Mr Fairless of Hexham.
Dimensions: HEIGHT: 38.2 cm. WIDTH: 40 cm. DEPTH: 11.5 cm.

11. One arm of a cross head
Present location: In niche in north wall of modern nave of Hexham abbey.
Evidence for discovery: First mentioned in 1925. No record of discovery.
Dimensions: HEIGHT: 19.8 cm. WIDTH: 27.6 cm. DEPTH: 14 cm.

12 Cross head
Present location: In niche in north wall of modern nave of Hexham abbey.

Evidence for discovery: Possibly referred to in 1861, first clear reference 1865. No record of discovery.
Dimensions: HEIGHT: 58.4 cm. WIDTH: 30.8 cm. DEPTH: 16.5 cm.

13. Grave marker (Tundwini)
Present location: In niche in north wall of modern nave of Hexham abbey.
Evidence for discovery: Found January 1911 in digging foundations of a building in Beaumont Street, now the Unionist Club.
Dimensions: HEIGHT: 22.2 cm. WIDTH: 31.6 cm. DEPTH: 11.5 cm.

14. Fragment of grave stone with an inscription
Present location: Built into west wall of modern nave.
Evidence for discovery: First mentioned in 1907. Found during reconstruction of the nave but the find-spot was not recorded.
Dimensions: HEIGHT: 35 cm. WIDTH: 26 cm. DEPTH: built into the wall.

15. Grave marker
Present location: Now built into west wall of modern nave of Hexham abbey.
Evidence for discovery: First mentioned by Stuart (1867). No record of its discovery.
Dimensions: HEIGHT: 35 cm. WIDTH: 42.2 cm. DEPTH: built into wall.

16. Grave marker
Present location: In niche in north wall of modern nave. It is built in and is hidden by a hogback.
Evidence for discovery: First noticed by G. Trayhurn and T. Middlemass, April 1972, when a hogback was moved out for photography. No record of its discovery.
Dimensions: HEIGHT: 30.5 cm. WIDTH: 25.4 cm. DEPTH: in wall.

17. Grave cover
Present location: In western bay of the south aisle of the choir of Hexham abbey.
Evidence for discovery: Found May 1908 close to large stone coffin which lies almost touching the S.E. wall of the apse of St Wilfrid's church.
Dimensions: LENGTH: 157 cm. WIDTH: 37 cm. DEPTH: 11.5 cm.

18. Grave cover
Present location: Standing against the north wall of the nave of Hexham abbey at the east end.
Evidence for discovery: No record of its discovery. First mentioned in 1888.
Dimensions: LENGTH: 154 cm. WIDTH: 48.6 cm. DEPTH: 13.4 cm.

19. Hogback
   Present location: In niche in north wall of modern nave of Hexham abbey.
   Evidence for discovery: Found by Hodges, 18 April 1907, lying on its side on upper surface of the south wall of the nave. Used as a filling stone in the core of the wall.
   Dimensions: HEIGHT: 38.7 cm. WIDTH: 96.2 cm. DEPTH: 23 cm.
   Two other recumbent grave covers which are in the hogback tradition have been assigned to the pre-Conquest period. The author however accepts J. T. Lang's assessment of these as post-Conquest.

20. Figural slab
   Present location: In a specially made case against the south wall of the modern nave at the west end.
   Evidence for discovery: Found March 1907 in hole about four feet across, about the centre of nave near the west end.
   Dimensions: As described in Appendix III.

21. Fragment of ? step
   Present location: in the south aisle of the choir of Hexham abbey.
   Evidence for discovery: No record. First noticed by R. J. Cramp in 1972.
   Dimensions: HEIGHT: 19 cm. WIDTH: 23.5 cm. DEPTH: 11.5 cm (broken).

22. Three fragments of one or more carved slabs
   Present location:
   (a) In niche in north wall of modern nave of Hexham abbey.
   (b) In the Chapter Library, Durham. Catalogue no. VIII.
   (c) In the Chapter Library, Durham. Catalogue no. IX.
   Evidence for discovery:
   (a) First drawn and mentioned in 1888. Described by Hodges as found on Campy Hill N.E. of the church.
   (b) First drawn and mentioned in 1867. Bought by the Chapter Library from Mr Fairless.
   (c) First drawn and mentioned in 1865. Bought from Mr Fairless and said by Greenwell to have been found on the site of the nave.
   Dimensions:
   (a) Fragment. HEIGHT: 30.5 cm. WIDTH: 40.6 cm DEPTH: 16.5 cm.
   (b) Catalogue no. VIII. HEIGHT: 34 cm. WIDTH: *c.* 30 cm. DEPTH: *c.* 21 cm.
   (c) Catalogue no. IX. HEIGHT: 18 cm. WIDTH: 52.5 cm. DEPTH: *c.* 16 cm.

23. Panel or slab
   Present location: Built into niche in north wall of modern nave of Hexham abbey.
   Evidence for discovery: Built into the floor of the triforium in the

south transept where it was first noticed by Canon Greenwell and regarded by him as part of St Wilfrid's church.
Dimensions: HEIGHT: 53.5 cm. WIDTH: 63.8 cm. DEPTH: built into the wall.

24. Fragment of string course
Present location: On a ledge on the north choir aisle of Hexham abbey.
Evidence for discovery: First mentioned in 1925. No record of its discovery.
Dimensions: HEIGHT: 14 cm. WIDTH: 22.9 cm. DEPTH: 10.1 cm.

25. Fragment of string course
Present location: In the Chapter Library, Durham. Catalogue no. XIa.
Evidence for discovery: Found on the site of the destroyed nave of Hexham abbey.
Dimensions: HEIGHT: 14 cm. WIDTH: 49 cm. DEPTH: 15.2 cm.

26. Fragment of string course
Present location: In the Chapter Library, Durham. Catalogue no. XIb.
Evidence for discovery: Found on the site of the destroyed nave of Hexham abbey.
Dimensions: HEIGHT: 14 cm. WIDTH: 26.7 cm. DEPTH: 13.5 cm.

27. Fragment of string course
Present location: In the Chapter Library, Durham. Catalogue no. XIc.
Evidence for discovery: Found on the site of the destroyed nave of Hexham abbey.
Dimensions: HEIGHT: 14 cm. WIDTH: 28.5 cm. DEPTH: 15.8 cm.

28. Fragment of string course
Present location: Built into west wall of modern nave of Hexham abbey.
Evidence for discovery: Found during reconstruction, 1899-1908.
Dimensions: HEIGHT: 14 cm. WIDTH: 33.7 cm. DEPTH: built into the wall.

29 Fragment
Present location: In niche in north wall of chancel.
Evidence for discovery: First mentioned in 1925. No record of discovery.
Dimensions: HEIGHT: 21 cm. WIDTH: 19 cm. DEPTH: 12 cm.

30. Impost
Present location: In the Chapter Library, Durham. Catalogue no. X.
Evidence for discovery: Found on the site of the destroyed nave of Hexham abbey.

Dimensions: HEIGHT: 40 cm. WIDTH: 26.5 cm. DEPTH: 12 cm.

31. Part of frieze
    Present location: In the south aisle of the choir of Hexham abbey at the east end.
    Evidence for discovery: Discovered in the tower restorations of Hexham abbey in 1966.
    Dimensions: HEIGHT: 18 cm. WIDTH: 35.5 cm. DEPTH: 29 cm.

32. Impost
    Present location: In niche in north wall of modern nave of Hexham abbey.
    Evidence for discovery: First mentioned in 1919.
    Dimensions: HEIGHT: 17.8 cm. WIDTH: 31.4 cm. DEPTH: 14.2 cm.

33. Impost
    Present location: Built into west wall of modern nave inside.
    Evidence for discovery: Found during the reconstruction 1899-1908, used as tread of a stair in the medieval newel stair in the west wall.
    Dimensions: HEIGHT: 21.5 cm. WIDTH: 29 cm. DEPTH: built into wall.

34. Stripwork
    Present location: Built into west wall of modern nave.
    Evidence for discovery: Found during reconstruction 1899-1908.
    Dimensions: HEIGHT: 13 cm. WIDTH: 43 cm. DEPTH: built into wall.

35. Stripwork
    Present location: Built into west wall of modern nave, middle row.
    Evidence for discovery: Found during reconstruction 1899-1908.
    Dimensions: HEIGHT: 14 cm. WIDTH: 40 cm. DEPTH: built into wall.

36. Impost
    Present location: In niche in north wall of modern nave.
    Evidence for discovery: Found on Campy Hill to the north of the chancel
    Dimensions: HEIGHT: 20.3 cm. WIDTH: 31.1 cm. DEPTH: 15.5 cm.

37. Stripwork
    Present location: Built into west wall of modern nave.
    Evidence for discovery: Found during reconstruction 1899-1908.
    Dimensions: HEIGHT: 20.2 cm. WIDTH: 22.3 cm. DEPTH: built into wall.

38. Fragment
    Present location: Built into west wall of modern nave.
    Evidence for discovery: Found in the gable of the north transept in 1905.
    Dimensions: HEIGHT: 22 cm. WIDTH: 16 cm. DEPTH: built into wall.

39. Fragment of pilaster.
    Present location: Lost.
    Evidencce for discovery: Found April 1907 on the site of the nave.
    Dimensions: Not given.

40. Base for pier or half column
    Present location: In niche in north wall of modern nave.
    Evidence for discovery: In the garden of Hexham House, moved into the church in 1888.
    Dimensions: HEIGHT: 33.5 cm. WIDTH: 42.5 cm. DEPTH: 19.5 cm.

41. Impost
    Present location: Built into the north jamb of the modern west door of the nave.
    Evidence for discovery: First mentioned in 1919.
    Dimensions: HEIGHT: 14 cm. WIDTH: 75 cm. DEPTH: 54 cm.

42. Impost
    Present location: Built into the south jamb of the modern west door of the nave.
    Evidence for discovery: First mentioned in 1888.
    Dimensions: HEIGHT: 14 cm. WIDTH: 47 cm. DEPTH: 21.3 cm.

43. Frith stool
    Present location: In the chancel of Hexham abbey.
    Evidence for discovery: First mentioned by Prior Richard of Hexham (1142-74) when it stood against the altar.
    Dimensions: HEIGHT: 59 cm. WIDTH: 80 cm. DEPTH: 54.5 cm.

44. Columns
    Present location: Built into the outer face of the north wall of the nave.
    Evidence for discovery: First mentioned in 1919.
    Dimensions: (a) Part of a half round attached column.
              (b) and (c) Two pieces of freestanding circular columns.

45. ? Piscina
    Present location: In a niche in north wall of modern nave.
    Evidence for discovery: None. Previously unpublished.
    Dimensions: HEIGHT: 13 cm. DIAMETER (external): 21.5 cm.

FRAGMENTS WHICH HAVE BEEN REJECTED AS OF ANGLO-SAXON DATE

46. An incomplete grave cover with tegulated roof and modern inscription
    11th-12th century. E. Okasha (1971) plates 53a and b.

47. Hogback with cruciform terminals and intersecting arcade ornament. Late 11th to 12th century. Collingwood (1925) fig. 19. (I am grateful to Mr J. T. Lang for his opinion of the dates of 46 and 47).

48. Panel thought by Collingwood to show an angel identified by Mr John Phillips as a Roman Victory. Collingwood (1925) fig. 5t.

49. Fragment of moulding with chevron and cable ornament. Roman. Collingwood (1925) fig. 4a.

50. Fragment with deep pellets and chequers. Roman. Collingwood (1925). Fig. 5m.

51. Portion of a capital? Unpublished.

52. Bulbous capital. Late eleventh century. Rivoira (1910) II. Fig. 536.

53 Stoup with intersecting arcade ornament. Late eleventh century. Unpublished.

54. Part of a re-used capital with spiral form ornament. Late eleventh century. Hodges and Gibson (1919) 68-9.
No illustration.

Acknowledgments

I would like to thank the Rector of Hexham and the Bishop of Ripon for permission to examine the monuments in their churches on many occasions, the Dean and Chapter of Durham, and Dr David Wright for permission to use some of their photographs, and the Verger of Hexham, Mr G. Trayhurn, for his constant helpfulness, in particular in locating the sculptures.

In addition, from the department of Archæology in Durham, I would like to thank Miss E. Coatsworth and Mrs B. Glover for their help with the preparation of the text, and Mr T. Middlemass whose photographs, specially produced for this article, form the bulk of the illustrations.

Appendix III

TWO EXAMPLES OF THE CRUCIFIXION AT HEXHAM

E. Coatsworth

I *Fragments of one or more carved panels*

Eight fragments from one or more carved panels are now preserved in a specially made case at the west end of the south wall of the nave of Hexham Abbey. It is possible to open the case but not to remove the pieces for detailed examination as they seem to be embedded in plaster of paris. In this discussion, the pieces are referred to by the numbers which accompany them in the display case (plate XIIIc and d): the unplaced pieces have been given the numbers 7 and 8. Fragments 1-4, the remains of a robed figure, have been discussed together. The depth given for each piece is the depth rising above the plaster setting and cannot be regarded therefore as an accurate measurement.

Fragments 1 and 2 (joining fragments) are 19 cm wide at the lower edge, widening to more than 20 cm at the top. The maximum depth is 5 cm and the maximum height is 16.5 cm. Fragment 3 is uniformly 19 cm wide, 2.5 cm deep and 12 cm high. Fragment 4 is 11 cm wide, 2.5 cm deep and 10 cm high.

The robe hangs in deep U-shaped folds which appear to be curving out towards the top. The moulded border, which can be seen most clearly on 3 and 4, has the appearance of being the outer folds of the dress. Pieces 1 and 2 have been partially defaced; the upper surface would probably have originally been smooth, like 3. The side edges of 3 are dressed smooth, but those of 1 and 2 are rather broken, and the moulded border or outer fold does not seem to be continuing upwards as a straight line. The slight extra width noted in the measurements seems to be accounted for by a widening at this side, and it is here that the careful dressing of the side edges is least in evidence. Taylor[1] considered these pieces to be the remains of a pilaster or vertical feature carved into human form and with parallel sides, but that the figure had arms remains a possibility: the pieces seem to be thicker as well as wider at the top and the fragments most clearly suggest the torso of a figure broken off at the point where the widening for shoulders and arms would start. Unfortunately the setting of the stones makes it impossible to see the back of these pieces, and therefore to determine whether they were part of the relief of a panel or the remains of a separate figure.

Fragment 4 is probably rightly assigned to its present position, though the border on the dexter side is slightly narrower than that on 3: this piece will be discussed again later.

Fragment 5 has the foot of a cross with a straight shaft curving out to a wider base. The remains of a pair of feet are placed side by side on the cross. The piece is *c.* 18.2 cm wide, 2.5 cm deep and *c.* 19 cm high. The relief stands out to a further 3 cm. This fragment is most clearly part of a carved panel representing the Crucifixion.

Fragment 6 is the tip of a wing, the feathers indicated by deeply cut grooves. The wing rests against a curved border, dressed smooth on the outside, and clearly representing the border of a panel. The fragment is 9 cm wide, 6 cm deep at the border and 13 cm high. The wing stands out to a maximum depth of 4.5 cm.

Fragment 7 is a piece from the corner of a panel. It is 5.5 cm wide, 2.5 cm deep at the border and *c.* 4.2 cm high. Fragment 8 is *c.* 4 cm wide, 4 cm deep at the border and *c.* 6 cm high. The fragment of the inner surface of the panel is 2.5 cm deep.

The questions raised by these pieces are three in number: how many carvings in fact are represented; how should they be reconstructed; and what evidence is there for assigning to them an early date?

Three of the fragments—6, 7 and 8—indisputably have borders, and all are different in depth, width and also in profile. The border of 6 is square in section, with a flat top. The border of 7 is rolled and scarcely rises above the level of the background. Number 8 is rolled also but is deeper than 7 and tapers from 2 cm wide at the level of the background to about 1 cm at the top. These differences suggest a series of panels: but another explanation is that they belong to one panel of which the frame widens and thickens as it nears the curved top, so increasing the arch- or canopy-like effect of that part of the frame represented by number 6.

The fragments have been variously reconstructed: the earliest descriptions did not include any drawing and have been taken to show that three more pieces were found than are now represented. The finders[2] described the pieces as the remains of two terracotta plaques. One was of the Crucifixion to which were ascribed no. 5, with the pair of feet resting on the base of a cross; no. 6 with the wing tip and border and a small piece which apparently had the upper part of the dexter arm of the cross, with the end of the arm described in terms which suggest it was of the same form as the foot. Taylor regarded this piece as missing: I believe it to be represented by fragment number 4 which was placed in its present position by both Collingwood and Taylor. If viewed in isolation it can be interpreted as the remains of a cross arm of a similar shape to the foot, though not quite the same, and with only the border and not the whole arm in relief. The second plaque described by Savage and Hodges was considered to represent the remains of an ecclesiastic in a chasuble, possibly Wilfrid. They describe it as 11″ (28 cm) by 7½″ (19 cm) which accounts for fragments 1, 2 and 3, but cannot include 4 as this would bring the total length to about 15¼″—an additional reason for believing this was the piece thought to be the arm of a cross. The description of the discovery accounts for only six of the remaining eight pieces.

Hodges and Gibson[3] give the same measurements and interpretation as above but now describe them more correctly as the remains of two painted oolite slabs.

Collingwood[4] also describes the material as oolite, and not a local stone. He suggests that the carving had been imported. His reconstruction differs considerably from that of Hodges: he uses the six pieces originally described and placed by Savage and Hodges but instead of two panels he considered that only one was in question, and that one represented the Crucifixion. In his drawing, Christ is wearing some kind of long skirted garment, though whether he thought it a long skirt or full length robe is left vague: pieces 1-4 are interpreted as the remains of the skirt, from about hip level to feet. The wing tip he placed on the right, as the wing of an angel above the cross arm on that side. He drew the remaining fragment of border as if it were straight with the curve of an arch beginning at the point where the margin is broken: in fact the margin itself appears to be curved, and to fit an arch most happily the other way up, as it is displayed at present. Collingwood's drawing is in fact very vague: he seems to have thought that the angels on either side of Christ's head each had a separate arch, and compared this to the arched frame over the arms of the Crucifixion on the Spital Cross.[5] In fact this has no arched frame at all, the idea of an arch only being suggested at a casual glance because of the curving splayed sides of the upper arm of the cross. His reconstruction makes no attempt to show how the whole panel was bordered.

The fragments are mentioned briefly again by Hodges,[6] and he first makes the suggestion that the limestone of which the pieces were composed could have come from Northamptonshire where Wilfrid had possessions. As he makes this suggestion in the same year in which Collingwood first wrote about the stones, one wonders if they were, in fact, examined by a geologist. Taylor[7] makes the same suggestion of a Northamptonshire origin, and for the same reason. Before Taylor wrote about the stones in 1966, the fragments had been put away and forgotten, and their rediscovery is due to Taylor's efforts. He described and re-interpreted the stones, reverting to Hodges' original suggestion that there were two slabs, one of the Crucifixion, and one of an ecclesiastical figure. He placed the angel's wing on the upper left edge of the frame of the Crucifixion panel. He followed up Hodges' suggestion of an analogy with the Crucifixion scene in the Durham Gospels[8] and drew his reconstruction on that model. The description of the so-called lost cross arm, apparently of the same shape as the foot, he regarded as additional supporting evidence for this interpretation. The arched border in his view extended over the top of the whole panel. He rejected the idea that the fragments of the robed figure belonged to the crucified on the grounds that robed Crucifixions of the Durham Gospels type did not have drapery falling in these deep U-shaped folds, and also because he considered the remains consistent with a carved pilaster or vertical feature, with the function perhaps of dividing two panels. He did not attempt to place pieces 7 and 8.

It seems, then, that at present the number of panels represented by these fragments must remain an open question: the border pieces could suggest two or three panels, or one panel with a rather elaborate frame. It is possible to interpret the robed figure, not as a vertical feature with parallel sides, but as a figure with arms, broken off just at the point where the arms would be. A large proportion of the seventh- and eighth-century Crucifixions are robed and the robes exhibit a considerable variety of forms. Some metal crucifixes from Hungary, for example, show Christ dressed in a long robe with a vertical fold down each side while the central panel of the dress has folds draped in a way rather similar to the Hexham fragments.[9]

If we omit the robed figure as an existing element of the Crucifixion scene, however, the dating of the fragments still relies on the shape of the cross foot, though a missing cross arm of the same shape can no longer be adduced as additional evidence for the shape of the whole cross. In spite of this, the nearest parallel still seems to be the Durham Gospels[10] and a bronze plaque from Athlone, both of which show the Crucifixion on a cross with arms of this shape. The former is of the early eighth century, the latter has been dated to *c.* 800.[11] I can find no parallels for a cross of such a shape used as the cross of the crucified painted or in relief later than these two examples, and the type does not appear in Crucifixion scenes outside the Hiberno-Saxon area at all. Ringheaded crosses with cross arms of a similar shape, used as the background for the Crucifixion do appear in the Northumbria of a later date after the period of the Viking Invasions;[12] but though the influence of Ireland may suggest a connexion between the two types, these later carvings are crude indeed compared with the Hexham fragments. If the wing tip of the angel be allowed to belong to the upper left edge of the panel, then this provides an additional link with the iconography of the Durham Gospels: angels on either side of Christ's head are a common feature, but the tip of the wing raised rather than drooping, even when the whole wing is raised, seem to be found only at Hexham and in this one manuscript.

The Spital Cross

This cross is so called because it was first noted when it was standing on the grounds of the Spital near Hexham. A footnote in the earliest account suggests it came from Warden originally, but there is no firm evidence for this.[13]

Collingwood[14] suggested that the rood panel might have been the model for this scene on the Spital Cross, but the remains we have do not suggest direct copying, though similar or related models might lie behind both. The details of the dress suggest a robed model rather than one with a loincloth, though the robe has been shortened to a tunic: this development can be paralleled, for example, in reliquary casket from Warden ascribed to the eighth century.[15] A large number of examples of the Crucifixion from the sixth to the eighth centuries showed Christ in a long robe, standing upright and with his arms stretched out as on the Spital Cross, with his head turned to his right so that his hair falls on his left shoulder. The earliest example of this is the Rabula Gospels,[16] but the powerful influence of the type is shown by such creations of Hiberno-Saxon art as the eighth century St Gall Gospels, where the interlace-like robe is still reminiscent of the traditional colobium and the hair hangs on the left shoulder, even though the head has not been drawn turned to the right.[17]

A feature of early Hiberno-Saxon Crucifixions is the reduction of the possible accompanying figures from the biblical narrative to the two soldiers. Only the Carndonagh slab and the St Andrew Auckland Cross do not have these last two figures. The rather large heads, turned to the spectator, are found in the Durham Gospels, the St Gall Gospels, and on the bronze plaque from Athlone mentioned earlier and the Moone Cross.[18] An eighth century date therefore seems likely without the supporting evidence of the vinescroll.

Other features which could suggest an early date are the position of the scene on the cross shaft and the splayed arms of the cross. Both of these features occur again however in later centuries, so although it is true that they occur on early crosses, they cannot be taken alone as supplying evidence of date: they only provide supporting evidence.

Notes

[1] H. M. Taylor, 'Rediscovery of Important Anglo-Saxon Sculpture at Hexham', *AA* 44 (1966), 49-60.

[2] Savage and Hodges, 42-3.

[3] Hodges and Gibson, 84.

[4] Collingwood, 29 and fig. 36.

[5] W. G. Collingwood, 'Early Carved Stones', 73 and fig. 6.

[6] C. C. Hodges, 'Simonburn Church', *AA* I (1925), 183.

[7] H. M. Taylor, 'Rediscovery of Anglo-Saxon Sculpture at Hexham', 53. Taylor did have the stones examined.

[8] Durham Chapter Library, MS. A II 17.

[9] K. Wessel, 'Die Entstehung des Crucifixus', *Byzantenische Zeitschrift*, LIII (1960), plates II, fig. 4, and IV, figs 8, 9 and 10.

[10] O. K. Werckmeister, 'Three Problems of Tradition in Pre-Carolingian Figure Style, *Proc. of the Royal Irish Academy* 63, C (1962-4), plate 33.

[11] F. Henry, *Irish Art in the Early Christian Period to A.D. 800* (London, 1965), 100 and plate 46.

[12] *e.g.* at Kirklevington, Yorkshire. Collingwood, 104 and fig. 29.

[13] W. H. D. Longstaffe, 'Hexham Church', *AA* 5 (1861), 158.

[14] Collingwood, 99 and fig. 37.

[15] J. Hubert, *Europe in the Dark Ages*, plate 294.

[16] D. Talbot Rice, *Art of the Byzantine Era* (London, 1963), fig. 26.

[17] St Gall Stiftsbibliothek, MS. 51, illustrated by F. Henry (1940), *Early Christian Irish Art* (Dublin, 1963), plate 45.

[18] F. Henry, *Irish Art in the Early Christian Period*, 141-2 and plate 68.

Appendix IV

ANGLO-SAXON COINS FOUND AT HEXHAM

H. E. Pagan

In his survey of the Hexham hoard Adamson estimated the number of coins to be in the region of 8,000.[1] Some 5,000 of these were available to him for study. All were base metal coins of ninth-century kings of Northumbria and archbishops of York or coins imitative of such and Adamson stated that about 2,000 were of King Eanred, a similar number of King Æthelred, 100 of King Rædwulf, 60 of Archbishop Eanbald and about 800 of Archbishop Wigmund.[2] He also noted the presence of a few coins of King Eardwulf and a single coin of King Ælla, but the first were in reality coins of Eanred carrying the name of a moneyer, Wulfheard, and the coin he assigned to Ælla was an imitative piece with garbled legend struck in the reign of Eanred or Æthelred.

The coins were widely dispersed on discovery and it is not now possible to reconstruct the hoard *in toto*. What can be done is to gain some idea of the structure of the hoard from available literary and physical evidence and on that basis to offer some remarks on its content, date of deposit and importance for the political and numismatic history of the period.

A starting point is provided by Adamson's paper. The text of this is not in fact of much assistance, as he generally avoids statements of an arithmetical kind about the coins found and his identifications of individual specimens are unsound, but there are carefully executed accompanying plates and on these 944 of the coins are illustrated. The principle on which Adamson's draughtsman was operating was apparently that he should draw all varieties of inscription and type. This means that the plates cover the whole range of the material found, which is satisfactory, but means also that they do not quite mirror its arithmetical composition, die-duplicates being in general omitted and more coins being drawn of reigns and moneyers where marked variations of inscription and type occur than where variations are comparatively slight. In the absence of any larger or more representative selection of coins from the hoard, however, the coins reproduced in the plates can profitably be listed below. The officially struck coins are arranged either by reign or by other defined period of issue in chronological order, with a note of the number illustrated of each moneyer.[3]

Coins from the Hexham hoard engraved for Adamson
A. KINGS OF NORTHUMBRIA
    Æthelred. Early Group.

185

Ceolbald 2; Cuthhard 1; Eadvini 1; Hnifula 2   6
Eanred. Series A.

Cunwulf 28; Cuthhard 3; Dægberct 21; Eadvini 35; Eadwulf
1; Herreth 23 (including some possibly imitative pieces);
Hwætred 3; Tidvini 5; Wilheah 9; Wulfheard 25; miscellaneous 3   156
  Series B.

Aldates 5; Badigils 4; Brother 33; Erwinne 1; Ethelweard 1;
Folcnoth 12; Fordred 25; Gadutels 14; Monne 42; Odilo 6;
'Teveh' 1; Wihtred 9; Wulfred 6; miscellaneous 2   161
Æthelred. First reign.

Alghere 14; Brother 13; Cœnred 1; Cunemund 8; Eanred 65;
Erwinne 2; Fordred 55; Hunlaf 1; Leofthegn 96; Monne 72;
Odilo 3; Wendelberht 11; Wihtred 19; Wulfred 17; Wulfsig 4;
miscellaneous 3   384
Rædwulf

Alghere 3; Brother 5; Cœnred 2; Cuthberht 4; Eanred 2;
Fordred 8; Hunlaf 1; Hwætnoth 4; Monne 5; Wendelberht 3   37
Æthelred. Second reign.

Eardwulf 9; Fordred 1; miscellaneous 1   11

B. ARCHBISHOPS OF YORK
    Eanbald

Cunwulf 10; Eadwulf 38; Ethelweard 11   59
Wigmund

Cœnred 22; Ethelhelm 9; Ethelweard 27; Hunlaf 20; miscellaneous 2   80

C. IMITATIVE
                                                            50

The principles behind the arrangement are familiar enough to numismatic specialists but it is convenient to note here the three main considerations on which it is founded. First, documentary evidence shows
that towards the middle of the ninth century Northumbria was ruled suc-
cessively by Eanred, Æthelred and Rædwulf, on whose death Æthelred,
who had been deposed, began a second reign, and that Eanbald and Wigmund were archbishops of York and held the see in that order. Second,
coins of Æthelred Early Group, Eanred Series A, and Archbishop Eanbald
are of higher silver content than the rest of the coins of which there were
examples in the hoard and are not linked with these by moneyers' names,
style, or die-identity, and the most likely explanation for this is that they
belong to a phase of coinage separate from and presumptively earlier than
that in which the rest were struck. Third, hoards of Northumbrian coins
found in 1695 at Ripon, in 1808 at Kirkoswald (Cumberland), in 1842 at
York, and in 1846 and 1967 at Bolton Percy (Yorkshire) contained a range
of coins similar to that recorded in Adamson's plates except that in these
hoards far fewer coins of higher silver content occur and the coins of
lower silver content are supplemented by numerous coins of Æthelred

from dies unrepresented in Hexham and by coins in the names of King Osberht and Archbishop Wulfhere, known from documentary evidence to have been the successors of Æthelred and Wigmund; such hoards will have been deposited during or just after Osberht's reign. Their evidence confirms that the coins of higher silver content are the earlier in date and enables the numismatist to recognise the coinage of Æthelred's second reign and to identify some examples of it among the coins found at Hexham.

The reliability of the plates as a guide to the composition of the hoard as a whole can be measured to some extent by a comparison with a parcel of 91 coins that was in the possession in the 1930s of Sir Carnaby Haggerston, Bt, a Northumberland landowner, and clearly derived from Hexham.[4] They were divided as follows:

REGAL		ARCHIEPISCOPAL	
Æthelred. Early group	None	Wigmund	19
Eanred. Series A	19	Eanbald	1
Series B	17		
Æthelred. First Reign	34		
Rædwulf	1		
Æthelred. Second Reign	None		

The higher proportion of coins of Archbishop Wigmund in the Haggerston parcel is attributable to the inclusion in that of die-duplicates—Æthelhelm, a moneyer whose coins are common but struck from a very limited number of dies, is the moneyer of Wigmund best represented in the parcel but worst represented on Adamson's plates—but such a factor cannot account for the good representation of coins of Eanred Series A. It may perhaps be that they were picked out specially for the parcel on account of their higher silver content and consequent attractive appearance, which is a reminder of the limitations of this method of checking the plates' evidence. It can serve as a reminder too that the composition of the Hexham hoard as originally put together may have owed something to an individual or local attachment to coins of higher silver content and that it may not provide an accurate cross-section of the coinage then circulating in Northumbria. There is certainly a dramatic difference between the 156:161 ratio for coins of Eanred of Series A and Series B in Hexham and the 5:207 ratio that obtained for the same classes of coin in the 1967 Bolton Percy hoard and that difference need not be solely due to the Bolton Percy hoard's later date of deposit.[5]

Dating the coins has its difficulties. The Hexham hoard was evidently deposited during the second reign of Æthelred, and it is possible by comparing its content with that of later hoards to calculate its relative date in that reign. In the 1967 Bolton Percy hoard there occurred 166 indubitably regular coins of Æthelred's second reign, of which 149 were of the same general character as those of this reign from Hexham and 17 were of another character. Of the 149 only 21 were struck from dies produced before the deposit of the Hexham hoard and that must mean that Hexham was deposited before the main second reign coinage was far advanced. On any chronological scheme, the Hexham hoard is likely to date from the first twelve or eighteen months of the second reign of Æthelred.

The hoard's absolute date is the problem. According to a chronology for the years 808-67 supplied by the twelfth-century historian, Symeon of Durham, and the thirteenth-century historian, Roger of Wendover, Æthelred's second reign belonged to the years 844-848/9, and that would imply a date of c. 845 for Hexham. On an alternative scheme recently advanced by the present writer, Æthelred's second reign would belong to the late 850s and early 860s,[6] and the Hexham hoard might have been deposited c. 859. It is not feasible to set out the arguments for and against these datings in a brief compass—the alternative chronology stems from doubts about the reliability of the documentation of which Symeon of Durham and Roger of Wendover made use and from such considerations as the fact that though Osberht is supposed to have reigned from 848/9 to 867 the extant coinage in his name is of a scale to suggest a reign for him of three or four years only and it is enough to note that argument over the coins' absolute dating does not have any marked bearing on their relative dating and arrangement.

One consequence of adopting the later chronological scheme deserves mention. It is known that Northumbria was ruled in the early ninth century first by King Eardwulf (796-806) and then by King Ælfwald (806-808). Symeon of Durham and Roger of Wendover name as Ælfwald's successor Eanred (808-41).[7] This is not easy to reconcile with evidence from a contemporary Frankish source to the effect that Eardwulf began a second reign in Northumbria in 808;[8] but, if the end of Eanred's reign could be dated later—in line with the later dates suggested for Æthelred and Osberht—then it need not necessarily have begun in 808 and there might have been a period after 808 into which a second reign for Eardwulf would fit. The possibility of such a period might provide an explanation for the existence of the coins of higher silver content in the name of a King Æthelred described above as coins of 'Æthelred Early Group'. Their presence in the Hexham hoard suggests that they are of ninth-century date and not coins of Æthelred, king of Northumbria 790-96; and if of ninth-century date they can be accounted for on the revised chronology as the coinage of a king who has slipped out of all the written records but who reigned after Eardwulf's second reign and before Eanred. This king may or may not have been identical with the Æthelred who later on held the kingship twice—the writer's own view is that he was a different person, though probably a relative of Eanred and the later Æthelred—and it is not impossible that his reign may have overlapped with the early part of Eanred's reign, for his coins are not of uniform character and of the coins from Hexham only those of the moneyer Ceolbald obviously antedate those of Eanred's moneyers.

The importance of the Hexham hoard lies in its size; in the extensive representation in it of coins of higher silver content, which do not occur in such numbers in other hoards; in the grounds it provides for associating coins with an otherwise unknown Northumbrian king Æthelred, of the early ninth century, and for identifying early issues of the later Æthelred's second reign; and in the light it sheds, subject to a *caveat* already entered, on the character and age structure of the coins in use in Northumbria at the time of its deposit. The uncertainty about the actual year of its deposit makes it difficult to relate this to external political or economic developments, but if the cause of its deposit was, as seems inherently likely, a Viking raid, this would be evidence that early in Æthelred's second reign Vikings were penetrating into the Northumbrian hinterland. At the same time the numismatic evidence that second reign coins of the same character as those present on the Hexham hoard continued to be struck for some time after its deposit shows that the mint of the Northumbrian kings at York was not at this point affected by external pressures, and that in turn says something for Æthelred's rule.[9]

Notes

[1] J. Adamson, 'An account of the discovery at Hexham, Northumberland, of a brass vessel containing a number of Anglo-Saxon coins', *Arch.*, 25 (1834), 279-310. The plates of the paper were reprinted for the third edition of R. Ruding, *Annals of the Coinage of Britain* (London, 1840), and are best known to numismatists in that context. There has been no subsequent paper on the hoard as such but there is a discussion of it and an analysis of Adamson's plates in C. S. S. Lyon's pioneering account of the coinage of the period (C. S. S. Lyon, 'A Reappraisal of the Sceatta and Styca Coinage of Northumbria', *BNJ* 28 (1955-7), 227-42). For the coinage in general, see also the remarks by Lyon in his 1967 Presidential Address to the British Numismatic Society, *BNJ* 36 (1967), 215-18, and by H. E. Pagan, 'Northumbrian Numismatic Chronology in the Ninth Century', *BNJ* 38 (1969), 1-15.

[2] *Op. cit.*, p. 280.

[3] The figures given here and given by Lyon, *loc. cit.*, involve much silent correction of identifications made in captions to the plates. The present figures are an improvement on those given by Lyon as they include imitative coins, which he omits, and correct a number of minor errors in his arrangement and classification. Of the moneyers' names given, one, 'Teveh', is printed within apostrophes to show that though a coin exists with this name it is improbable that there was such a moneyer. It is also improbable that the moneyer Cœnred, primarily an archiepiscopal moneyer, worked for Æthelred in Æthelred's first reign, and die-linkage suggests that the single coin of his for the king stems from the whim of an engraver. In accordance with past custom the moneyers' names Eadvini and Tidvini have been transcribed exactly as they appear on the coins, though these are doubtless genitive forms of Eadwine and Tidwine.

[4] J. Allan, 'A collection of Northumbrian stycas in the possession of Sir Carnaby Haggerston', *History of the Berwickshire Naturalists' Field Club* 29 (1937), 289-91.

[5] The 1967 Bolton Percy hoard is unpublished and will be the subject of a forthcoming paper by the writer. There is a brief account of it in an introductory note to the catalogue of a sale held by Sotheby's on 23 June 1971 at which the major portion of the hoard was dispersed.

[6] H. E. Pagan, 'Northumbrian Numismatic Chronology in the Ninth Century', 9.

[7] Roger of Wendover actually places Eanred's accession in 810, but this does not accord with the reign length of thirty-two years which he assigns Eanred and it is

clear that on his chronology he should have dated the start of Eanred's reign 808 (cf., 'Northumbrian Numismatic Chronology in the Ninth Century', 4-6).

[8] *Annales Regni Francorum*, ed. F. Kurze, *Ss rer germ* (Hanover, 1895), 126-7.

[9] I have to express my thanks to the photographic department of the Ashmolean Museum, Oxford, for the illustrations that accompany this paper. I might perhaps also be allowed to express a personal pleasure at having been asked to write on this subject, as my great-great-great grandfather, John Fenwick (1787-1867), a Newcastle solicitor and antiquary, was both a Hexham man by birth and a friend of Adamson, and took a close interest in the original discovery.

INDEX

Aachen, 109
Abercorn, 9, 51, 66
Aberlady, 134
Abingdon, 64, 161
Acca, bishop of Hexham, 6, 9, 24ff., 38, 45, 57, 63, 75, 81ff., 115ff., 141, 162, 172
Acha, queen, 18
Adulualdi, 6
Æbbe, abbess of Coldingham, 26, 27, 46, 49
Ælfflæd, abbess of Whitby, 19, 20, 22, 24, 54
Ælfric, archbishop of York, 170
Ælfsige, abbot of Ely, 91
Ælfwald, king of Northumbria, 188
Ælfwine, sub-king of Deira, 45, 61, 63, 73
Ælfwold, king of Northumbria, 16, 25, 27
Ælla, king of Northumbria, 26, 185
Ælle, king of Deira, 17
Æthelbald, king of Mercia, 71, 78 (n. 68), 100
Æthelberht, son of Aistulf, king of Wight, 32 (n. 72)
Æthelfrith, king of Northumbria, 17, 18
Æthelhelm, moneyer, 187
Æthelred, king of Mercia, 22, 50, 53, 54, 62, 63
Æthelred, king of Northumbria, 25, 26
Æthelred, hitherto unknown king of Northumbria, 186, 188, 189
Æthelred, king of Northumbria, son of Eanred, 26, 185, 186ff.
Æthelric, father of Æthelfrith, 18
Æthelthryth, queen, 45, 46, 52, 61, 72, 73, 81, 91, 99, 100, 139 (n. 34), 169
Æthelwald, bishop of Lindisfarne, 2
Æthelwalh, king of the South Saxons, 50, 62

Æthelwold, bishop of Winchester, 91, 98-9
Æthelwulf, monk, 15
Ætstanforda, 42, 61
Agatho, pope, 48, 63, 76, 77 (n. 26)
Agilberht, bishop, 12, 42, 44, 70
Aidan, bishop of Lindisfarne, 2, 7ff., 14-15, 28, 35, 38, 40
Ailred, abbot of Rievaulx, 68, 81, 82, 93, 95, 108
Alchfrith, son of Oswiu, 8, 9, 24ff., 42ff., 61, 72, 73
Alchred, king of Northumbria, 25
Aldfrith, king of Northumbria, 10, 12, 16, 19, 20ff., 51, 54, 62, 64, 69
Aldgisl, king of the Frisians, 48
Aldhelm, 53
Aldingbourne, 62
Alhflæd, 22
Allendale, 170
Alnmouth, 137
Ambrose of Milan, 42
Anna, king of East Anglia, 46
Annemundus, archbishop of Lyons, 40, 41, 42, 48
Ardagh, 153
Athlone, 183
Auckland, 184
Audubaldi, 6
Augustine, archbishop of Canterbury, 2, 3, 14, 44, 57, 63, 68
Austerfield, 37, 52, 56
Auxerre, 65, 97

Bamburgh, 7, 26, 44, 54
Bangor-is-Coed, 67
Basse Œuvre (Beauvais), 102
Bawtry, 52
Becket, Thomas, 55
Bede, the Venerable, 1ff., 13ff., 20ff., 29, 35ff., 69ff., 82, 91, 92, 107, 115, 127, 128, 161, 162, 169
Beeston Tor, 160
Benedict Bishop, 40, 64, 66, 68, 69

THE PLATES

PLATES I & II. Pages from a MS of The Life of St. Wilfrid by Eddius Stephanus.
(*British Musuem*).

confirmante abbatē ordinatū accepunt·

q̄ pro amore patrīſ ſui ſc̄i pontificiſ n̄r̄ multa
bona facere conſueuit; Hā om̄ı dıe p̄ eo miſſā
ſingularē celebrare· & om̄ı ebdomada q̄ntā
ferıā ınq̄ obııt q̄ ſı domınıcā ınepulıſ uenerare·
& annıuerſarıa dıe obıt̄ ſuı umıūſaſ decımarū
parteſ de arm̄tıſ & de gregıb; pauṗıb; popt̄ı ſuı
dıuıdere om̄ıb; dıeb; uıtę ſuę adglorıā d̄i con—
ſtıtuıt· abſq; hıſ elemoſınıſ· q̄ ſ om̄ı dıe ṗ ſe & pro
anıma ep̄ı ſuı ſēṗ nomınatū ſımul ındıgentıſ & deo—
dabat;

O̅R̅S itaq; n̄r̄ ſc̄m pontıficē magnū   Ca̅: IX·r̅ı
uırū & fıdelem ſeruū ſı̄c credımuſ· apud ſe ınter
ſuoſ ſc̄oſ mıraculorū uırtutıb; homınıb; declarauıt;

Hā quadā dıe abbateſ undıq; aduenıenteſ· ſc̄m corp̄
pontıficıſ ın curru deducentıb; abııſq; p̄eentıb; teſ
ſc̄m corp̄uſ lauare· & dılıgenter honorıfice q;
ınduı· ſı̄c dıgnū erat· lıcentıā ṗ p̄erauerunt;

Tunc enī q̄dā exabbatıb; nomıne baculā ındoné
ſuā ſupra facıē t̄re expandıt· & ſup eā ſc̄m corp̄
depoſuerunt fr̄ſ ſuıſ manıb; lauanteſ· ecclaſtıceq;
ınduenteſ· & ad p̄fınıtū locū cū hymnıſ & cantıcıſ
cū tımore deı portabant· & ſup domū quaſı reſıden—
tıū auıum cū ſonıtu ıt̄ um audıerit· & ſtatī ıt̄ um
auolantıū ın celū· cū ſuaui modulamıne penna
rū; Sapıenteſ aut̄ q̄ıllıc aderant dıxerunt·
certe ſe ſcıre angt̄ox choroſ cū mıchahel eo

PLATE III. Hexham, ante-chamber B looking north.
(*Photo. Bruce Allsopp*).

PLATE IV.   Apparent traces of spiral or newel stair in the south
passage of the crypt.
(*Photo. Dept. of Archaeology, Durham University*).

a

PLATE V.

a The exterior of the south wall of the nave during excavations 1905— (*from Savage & Hodges, Photo. Gibson*).

b The interior of the south wall of the nave during excavations (*ibid.*).

b

a

PLATE VI.

a The interior of the west wall of the nave with wall passage and newel showing also the respond at the west end of the north nave arcade. Note the double hollow bases.

b The exterior of the north aisle wall of the nave during excavation (*Photos. ibid.*).

b

a

b

d

c

PLATE VII.   *a.*   Panel with rosette, Hexham 23. (*Photo. T. Middlemass*).

              b.   Part of a panel with a vintage scene, Hexham 22a. (*Photo. T. Middlemass*).

              c.   Part of a panel with an archer, Hexham 22b. (*Copyright, Dean and Chapter, Durham Cathedral*).

              d.   Part of the base of a panel with plant scroll, Hexham 22c. (*Copyright, Dean and Chapter, Durham Cathedral*).

a   *b*

c

d

PLATE VIII.   *a.*   Baluster and cable impost, west door, Hexham 42.
                    b.   Roman type, impost, west door, Hexham 41.
                    c.   Baluster frieze, Jarrow, north porch.
                    d.   Late baluster frieze, Jarrow, north porch. (*Photos. T. Middlemass*).

a

b

c

d

PLATE IX.   *a.*   Part of animal frieze, Hexham 31.

                b.   Face of boar impost, Hexham 32.

                c.   Side view of Hexham 32.

                d.   Lion impost, Hexham 33.   (*Photos. T. Middlemass*).

a

b

c

d

PLATE X.   *a.*   Impost or frieze, Hexham 37.

               b.   Part of a cross arm or windowhead, Hexham 38.

               c.   Part of a decorated step or frieze, Hexham 21.

               d.   Part of a decorated frieze, Saxon or Roman, Hexham 29.

(Photos. T. Middlemass).

a

b

d

c

e

f

PLATE XI.   a.   Interlace impost, Hexham 36.   (*Photo. T. Middlemass*).
              b.   Interlace impost, Hexham 35.   (*Photo. T. Middlemass*).
              c.   Interlace impost, Hexham 34.   (*Photo. T. Middlemass*).
              d.   Two interlace imposts, Ripon Cathedral, north wall. (*Photo. T. Middlemass*).
              e.   Lost pilaster, Hexham 39.   (*after Gibson*).
              f.   Pilaster strip from Ledsham parish church.   (*Photo. R. Cramp*).

a

b

c

d

e

PLATE XII.　　*a.*　Chamfered impost, Simonburn church porch. (*Photo. R. Cramp*).

　　　　　　　　b.　Frontal view of base, Hexham 40. (*Photo. T. Middlemass*).

　　　　　　　　c.　Impost capital, Hexham 30. (*Copyright, Dean and Chapter, Durham Cathedral*).

　　　　　　　　d.　Side view of Hexham 30. (*Copyright, Dean and Chapter, Durham Cathedral*).

　　　　　　　　e.　Side view of base, Hexham 40. (*Photo. T. Middlemass*).

13

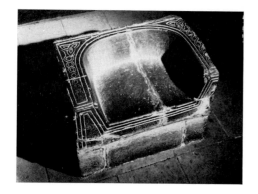

a   b

e

c   d

PLATE XIII.   *a.*   Frith stool, Hexham 46. (*Photo. T. Middlemass*).

                b.   Reconstructed chamfered impost, Ledsham. (*Photo. R. Cramp*).

                c.   Fragments of Crucifixion panel, Hexham 20. (*Photo. T. Middlemass*).

                d.   Fragments of draped figure, Hexham 20. (*Photo. T. Middlemass*).

                e.   Undecorated column, Hexham 51. (*Photo. T. Middlemass*).

14

a

b

c

d

PLATE XIV.   *a.*   Impost with baluster and rail decoration, Hexham 25. (*Copyright, Dean and Chapter, Durham Cathedral*).

              b.   Imposts with baluster and rail decoration, Hexham 26 and 27. (*Copyright, Dean and Chapter, Durham Cathedral*).

              c.   Impost with baluster and rail decoration, Hexham 28. (*Photo. T. Middlemass*).

              d.   Baluster impost, Hexham 24. (*Photo. T. Middlemass*).

a

b

c

d

e

PLATE XV. *a.* Head or footstone with cross, Hexham 15.
 b. Grave corner with cross, Hexham 17.
 c. Grave marker with cross and rosettes, Hexham 16.
 d. Inscribed grave marker, Hexham 13.
 e. Hogback grave corner, Hexham 19.

(*Photos. T. Middlemass*).

16

a   b   c   d

PLATE XVI.   *a.*   Acca Cross, Hexham 1, east and north faces.

                 b.   Hexham 1, north and west faces.

                 c.   Hexham 1, west face.

                 d.   Hexham 1, west and south faces.   (*Photos. copyright David Wright*).

17

PLATE XVII.
a. Hexham 1, detail of the head. (*Copyright David Wright*).
b. Hexham 1, central portion of the inscription. (*Photo. T. Middlemass*).
c. Hexham 1, detail of west face. (*Copyright David Wright*).
d. Hexham 1, detail of the north face. (*Copyright David Wright*).

b

c

a

PLATE XVIII.   *a.*   Hexham 1, west face, full length.   (*Photo R. Cramp*).

b.   Hexham 3, broad face.   (*Copyright, Dean and Chapter, Durham Cathedral*).

c.   Hexham 3, broad face.   (*Copyright, Dean and Chapter, Durham Cathedral*).

a

b

PLATE XIX. *a.* Hexham 2, broad face a. (*Photo. T. Middlemass*).

       b. Hexham 2, broad face b. (*Copyright David Wright*).

c

d

c. Hexham 2, narrow face a. (*Copyright David Wright*).

d. Hexham 2, narrow face b. (*Photo. T. Middlemass*).

a   b

c   d

PLATE XX.   a.   Lowther, Westmorland. Broad face showing medallion vinescroll and side face with the typical west Northumbrian trail with spiral tendril.

                  b.   Lowther, Westmorland with counterpointed vinescroll with internal leaves.

                     (*a. and b. by kind permission of the Royal Commission on Historical Monuments*).

                  c.   Stamfordham, Northumberland. Part of the broad face showing tangled trellis vinescroll.

                  d.   Stamfordham, Northumberland. Vine trail.

                     (*c. and d. copyright, Dean and Chapter, Durham Cathedral*).

PLATE XXI.   *a.*   Hexham 4, base. Panel face 1.   (*Photo. T. Middlemass*).

                 b.   Hexham 4, general view.   (*Photo. T. Middlemass*).

                 c.   Hexham 4, upper surface.   (*Photo. T. Middlemass*).

                 d.   Hexham 5, carved face.   (*Copyright Dean and Chapter, Durham Cathedral*).

PLATE XXII. *a.* Northallerton cross shaft with tree scroll vine.
b. Northallerton cross shaft with medallion vine scroll.
c. Northallerton cross head. Face a.
d. Northallerton cross head. Face b.
e. Northallerton cross head. Side view with baluster ornament.
f. Jarrow. Cross head with zig zag ornament on the face and baluster ornament on the side.

(*Photos. T. Middlemass*).

24

a

b

c

d

PLATE XXIII.   *a.*   Ripon, possibly an altar-pillar. General view. (*Photo. T. Middlemass*).
                   b.   Ripon. Altar-pillar, carved face. (*Photo. T. Middlemass*).
                   c.   Hexham 10. Cross head with rosette. (*Copyright, Dean and Chapter, Durham Cathedral*).
                   d.   Hexham 11. Plain cross head. (*Photo. T. Middlemass*).

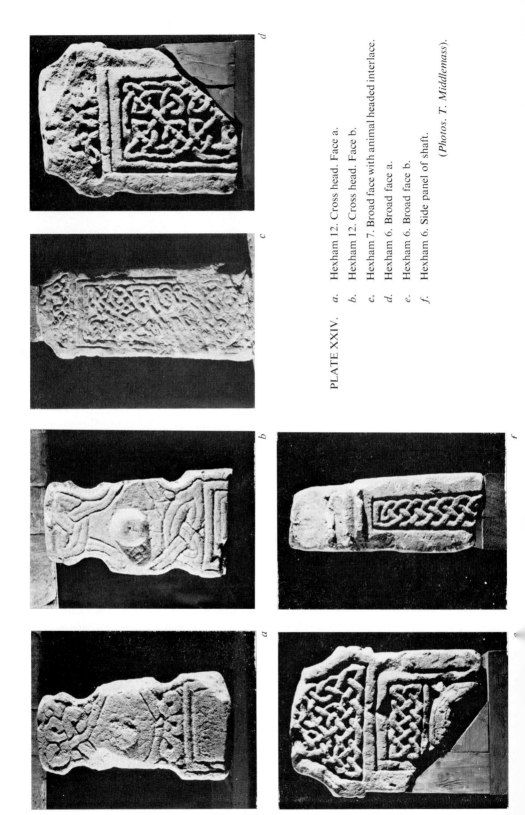

PLATE XXIV. *a.* Hexham 12. Cross head. Face a.

b. Hexham 12. Cross head. Face b.

c. Hexham 7. Broad face with animal headed interlace.

d. Hexham 6. Broad face a.

e. Hexham 6. Broad face b.

f. Hexham 6. Side panel of shaft.

(*Photos. T. Middlemass*).

b. The Oseberg bucket.
(*Univeristets Oldsaksamling, Oslo*)

PLATE XXV.   a.   The Hexham bucket.
(*British Museum*)

27

a

c

b *d* *e*

PLATE XXVI.

a.–c. Details of the Hexham bucket. (*British Museum*).
d. and *e.* The Gausel escutcheon. (*Historisk Museum, Bergen*).

a

b

PLATE XXVII.

a. Base of the Hexham bucket.

The Hexham Plaque.

b. face.

c. reverse.

(*British Museum*).

c

29

PLATE XXVIII.

The Hexham/Corbridge Ring. (*Photos. T. Middlemass*).

a

b

c

PLATE XXIX.

a.
The Hexham Chalice.
(*Photo. A. Wiper*).

b.
Grave chalice of
Archbishop Poppo
(gest. 1047) from Trier.
Height 5 cms.
(*Photo. Haas, Trier*).

c.
Grave chalice of Bishop
Hezilo (gest. 1079) from
Hildesheim.
Height 6·2 cms.
(*Niedersächsische
Landesgalerie,
Hannover*).